Herman Witzel
A Pragmatic Approach to Agency in Group Activity

Practical Philosophy

Edited by
Herlinde Pauer-Studer, Neil Roughley,
Peter Schaber, and Ralf Stoecker

Volume 23

Herman Witzel

A Pragmatic Approach to Agency in Group Activity

—

DE GRUYTER

ISBN 978-3-11-062811-1
e-ISBN (PDF) 978-3-11-062862-3
e-ISBN (EPUB) 978-3-11-062908-8
ISSN 2197-9243

Library of Congress Control Number: 2019951615

Bibliographic information published by the Deutsche Nationalbibliothek
The Deutsche Nationalbibliothek lists this publication in the Deutsche Nationalbibliografie;
detailed bibliographic data are available on the Internet at http://dnb.dnb.de.

MIX
Papier aus verantwor-
tungsvollen Quellen
FSC
www.fsc.org   FSC® C083411

Preface

"A pragmatic approach to agency in group activity" is my philosophical contribution to the research field of group action, group intentionality and action theory in general. The results presented are relevant for philosophers, sociologists, business ethicists and all people who create, organize or manage groups. Accordingly, I kept the text self-contained with all technical terminology highlighted and explained as well as properly referenced for background reading.

My approach builds towards a theory of agency which bridges individual agency and agency in groups, but it does so by starting from practical insights about group activity, rather than from our understanding of individual agency. Interactions and structures within group activity are often out in the open, ready to be observed and analyzed. Many philosophers have exploited this accessibility to provide deep insight about agency in group activity. To my knowledge, however, none have given these insights priority over how we think individual agency works. In this sense, I turn the direction of building action theory around, and the result is a practical view of agency that respects the large variety of expressions of agency, combined with a clean approach to relevant terminology and concepts.

My personal motivation for the research presented here is both practical and theoretical. The practical motivation comes from my time at a management consulting firm where I served various companies over several years. As a consultant, I found myself in a strange position: we had enormous influence on the decisions made, yet we rarely ever actually made the decisions–our clients did. We also rarely took responsibility for these decisions and we rarely ever carried out the decisions and lived through the consequences. What exactly was our role in these situations? How did our actions and decisions relate to what happened in these companies? What was our "share" of responsibility? I am certain many people in all kinds of businesses–from employees to managers–ask these questions themselves at least occasionally. As for myself, I found the answers presented in this thesis to be helpful and actionable.

My theoretical motivation comes from a completely different direction: my first academic contact with philosophy during my studies of physics took me into discussions about free will and ethics. For both topics, an understanding of action and agency is crucial; free will is ultimately expressed in free agency, and ethics must relate our actions to the things we are responsible for. The main positions of action theory, in turn, have a strong focus on individual human agents and, more particularly, on what is happening in the minds of these agents. This focus is as understandable as it is elusive; we know very little about how our minds work, while the things we do know scientifically often leave us puzzled. To me, this

https://doi.org/10.1515/9783110628623-202

was never a good theoretical foundation. Accordingly, I developed an approach to action theory that leaves me much more confident to take its lessons to other areas of philosophical discussion.

With these ideas and motivations, I was determined to start my work on "A pragmatic approach to agency in group activity," but more was required. I was fortunate to find an extremely helpful and good-willed environment both professionally and personally. Special thanks go to Ralf Stoecker. He supported my transition from being a physicist and consultant to being a philosopher. His engagement, inspiration, advice, philosophical intelligence and insight were invaluable to me personally and to the quality of my work. I could not have wished for a better supervisor, and I am deeply thankful for this. I also want to thank Johanna Wagner for sharing an office with me, enabling countless philosophical discussions, and for just being the kind, open-minded person she is. This creative environment was complemented by inspiring colleagues like Christian Neuhäuser, Christian Nimtz, Almut von Wedelstaedt, Peter Schulte, Pia Becker and many more. I am also very grateful to Bielefeld University. The dissertation, published here as an improved version, was successfully completed and defended at its Departement of Philosophy.

Outside of my home university, I also found a thriving and inspiring scientific community. I am grateful for the exchanges with countless truly committed philosophers. Special moments of insight and clarity of approach were inspired by conversations with Michael Bratman, Stephen Butterfil and Bence Nanay, even though they might not be aware of it. Ultimately, I hope that in publishing this work, I give back a little of what I received from this community.

Finally, none of this would have been possible without the unwavering support of my family and friends. My wife enabled me to pursue philosophy when we adapted to our new life as a family. I am deeply thankful for her gifts of love, happiness and both a daughter and son, who have inspired me in their own right. My friends helped me to keep things in perspective, brainstorm, think outside myself and bounce around ideas. I look forward to continuing life's adventures with them by my side.

Contents

1 Introduction

"U.S. strikes ISIS camp in Lybia," "How ISIS recruits children then kills them," "Uber losing 1$B a year in China," "Ford plans four new SUV models," "Apple rebuffs FBI, sparks anger and praise." These headlines are taken from the arbitrarily chosen day February 19th, 2016 from the CNN website (Botelho and Starr, 2016; McLaughlin, 2016; Yan, 2016; Isodore, 2016; Botelho et al., 2016). They are completely comprehensible as long as one knows the groups in these statements, e.g., the U.S. and China are governmental states, ISIS is a terror organization, Ford, Uber and Apple are business corporations, FBI is an intelligence agency. Headlines like this are also ubiquitous. Looking at any other news website on any other day yields similar statements.

The ubiquity is owed to the tremendous importance of groups and their activity in our society–especially in our time (French, 1995, for a historic perspective). The comprehensibility, in comparison, is not so easily explained. At face value, the headlines state that the respective groups display agency. They perform actions and they interact with each other. The headline about Apple and the FBI even suggests they can be praised or blamed for their actions. When taken literally, such statements refer to groups as if they were agents engaged in full-blown agency.

The literal interpretation, however, is problematic: groups are not beings themselves; they are groups of human beings. Human beings, on the other hand, are agents. The immediate suggestion is that groups are not really agents themselves, but merely groups of agents. Saying a group acts, consequently, is a simpler way of saying the members of the group act. The appearance of group names in these statements is merely for abbreviation (Ludwig, 2014, for such a claim in more technical detail). The abbreviation-interpretation, too, is immediately challenged. The first headline from above, for example, could easily read 'U.S. pilots strike ISIS camp in Lybia', but this would be ambiguous: U.S. pilots might strike an ISIS camp without the U.S. striking the camp–maybe they have gone rogue, or they are striking the ISIS camp for another state like Iraq with Iraq military equipment allowed by the U.S. government. Even if the U.S. pilots strike the ISIS camp within their regular duty, they only perform the very last stage of the strike, namely actually dropping the bombs. Other agents gathered relevant intelligence, decided the strike and prepared it. It is not immediately obvious how the overall activity of striking the ISIS camp can be understood solely in terms of the individuals' agency.

In either interpretation, literal or abbreviatory, a first glance at the statements does not provide a simple, easily comprehensible understanding. Accordingly, our practical reactions vary between the two interpretations. We make demands for compensation, for example, directed at the entire group, while we may also

https://doi.org/10.1515/9783110628623-001

demand that specific individuals resign from their positions within the group. We impose business restrictions on a company affecting all of its members, while, at the same time, we charge specific individuals who played an outstanding role in whatever happened. Sometimes the target of our practical reactions is the group as a whole, and sometimes it is individuals within the group. This is an immediate consequence of the difficulty to ascribe agency in group activity.

The clarification of agency in group activity is, therefore, an important and non-trivial task. Intuitively and philosophically, however, agency is first and foremost concerned with individuals. In particular, agency is almost unanimously thought to be characterized by intentionality since Elisabeth Anscombe's influential monograph "Intention" from 1957. Intentionality in agency, in turn, is usually associated with states of mind or a combination of states of minds in line with the equally influential 1963's paper "Action, Reasons and Causes" by Donald Davidson. Thus, the dominant view on agency characterized by intentionality is inherently individual.

Nonetheless, most theories of agency in group activity attempt to make sense of intentionality on a group level in order to recover continuity with the dominant view on individual agency. In fact, the major, bi-annual philosophical conference on the topic is called "Collective Intentionality" (Collective Intentionality X, 2016). On a group level, clearly, there is no direct equivalent to the states of minds of individuals, which are used to characterize intentionality in individual agency. Consequently, the explanation of intentionality on a group level forces philosophers to use alternative features readily accessible without a study of the human mind. Different proposals focus on different features for agency in group activity, for example, planning (Bratman, 1999), procedures for decision making (List and Pettit, 2013; French, 1995), forms of commitment (Gilbert, 1990), or basic individual social attitudes enabling us to make sense of intentionality on a group level (Searle, 1990; Tuomela and Miller, 1988; Tomasello et al., 2005). Notably, the features by themselves already provide powerful explanations of agency in group activity without direct reference to any form of intentionality. Indeed, the framing of the respective accounts in terms of intentionality for the sake of theoretical continuity usually adds little to their explanatory power.

While a continuity of individual agency and agency in group activity makes immediate sense, it is worthwhile to realize that the direction of continuity can go two ways. One option is to start with individual action theory, and then extend this to group activity. Another option is to start with group activity that seems to display features of agency. This comes with the pragmatic advantage that those features are out in the open: we need not look into the individual agents' minds to understand agency in group activity, but we can simply look at the practice of group activity. In a second step, the demand of continuity can be understood as a challenge to action theory for individual agency. The aim of this text, ultimately, is to push forward this pragmatic approach and offer a new way to think about agency in general and about agency in group activity in particular.

The structure of this thesis roughly follows the brief discussion up to now. In the second chapter, I show that the challenge of ascribing agency in group activity comes from a fundamental disruption of individual agency in group activity. Statements like "Ford plans four new SUV models" suggest that the explanation of group activity cannot refer to individual agency alone. Indeed, when agents engage in group activity, they face a coordination problem: they must properly coordinate their interaction for successful group activity. When an individual agent only interacts with her environment, she can adjust her actions and decisions to circumstances. In group activity, in contrast, the agents can influence each other even before anything has happened. This responsiveness enables agents to link their respective actions together by linking their agency together, i.e. the agents do not simply adjust their own actions to what the other agents do, but they already influence each other on their way to action.

In order to understand the challenge for the ascription of agency in group activity, thus, I analyze various examples of how agents usually coordinate themselves in group activity and how this affects the agents' agency. I uncover a general coordination principle, which is the basis for all forms of coordination. In order to coordinate, agents need to create some form of external link between them relevant for their respective agency. This can be as simple as external information flows, e.g., established by verbal or non-verbal communication, which carries relevant information for the mutually depended action decisions, a definition of roles settling what to expect from each other, or a set of simple rules to which agents agree and adhere to. By doing so, the individual agent's agency is no longer self-sufficient, but rather relies on external factors. This by itself does not necessarily pose a problem for agency. Even in the absence of other agents an agent is dependent on external factors. In more complex group activity, however, this principle does impact individual agency in a fundamental manner.

In large groups with complex goals, this becomes particularly evident. Companies, for example, usually persist through large time spans during which hundreds or even thousands of agents at each given time must be properly coordinated. The performance of such group activity, notably, is largely independent of agents leaving and entering the group. Furthermore, many agents do not necessarily know what the other agents are doing–or they do not even know many of the other agents at all, yet, they contribute to the same overall activity.

The respective coordination problems in such group activity cannot be championed with simple information flows or simple rules. Rather, the methods for coordination have to ensure successful group activity largely independent of the specific individual agents. This is also achieved by establishing external links between the agents. In contrast to simpler forms of group activity, however, the links are not merely relevant or helpful for the individual agents, but crucial to the exercise of agency: structures of goals and means are defined on a group level, and the group organization is set up accordingly; the individuals are provided with incentives to contribute to the group activity irrespective of their endorsement of the group activity; procedures are defined to ensure reliability and consistency in execution and so on and so forth. In consequence, the agents in such group activity often do things that they did not decide to do; they bring about goals that are not their own goals; even the way how they do things often is prescribed by working procedures, or heavily restricted by policies. In short, features crucial for agency are established on a group level, and the individual agents draw from these resources for their performance. As a consequence, it is not possible anymore to describe the display of agency in group activity solely on the individual level. Instead, one has to invoke group level features to explain agency in group activity. This is the fundamental disruption of individual agency in group activity.

The disruption of agency in group activity presents a challenge for action theory. It is not clear how exactly individual agency is eroded in group activity, or simply takes another form. What is obvious, however, is that the disruption of agency in group activity is gradual and not an all-or-nothing matter. In simple cases of group activity, the results can be fully explained with recourse to the individual agents' agency added by some helpful external mechanisms. In more complex cases, key features of agency are established on a group level, while others remain with the individuals. Developing a convincing theory of agency for these dynamics is challenging, but they also present the opportunity to think about agency from a new perspective. The coordination in these group activities replaces key features of agency on the individual level by respective features on the group level. In doings so, those features are directly observable. Understanding group activity, therefore, provides an independent access to agency or, at least, to the various features relevant for agency.

Hence, in chapter three, I analyze group activity independently of concepts of individual agency in order to provide an original basis for the study of agency in group activity. To help with the clarity of the explanatory scope and the structure of research, I draw a research map for group activity. The research map contains distinct types of group activity in need of explanation especially with respect to agency. I characterize the different types of group activity using untainted concepts independent of existing accounts of agency or group activity. This way, the research map remains neutral with respect to theory building, but highlights the basic concepts needed for understanding group activity. I subsequently discuss different positions on group activity to find out about features of agency most relevant to group activity.

In order to draw the research map, I analyze the different meanings of 'together' as they appear in descriptions of group activity. Agents do many things 'together', but there are different reasons why we describe it this way. Indeed, the analysis reveals distinct types of group activity based on equally distinct concepts. For example, agents work together towards the same goal and recognize each other in doing so. This alone usually suffices to say that two or more agents do something together. However, agents do not need to have the same goal to do something together. They may only coordinate themselves in order to realize, for example, a common means to their different personal goals. Neither of the two, goals or coordination, is required when agents do something together simply for the sake of doing it together rather than alone.

Naturally, combinations are possible as well. Many times, agents coordinate to achieve a common goal, and they may even do so partly because they enjoy doing it together. The range of group activities from this analysis alone, consequently, is rather wide. More importantly, the differentiating characteristics are completely distinct, which implies that research on agency in group activity requires a differentiated approach as well. To make matters worse, group activity is not restricted to things agents do 'together' in any of the above meanings. Indeed, group activity is not always properly described as doing something 'together', i.e. there are important cases where multiple agents bring about some result in a non-incidental manner, yet, they do not do it together.

Authority, for example, empowers individual agency by forcing other agents into joint activity. An agent in authority quite literally extends the reach of her agency using other agents. The involved agents do not bring about a result together, but the agents under authority do something *for* the agent in authority–not *with* them. On the other hand, authority can, indeed, be used as a helpful coordination method when acting 'together' in a proper sense. Eventually, a mix of the two cases gives rise to a new form of group activity: individual agents may do something *for* the group, but do not do it *with* other members of the group at the same time. The authority, so to speak, comes directly from the group to empower the group activity. Authority, therefore, walks the lines between individual agency, acting together and a form of group activity that goes beyond acting together. The same is true for the related principle of authorization. Agents may authorize other agents to act in their name to expand the reach of their individual agency, or agents authorize each other to be more efficient in doing something together, or the group establishes a structure such that individual agents are authorized to act in the name of the group in a way that goes beyond acting together with the other group members.

The important insight about authority and authorization is that agency–even in the individual case–can disassociate from the agents in non-mysterious ways. All an agent in authority actually does is giving orders, yet, the result of what another agent does when following the order is traced back to the agency of the person in authority. Clearly, the reason is that the explanation of what is happening in terms of agency must refer mainly to the person in authority: she orders what to do based on a decision that she made, presumably to serve her goals–the executing agent does not contribute much to the story of agency. This is in line with the discussion of the disruption of agency in the second chapter: when fundamental aspects of agency are established on a group level, then agency cannot be described solely on the basis of the agents actually executing the actions. Accordingly, I pick up group activity so characterized for the research map under the header of corporate activity. I provide examples for corporate activity that are not as ambiguous as cases of authority and authorization to show that, indeed, corporate activity deserves treatment in its own right.

With the discussion of group activity that cannot be described as doing something 'together', the research map for group activity can be completed. In the next step, I discuss several positions on agency in group activity. The literature is still fragmented and unstructured, and little has been done to consolidate the field, yet. The research map, at least for the work at hand, helps clarify what exactly the respective positions explain and compare them appropriately. In fact, it turns out many of the positions, which appear to compete with each other at first glance, aim at different types of group activity. This, fortunately, helps the purpose of studying the literature. The aim is to find out about how philosophy of action accounts for the transfer of crucial features of agency onto the group level. Since many of the positions aim at different types of group activity, their ideas can complement each other instead of competing against each other.

The reason why many of the positions appear to compete lies in the common reference to some sort of 'intentionality' on the group level. In fact, group intentionality in one form or another is the focal point of philosophical discussion. The focus on intentionality is so prominent because intentionality is thought to be the very mark of individual agency. Naturally, the positions on agency in group activity drive for continuity with individual action theory. However, where intentionality in individual agency is usually understood in terms of an agent's mental life, any construction of intentionality on a group level is forced to spell out what exactly it means in terms of more basic non-mental concepts. As a positive consequence, the different accounts highlight different features on the group level and how they enable group activity or even group agency.

The most influential accounts on agency in group activity already propose very different features. Michael Bratman spells out what it means to plan something together, which is supposed to constitute shared intentionality (Bratman, 2014). Pettit and List describe how decision making in groups may go beyond the individual level (List and Pettit, 2013). Notably, their account does not put a form of group intentionality in the center of their discussion. John Searle argues for an inherent social motivation, which is the basis for 'we-intentions' on the individual level that enable agents to act together (Searle, 1990). In a similar manner, Raimo Tuomela and Kaarlo Miller describe a special 'we-mode' in an agents reasoning ultimately resulting in participatory 'we-intentions' (Tuomela and Miller, 1988). Margaret Gilbert introduces a 'joint commitment' on the group level that allows for 'joint intentions' (Gilbert, 1990). Those five positions shape the philosophical discourse, but there is a host of alternative positions of which I select a few particularly inspiring. Peter French discusses how organizational structures in corporations make them agents (French, 1995). David Schweikard synthesizes and supplements existing positions and highlights the specific relations between the individuals' intentions enabling elaborate group activity (Schweikard, 2011). James Butterfill, Elisabeth Pacherie and Michael Tomasello provide insight for simpler forms of group activity by focusing on the explanatory power of predictions and expectations (Butterfill, 2012), basic forms of team reasoning that enables a less sophisticated notion of shared intentionality (Pacherie, 2013), and a basic motivation to share emotions as a stepping stone towards sharing intention (Tomasello et al., 2005), respectively. Finally, there are insightful contributions on the topics of authority and authorization used in group activity by Abraham Sesshu Roth (Roth, 2014) and David Copp (Copp, 1979).

With so many fundamentally different concepts, most of which successfully explain at least some type of group activity, the common reference to intentionality is remarkable. Clearly, theoretical continuity between individual agency and agency in group activity is a sensible demand, but it is noteworthy that the construction of intentionality on the group level refers primarily to specific, comprehensible features that stand in their own right. To make sense of agency in group activity an investigation into intentionality and its relation to those features of agency is essential.

While the different positions on agency in group activity focus on specific features and the relation to the idea of intentionality in agency, there is another hidden champion for the explanation of agency in group activity. The idea that agents in group activity somehow have a common goal is taken for granted implicitly or explicitly in virtually all of the above positions and often plays a central role in the construction of group intentionality. The appeal of using goals as the basis for group intentionality is rooted in the intuitive assumption that goals are external to the agents. External things, in turn, are easily accessible to all the agents in group activity and, thus, goals can be 'shared' or 'achieved' together in a direct manner.

However, the research map clearly shows that there are cases of group activity in which the agents do not share a common goal; even most elaborate group activity is possible without the agents having a common goal. Furthermore, the ad-hoc characterizations proposed by the different positions of what it means for a group to have a goal, or even the basic concept of what it means to 'have a goal' or 'be a goal', are incoherent, if not contradictory. Unfortunately, research about the role of goals in agency is surprisingly sparse. Even in the above positions, the importance of goals is veiled behind the more prominent notion of intentionality and the various original features of group activity.

Consequently, in the fourth chapter, I examine the two major concepts in the discussion of agency in group activity, intentionality in agency and goals in agency. I show that a variety of at least six features are associated with intentionality in individual action theory, most of which are conceptually distinct and fulfill different explanatory roles with respect to agency. 'Goals' or 'having goals' is one such feature. Given that goals are essentially unanimously thought to play an outstanding role in group activity as shown in the third chapter, I also provide an analysis of the concept of a 'goal' or 'having a goal' in agency and discuss the possible relation between goals and intentionality in agency.

Intentionality in agency, according to the standard approach, comes in three variations. 'Acting intentionally' captures the intuitive feeling that there is a difference between lower forms of behavior and actually acting. 'Intending to act' captures the idea that we make plans and intend to do something in advance. 'Acting with an intention' captures the idea that we usually act in order to achieve something.

Upon closer inspection, I propose that the three standard forms of intentionality do not even cover all features usually associated with intentionality in agency. I argue for at least six such features of agency: first, agents experience a difference between acting intentionally and things happening to them like reflexes, or spastic movements. Second, acting intentionally also highlights the epistemic perspective of the acting agent, i.e. only specific aspects of a given action are intentional, while other aspects of the very same action may be unintentional. I do, for example, intentionally type this sentence, while I unintentionally make typing noises on my keyboard. Third, it is usually said that we bring about effects of our actions intentionally as soon as we know about them even when our action is not explicitly directed at that effect. This gives rise to the notorious discussion on the double-effect or side-effect (Harman, 1976; Knobe, 2003; McIntyre, 2019; Stoecker, 2014). Fourth, some of the effects of our actions are, indeed, intended, i.e. the agent intends a certain consequence of her action, not just the action itself. It is here that intentionality in agency and goals come together. Fifth, intentionality is also characterized by elaborate planning for the future, i.e. not only do we want to achieve something with single actions, but many actions are coordinated over time to achieve some greater end. Finally, sixth, there is the notion of intending particular actions, which usually comes down to having made a decision.

In a full display of agency, all forms of intentionality in agency are present, and they all revolve around one or more specific actions. Aside from this connection, however, the concepts are independent of each other. It is unclear how the idea of 'intentionality' as the single mark of agency can be recovered from these range features of agency. More importantly, it is unclear what the notion of intentionality in agency adds to the explanatory power of the associated features. To show-case this problem and connect the discussion to group activity, I focus on one of the features associated with intentionality in agency that also plays an outstanding role in accounts for group activity.

The concept of a 'goal' and 'having a goal' is virtually omnipresent in the discussion of agency in group activity, and it also corresponds to one form of intentionality in agency. Despite its obvious importance there is little to no explicit discussion in individual action theory and very few dedicated discussions in action theory for groups. The reason for this could be that the concept of a 'goal' appears to be so plain, almost trivial. However, it is not.

First, 'goal' and 'having a goal' cannot be separately discussed. Saying that something is a goal already implies an agent who has that goal. Second, when agents 'have a goal' they have some sort of representation of a state of affairs. Neither does one need to have a representation of a particular state of the world, nor a particular action of which the goal is an outcome. Rather, third, goals guide decision making with respect to the specific state to bring about and how to bring it about. This guidance, fourth, usually adheres to some normative constraints depending on the capabilities and opportunities of the agent. Finally, fifth, a goal comes with a commitment by the agent to actually do something about it. The concept of a 'goal', thus, is far richer than one would intuitively assume. In fact, many aspects of agency are readily explained with reference to goals and their functionality. What, then, is left for the idea of intentionality in agency?

Once more, the research on agency in group activity is helpful because features of agency on a group level are related to intentionality in order to ensure continuity with individual action theory. Goals, on most accounts, are located on the group level together with at least one other feature of agency taken to be key to agency in group activity. The link to intentionality usually takes one of two routes. On one approach, the group goal, or the group activity that achieves the goal, becomes the content of the intentions of the individual agents. On the other approach, the goal remains on the group level, but the individual agents intend actions that contribute to it. What exactly is the explanatory benefit of these approaches? Following the first approach, the group level features, e.g. group goals, are literally transferred into the agents' minds by the vehicle of intentions. This way, group activity can be explained with reference to a mindful agent, which satisfies the powerful pre-conception that agency requires a mind in some form or another. The second approach acknowledges that not all features of agency require a mind, and leave them at the group level. When it comes to actual intentional action execution, however, it turns back to the individual agents. This satisfies another powerful pre-conception of agency, namely that agency requires a physical body literally able to take action. The construction of intentionality for agency in group activity, therefore, serves the purpose to properly link group activity to minds and bodies. To challenge this is to challenge the pre-conceptions that agency requires minds and bodies.

Human agency without our minds and bodies is, indeed, inconceivable, but it is worthwhile to think about how exactly they actually figure in our agency. In the final chapter, I do exactly that and explore whether or not the explanation of agency in group activity has to fall back on the individual agents' minds and bodies. Fortunately, the role of at least aspects of our mind and body in agency are subject to empirical research. It is highly instructive to look at the results. I provide a selective review of empirical research on 'decision making' and 'execution control' as exemplary features of agency closely tied to our minds and bodies, respectively. The results strongly suggest that we must substantially review our intuitive concept of human agency and, thus, agency in general. This makes room for a theory of agency that not only provides a more accurate model of reality, but can also be applied to forms of agency beyond individual human agency.

Psychological research suggests that human decision making does not follow the ideals of rationality many action theories and our intuition would make us believe. Rather, most of our actions rely on sub-conscious, arational mechanisms, often called 'heuristics', which help us make fast and often sensible decisions. The dominion of rational deliberation is surprisingly small and seems to play a minor role in everyday display of agency. Thus, the role of the human mind in agency is deeply challenged. Clearly, human agency is realized to a great part through our specific biological mind, but only to a small part by way of conscious rational deliberation that has been at the center of action theory throughout the ages. This sheds a positive light on other realizations of deliberative structures as, for example, for agency in group activity.

Physiological and neurological research on execution control draws a similar picture. At least as far as specific body movements are concerned, conscious action control is severely limited. Most movements are executed according to motor programs generated by internal models, which run completely below consciousness.

In fact, if we do consciously intervene or merely attend to our body movements consciously, performance, quality and speed are reduced drastically. This suggests that conscious control in human agency has a teleological character, i.e. we do not consciously control the specifics of *how* something is done, but only *what* is being done. A lack of actual execution control, thus, seems irrelevant as long as an agent has teleological control. This, however, can easily be claimed for other displays of agency as well, for example, for agency in group activity.

While human agency seems introspectively accessible, our introspection cannot be trusted. Consequently, taking human agency as a blue-print and continuously expanding the theory of agency from there is a questionable strategy. Instead, I propose that agency should be explained in terms of the pragmatic concepts, i.e. features displayed in agency independently of their specific realization. If these features are properly realized in another form than the human biological form, we should embrace the idea of other kinds of agency than individual human agency.

Agency in group activity, therefore, should be understood as a form of agency in its own right. This does not mean that agency in group activity is independent of the human agents, but only that the human agents in a group can create a new form of agency mediated by various features of agency on a group level.

2 Disruption of agency in group activity

Companies, states and various other large and small groups shape the world in a way no individual can do on her own. This is acknowledged in everyday practice by ascribing actions to groups, which is captured by statements about group activity (GA) of the general form:

(GA) Group G did action A

The interpretation of such statements presents a challenge for understanding the concept of agency. Agency is associated first and foremost with individual agents, whereas statements of the form (GA) claim that groups act. Fortunately, the groups featured in such statements are usually made up of individual agents. This immediately offers an explanation strategy for (GA): group activity is nothing but the activity of the individuals who make up the group. Accordingly, the group as such does not act, but rather only the individuals are acting, and statements of the general form (GA) are abbreviations. The success of this explanation strategy, however, faces a serious obstacle. Group activity is more than individual agents acting alone. It is constituted by agents who act *and interact*. The interaction in group activity, in turn, affects the agency of the involved individuals in ways that makes it unreasonable to ascribe the results of the group activity to the individuals. If so, the explanation that statements of the form (GA) are abbreviated fails, and the reason for the failure is a disruption of agency by the interaction of agents in group activity.

The disruption of agency in group activity traces back to how the interaction of agents in group activity works. For successful group activity, the involved agents must *coordinate* their actions. In individual agency, the agent faces a similar challenge with regard to her own actions. Various features of the agent's constitution ensure that this challenge is properly met. I refer to these features as *agential features*. In group activity, actions of different agents have to be linked, but this cannot be achieved by the agential features realized within the individual agents. Instead, the agents have to *externally realize* agential features. External realization of agential features is the key to understanding the disruption of agency in group activity, and the sense in which (GA) is not just abbreviated.

External realization of agential features can be as simple as gazing or nodding to convey important information to each other in order to coordinate different actions. The information flow warranting proper coordination of different parts of an action in individual agency is externalized by means of some communicative act to ensure proper coordination. In more elaborate group activity, more profound

https://doi.org/10.1515/9783110628623-002

agential features are externally realized. A group may have goals without any of the individuals having these particular goals, but only sub-goals or personal goals appropriately linked to the group goals by a smart incentive system. Decisions in groups may go through a decision making procedure by-passing individual decisions, or at least substantially altering them (List and Pettit, 2013). Goals and decisions are central to the concept of agency. Consequently, their external realization disrupts individual agency in group activity in a way that makes it unreasonable to ascribe the results of the group activity to the individuals' agency in a direct manner.

The disruption of agency in group activity challenges action theory both theoretically and practically. From a theoretical point of view, the transfer of agential features from the individual level to the group level demands a review of the concept of agency and extension to group activity. If statements like (GA) cannot be readily explained with recourse to standard individual action theory, then a more general theory of agency is required. From a practical point of view, statements like (GA) are but a precursor for more important practices. If statements like (GA) really suggest that groups display some new form of agency, then society needs to think about how to interact with groups and hold them responsible. I focus on the theoretical aspect, but this discussion comes with implications for the practical challenges as well.

While the disruption of agency presents a challenge for action theory, it also presents an opportunity. The observation that agential features are externally realized in group activity also means that those features are easily accessible to analysis independently of the individual agents. The analysis of group activity, thus, is an independent source of insight for action theory. The agential features of groups are not integrated into a complex biological system, which is the case for human agents. Consequently, we do not need to rely on introspection, intuition or speculation about human nature to learn about key features of agency. The disruption of agency in group activity, therefore, offers an alternative starting point in thinking about agency in general.

In this chapter, I detail the line of thought just presented. I start by exposing the problem of group activity implied by statements of the form (GA). This is followed by an analysis of interaction of agents in group activity, which features the external realization of agential features as the core principle in group activity. I argue how agent interaction disrupts agency in group activity and discuss how this disruption can be used constructively to generate insight for agency in general.

2.1 Ascription of agency and agent responsibility

Statements of the form (GA)–'Group G did action A'–in our everyday talk seemingly ascribe agency to groups. This raises the question whether or not groups display a genuine form of agency. Since statements of the form (GA) already suggest a positive answer, they are not the best starting point for analysis. Fortunately, ascriptions of agency like (GA) come with a richer context that offers a more appropriate starting point.

Often, ascriptions of agency are merely used to describe something that happened. More importantly, however, ascriptions of agency express a relation between some event or state of affairs and an agent. If an action A leads to a result R in a straight forward manner, then the result R is also ascribed to the agent. The result R, however, is not necessarily ascribed to the agent as an action, but she is *responsible* for R in a basic sense. For the relation between an agent and an event or state of affairs that traces back to her agency, I will use the technical term '*agent responsibility*', or (AR):

> (AR) Agent responsibility is the basic responsibility an agent has for some event or state of affairs R resulting from her agency.

I do not include an action A in (AR) because agent responsibility does not require an action, but only that an event or state of affairs R can be properly ascribed to an agent by way of her agency. If an agent deliberately chooses not to do something, for example, she is also responsible for the results of her omission in the sense of (AR). Furthermore, agent responsibility (AR) may be ascribed for results that are not results of single actions, but many coordinated actions directed towards a single outcome.

This is also the reason why agent responsibility (AR) allows to describe the problem posed by statements about group activity (GA) in a more appropriate form. Group activity is activity of at least two agents who interact with one another. The results from their actions and interactions are the result of the group activity. In most cases, it will not make much sense to ascribe the action A from (GA) to any of the individual members directly. The more interesting question is whether or not the agent responsibility of the individual agents is sufficient to account for agent responsibility implied by (GA), i.e. whether or not the results of group activity can be properly traced back to the agency of the individuals.

In order to answer this question, it must be understood when an agent is responsible for something in the sense of (AR). There are unambiguous cases: when a result R is directly realized by one of my actions A, the action is often redescribed such that the result itself is my action A_R (Anscombe, 1957; Austin, 1956;

Davidson, 1963; Goldman, 1970; Feinberg, 1970; Bratman, 2006b), e.g. my action of blocking a door of a train, which results in a delay of the train, is re-described as my action of delaying the train. In such cases, agent responsibility and agency are two sides of the same coin. When the action A_R is rightly attributed to the agent, then so is agent responsibility for R. Unfortunately, the action A featured in group activity (GA) can usually not be re-described as an action that can be directly ascribed to individual agents.

When agent responsibility is not trivially linked to an agent's action, the conditions for agent responsibility are less clear, but we can draw from the discussion of responsibility in general. Indeed, agent responsibility is but a precursor for more substantial forms of responsibility, which have been thoroughly discussed in philosophical discourse. In particular, I draw on the insights from the discussion of moral responsibility to provide conditions for agent responsibility.

To see the close connection between agent responsibility and moral responsibility, John Mackie's famous "straight rule of responsibility" from his book "Ethics: Inventing right and wrong" (1977) is helpful. Mackie's straight rule reads: "an agent is responsible for all and only his intentional actions" (p.208). At face value, Mackie's straight rule of responsibility has a smaller scope than (AR) because it is limited to actions only, but Mackie proposes a broader understanding of intentionality in agency to overcome this limitation. He refers to Bentham's account of intentionality allowing to also include intended results of actions or accepted side effects into the concept of 'intentional actions' (Bentham, 1988). This interpretation of Mackie's straight rule is already close to the idea of agent responsibility.

The straight rule might still be misleading in its original formulation. Ralf Stoecker, for example, points out that "our own actions are almost the only things in the world we are never responsible for" (Stoecker, 2008, p.38). Indeed, a hooligan is usually made responsible for the pain of the victim and not the action, e.g. 'beating', itself. Additionally, omissions are a problem even for a broad interpretation of the straight rule. Omissions show that people are responsible for something they have let happen. To keep Mackie's straight rule of responsibility intact, one would have to show that omissions are actions, or at least intentional consequences of actions, but this leads into contested territory (Birnbacher, 1996; Foot, 1967; Thomson, 1976). What is true, however, is that a person omitting some action must have been at least able to consider taking action and perform it. Her not doing so is an expression of her agency and makes her responsible in the sense of (AR). Thus, while Mackie's straight rule does not turn out to be as straight forward as it first appears, the discussion only brings agent responsibility and moral responsibility closer together. Therefore, it seems to be a valid approach to draw on insights from moral responsibility and apply them to the more basic notion of agent responsibility.

The nature of moral responsibility, in particular it's appearance in the form of blame and praise, have been discussed for millennia. Aristotle discussed two main reasons to justify not blaming or praising agents, but react with "pardon, and sometimes also pity" instead. According to him, "[t]hose things, [...] which take place under compulsion or owing to ignorance" are excused(Aristotle, 350, 1109b). This and the following passages in Aristotle's "Nichomachean Ethics" are generally read as establishing a 'control condition' and a 'epistemic condition' for moral responsibility (Fischer and Ravizza, 1998, p.13).

The control condition is not specific to moral responsibility. Indeed, it makes immediate sense for agent responsibility as well. If an agent is not in control of what she is doing, she is not exercising agency and, consequently, not responsible for the results. With regard to agency, two types of control are relevant. First, the agent needs *execution control* of some form. If an agent cannot reliably trigger or hold off the execution of something she wants to do, she has no execution control and, in consequence, is not responsible for the results of what she is doing. Second, the agent needs some form of *decision control*, which roughly means that she chooses what she wants to do or what she wants to choose and does so without invasive external influence[1] (Frankfurt, 1971; Watson, 1975). If an agent is forced to do something by threat of life or as a result of some psychological deficiency, she is not responsible for it by way of her agency.

The epistemic condition, on the other hand, is specific to moral responsibility in the sense that it must be specified what an agent should know from a moral perspective. However, it can also be simplified and applied to agent responsibility (AR). For moral responsibility, the epistemic condition has at least two components. First, the agent needs to know what his actions or decisions will bring about. Second, she needs to be able to judge those results from a moral point of view. When the second part is removed, the first part still provides a sensible condition for agent responsibility: an agent brings about many things with her actions and lets many things happen by way of her inaction, but only those she actually knew about and considered can be traced back to her agency in the sense of (AR).

The epistemic condition as it stands only refers to actual knowledge of the agent. It is mute towards the things an agent should have known. Often, however,

---

1 Frankfurt proposes a model of higher order desires allowing agents to have desires about the desires they want to act on. This constitutes the required depth of decision making in agency to properly conceptualize freedom of will, responsibility and personhood in his view. Gary Watson developed another approach by proposing a "valuation system" from which agents draw practical reasons and gain control over their "motivational system" to some extent. Decision control as it is used here is neutral with respect to the depth of decision making in agency but contrasted to mere control about one's body.

we expect agents to know about certain facts and make them responsible because they did not know them. The implicit assumption, I believe, is that the agent is sophisticated enough to simply know certain facts or possibilities and consider them when taking action. When a small child throws a rock from a balcony to see what happens when it hits the ground, we do not expect the child to know that someone could walk by and get hurt. When an adult or older child does it, we cannot help but believe she acted grossly negligent, possibly with malice, because she must have known about this possibility. As soon as an agent neglects or embraces a possible consequence of her actions or decisions, however, the result can be explained within the context of her agency and, consequently, she is responsible for it as an agent.

The adaptation of the discussion of moral responsibility results in two control conditions and one epistemic condition for agent responsibility (AR):

(CAR) Conditions for agent responsibility for a result R:

(ExCC) Execution control condition:
The agent has control over the execution or non-execution of her action decisions that eventually result in R
(DeCC) Decision control condition:
The agent has control over her decisions that eventually result in R
(EC) Epistemic condition:
The agent knows that her decisions and actions result in R, or at least knows that R is a possible consequence.

The conditions for agent responsibility (CAR) help decide whether or not an agent is responsible for some event or state of affairs R by way of her agency. With the notion of agent responsibility and the respective conditions for agent responsibility, the problem posed by statements (GA), which seemingly ascribe actions to groups, can be restated in a neutral manner. The question is whether or not the agents in a group are responsible for the results of the group activity by way of their agency.

2.2 Responsibility voids in group activity

Three claims are possible with respect to the question whether or not agents are responsible for the results of group activity by way of their agency. Either, agents are always responsible for the results of group activity, or they are never responsible for the results of group activity, or they are sometimes responsible for the results of the group activity. The third claim only requires proof that both cases exist; the first two claims are thereby automatically disproved. I take it as given that sometimes the agents are responsible for the results of the group activity. I believe it is more controversial whether or not there are cases in which the individual agents in a group are not responsible for the results of the group activity.

In order to demonstrate that an agent is not responsible for something by way of her agency, in general, one needs to show that at least one of the conditions for agent responsibility (CAR) is not fulfilled. This makes the analysis instructive not only for the question itself, but the explanation reveals how specifically the agency of the agent is disrupted with respect to R.

In the discussion of agent responsibility in group activity, therefore, it is instructive to look at cases that display what is sometimes referred to as a *responsibility voids* (Braham and van Hees, 2011, e.g.). Using the terminology introduced above, responsibility voids can be understood as:

> (RV) Responsibility voids occur whenever no agent is responsible for some event or state of affairs by way of her agency.

When only one agent is involved, the explanation of responsibility voids is nontrivial though, at least in theory, straight forward. We merely have to check whether or not the conditions for responsibility (CAR) are obtained. If they are not obtained, we face a responsibility void, and the agent is excused based on a specific disruption of her agency. In group activity, when more agents are involved, the analysis of responsibility voids is more complicated due to the interaction of multiple agents. Indeed, I show that the distinctiveness of responsibility voids in group activity is given by how the agents interact with each other, which is fundamentally different from interaction with mere objects in the environment in individual cases.

I start with an analysis of minimal interactions and introduce more complex interactions step by step.

2.2.1 Minimal interaction

I begin with a case that features three agents producing some result that none directly intended. Imagine a successful business with three accountants in different departments, each of which decide to embezzle money from the business for their own purposes. Taken together, they overdo it and ruin the business, while none of them intended to do so. Surely, the individuals are responsible for their individual acts of embezzlement, but who is responsible for ruining the business? The answer to this question depends on the relation between the fraudulent accountants.

First, it is possible that the accountants do not know of each other. In this case, there is no interaction at all, and we can simply assess the conditions for responsibility for each agent separately. The assessment may be difficult, especially with respect to the epistemic condition, i.e. the question whether or not the accountants should have known about the possibility of ruining the business. In order to be responsible for bankrupting the business, the agents have to be aware of the risk and have no good reason to believe the risk is neglectfully small. Given that the sum of the embezzlements are large enough such that three of them suffice to ruin the business, it is very likely that the accountants have considered the potentially devastating effect on the business. However, a full assessment requires the details of the case. No matter the result of the assessment, it is a mere contingency that the three accountants contributed to ruining the business.

The case becomes more interesting, when the accountants know of each other's activities. In particular, by introducing an element of overdetermination, a paradoxical situation arises when we compare a synchronous scenario with a progressive scenario. Consider the case that any two of the three financial frauds suffice to ruin the business, and they occur one after another. Given that the ruin is already a matter of fact before the last act of embezzlement has taken place, it is hard to argue that the last accountant is also responsible for the ruin. David Lewis discussed this type of 'causal preemption' in his 1973's paper "Causation" as a challenge for technical accounts of causal responsibility, but it challenges our intuition about agent responsibility as well. In the progressive case, we are inclined to say that the preempted accountant is not responsible for ruining the business, neither causally nor in any other way. By way of symmetry, the same logic should be applied to all of the accountants in the synchronous case. Our intuition about the synchronous case, however, usually does not follow this logic: if the three accountants recognize that each of them is cheating the business, yet, still go through with it, they are responsible. Why is there a difference between the synchronous case and the progressive case when the result is over-determined by the individual actions?

Notably, the difference vanishes, when we replace two of the accountants by some natural event, e.g., a hurricane that hits the main factory and inflicts heavy damage, which ruins the business. The remaining accountant is not responsible for the ruin of the business, which was already a matter of fact due to the hurricane. The hurricane tragically ruins the business, the accountant does not. This seems true for both, when the hurricane and the fraud occur one after another or at the same time. When we take the perspective of the third accountant in both progressive scenarios, it is a matter of fact that the business is ruined. The reason for the ruin, be it a hurricane or other fraudulent accountants, has little relevance. The replacement in the synchronous case, for some reason, does matter. Therefore, the solution to the paradox lies in the difference between natural events like hurricanes and agents, not so much in the difference of timing or causal structure.

Gunnar Björnsson observes the same problem in his 2011's paper "Joint Responsibility without Individual Control: applying the Explanation Hypotheses" from a similar example featuring three polluters and a lake. He suggests that "*[t]aken together* [the polluters] played a significant causal role in wiping out the fish; *individually*, they did not" and concludes that "the responsibility attributed to the three is fundamentally collective"(Björnsson, 2011, p.184). Indeed, a new fundamental type of responsibility for agents would solve the problem, but it is also a rather far reaching stipulation. I suggest looking at more accessible differences between hurricanes and agents to explain the paradoxical situations in cases of overdetermination.

When the hurricane and the single accountant harm the business, the options for the accountant are limited. If the hurricane does not hit, her fraud will not ruin the business. If the hurricane does hit and ruins the business, her fraud does not ruin the business either–it already is ruined from the hurricane's damage to the factory. Consequently, independently of the certainty of the hurricane's occurrence, she may proceed with her fraud without being responsible for ruining the business.

In comparison, when three accountants harm the business, there are more options. When the accountants realize that their embezzlements will ruin the business, they can refrain from embezzling or reduce the amount of damage done to the business *given that at least one other accountant does so as well*. The accountants have the option to interact with each other, conspire, to make sure their frauds do not ruin the business rendering them out of work and likely to be discovered. This requires that the agents are responsive to the considerations of one another. Hurricanes are not responsive in this way, but agents are. Indeed, this seems to be the essence of what this paradox implies: when agents do things together, their decisions need not depend only on the knowledge of the other agents' actual actions, but on the other agents' considerations as well.

The paradoxical situation, therefore, should vanish when we differentiate between a scenario in which it is possible for the agents to communicate their considerations and a scenario in which the interaction of the agents is severely restricted such that they must rely only on their knowledge about what the other agents are about to do.

In the first scenario, the accountants know about each other's action plans, but also about their background considerations. Maybe they checked the books, noticed some dubious figures and contacted one another. In their conversation, they find out eventually that each of them is willing to hold back on the frauds or reduce them so that the business is not ruined. The ability to adjust to each other's considerations allows the agents to exercise the sort of control required for agent responsibility. The agents must deliberately ignore or accept the ruin of the business in this scenario, if they went through with their embezzlements unchanged. This would make them responsible individually.

However, it is also plausible that the accountants do not have the opportunity to reveal their considerations to each other. They may have checked the books and noticed irregularities, but due to limitations of time, resources or fear of being discovered they do not contact one another to collaborate. In this case, the perspective from the individual accountant really is identical to the scenario of the hurricane: the knowledge about the indicated actions of the other two accountants gives her no reason to act differently with regard to the ruin of the business. If anything, she is motivated to hurry up and cover her tracks well to protect herself from certain investigation after the ruin of the business. This is perfectly compatible with the fact that none of the accountants wants to ruin the business and would be willing to reduce the fraud, or completely cancel it, given that at least one of the others would do so as well. In this scenario, indeed, none of the agents seems responsible for the ruin of the business by way of their agency given a good reason why they could not collaborate.

This conclusion is in line with the discussion of moral responsibility for random collectives by Virgina Held (Held, 1970). She claimed that random collections of agents like the accountants in the scenarios above are responsible for "forming [themselves] into an organized group" if a collaborative effort could prevent harm in an easily perceivable way (p.476). If forming an organized group is not possible or reasonable, consequently, the random collective is not responsible. The reason for responsibility voids in such scenarios of minimal interaction with an element of overdetermination, thus, is the inability of the agents to lift their interaction to a level beyond interaction of things. In fact, the discussion suggests that when the agents do start to interact in more substantial ways, then the responsibility voids disappear and the results of the group activity can be properly linked to the agency of the individuals.

Indeed, the introduction of more elaborate interaction allows the agents to exercise more control over what happens. As a consequence, it only makes sense that the reach of their agency increases. At the same time, however, the introduction of new interactions also introduces more complexity and new difficulties for the explanation of the results of group activity by way of the individual's agency, as I discuss next.

2.2.2 Simple coordination and collective agency

Situations in which agents cannot or do not communicate, while being close and even bringing about some effect together are possible, but atypical. Indeed, we might challenge the idea that the accountants from our example above ruin the business owner 'together' in any substantial sense. The way in which the word 'together' is used merely seems to be pointing out that more than one agent is somehow involved.

More typically, when we are doing something with someone else, we interact in many and possibly complex ways. In particular, when agents come together to bring something about in a joint effort, they start to coordinate themselves. The discussion of minimal interaction in the last sections has shown that we must set apart such coordination from cases in which agents merely adjust their actions to what they know is going on. Agents do that with inanimate objects, but it would be odd to say, for instance, that I coordinate my actions with the wind in order to successfully sail. Coordination, in contrast, aims at the different agents' considerations in order to produce effective interaction. Agents who coordinate do not merely adjust their actions to other agents' actions, but they already adjust their considerations which leads to properly coordinated actions.

I start with an analysis of simple coordination methods in group activity and discuss their impact on agency.

2.2.2.1 Plain split

One of the simplest coordination methods is to split a task into smaller tasks, which are distributed among the agents. Splitting up a task can take several forms; the most simple of which is a plain split into similar or identical tasks. Imagine, for example, a pile of construction material needs to be moved to another location. Several agents may simply agree to each carry some of the material. Alternatively, they form a chain and each of them carries the material a small distance. The split may also respect the different capabilities and availabilities of the agents. Strong women, for example, agree to carry heavy pieces, or women with free time in the morning offer to begin moving the pile, so that others can join in later. In either case, the task of moving the pile of construction material is split into more or less identical sub-tasks that directly contribute to the completion of the group task.

The plain split of a task already comes with significant practical advantages. Agents can cope with tasks that go beyond what anyone of them could do alone, and they are enabled to optimize performance with regard to the agents' individual capabilities or availabilities. In order to achieve this, however, the agents need to establish an information flow between them. They might nod, point, or simply talk to each other. This information flow will sometimes fail due to external circumstances. To illustrate, consider the following example: my wife and I decide to share the duty of watering our plants and take turns. To successfully coordinate the split of the task, we agree to remind each other and help out if one of us is unable to do it. On one particularly hot summer day, it is my turn. My wife wants to make sure that we manage to water the plants and asks whether or not I already watered the plants. Having not done it yet and being in hurry for a business trip, I quickly say 'Uh...yes, right...I did forget again. Can you do it? See you tomorrow. Bye, Love' and rush out. My wife is in the other room and not all words come through which is why she understands 'Yes...I did. Can you do it tomorrow? Bye, Love.' As a result, the plants do not get watered, and one of them dries up—was that a result of the agency of either myself, or my wife, or both?

Clearly, I forgot to water the plants, but that possible failure was covered by our coordination method to split the task: my wife would remind me and, if necessary, help me out. She did remind me and I responded properly leaving the watering to her. I did everything that one could expect me to do. She, on the other hand, also did not water the flowers, because she misunderstood what I said by no fault of her own. She, too, did everything that one could expect her to do. Neither of us knew that the plant would dry up due to our failure of watering it, and we took reasonable care. Thus, neither of us is responsible by way of our agency, but we simply misunderstood one another.

This example shows that even the simplest form of coordination bears the possibility of a responsibility void due to a failure in the information flow caused by a misunderstanding. The general idea of responsibility voids based on faulty information flows was noted by French in his book "Corporate Ethics" (1995) and used by, e.g., Neuhäuser in "Unternehmen als moralische Akteure" (2011)[2] to discuss collective responsibility. This idea is important because it is specific for group activity. What makes it specific to group activity is a core principle that enables effective group activity: as long as I water the plants myself, the information that relates my actions to each other belongs with me. As soon as I am part of a group, even if it is only a two person group, this internal information flow needs to be replaced by an external information flow. I refer to this principle by the technical term *external realization of agential features*:

> (ERAF) External realizations of agential features are agential features that are constituted by some mechanism, process or structure external to individual agents,

where an agential feature is broadly understood as:

---

2 French describes in detail several real world cases of company activity and how the involved agents were not responsible due to insufficient or faulty information flows, e.g., the Exxon Valdez oil spill (French, 1995, p.217–18) and the Hooker Chemical pollution of Love Canal (p.28–31). Neuhäuser applies Herbert Simon's concept of bounded rationality (Simon, 1979) to group activity and notes that the information reaching individual agents is in part optimized to reduce complexity leading to potentially flawed decision making (Neuhäuser, 2011, p.78).

(AF) An agential feature is any feature of an agent required for exercising a particular instance of agency.

Agential features by this definition are not a fixed set of features necessary or sufficient for agency, but merely features without which a particular action or a particular display of agency in general would not be possible. Some agential features are always necessary for successful agency. Such is the case with basic information flows between the different faculties of an agent, but often times the features will enable the execution only of a specific action, or be merely supplementary for a more comfortable or simpler execution.

Consequently, the external realization of agential features does not necessarily undermine the agency of the individual agent. What we have seen from the discussion of one of the simplest methods of coordination, however, already shows how the external realization of agential feature affects the agency of agents in group activity with non-trivial interactions. The agents externalize the information flow required for coordinating the actions of different agents. As long as the external information flow works flawlessly, we may not even notice the fundamental change of how we act. However, as soon as the information flow is corrupted, we realize that an important enabling feature of our agency is no longer part of our individual agency. This is how I propose to understand the disruption of agency in group activity.

2.2.2.2 Procedural split

The splitting of tasks may also take more complicated forms. For an elaborate action, an agent usually engages in deliberation preceded by interpretation of observations and climaxing in a decision that is carried out by the agent. In groups, this procedure can be split up and distributed among the agents. When we think back to the pile of construction material that needs to be relocated, for example, it may be the case that picking up some of the pieces without care can cause a dangerous collapse. Therefore, one of the experienced agents becomes the forewoman and carefully chooses which pieces to pick, while the other agents do the heavy lifting without making any decisions. Another agent may direct the construction of the new pile without instability issues. The idea is that the agents focus only on particular parts of the activity and need not worry about the other parts. Naturally, the parts must be linked in some efficient way.

As before, an external flow of information is required that is at least as disruptive for agency as before and, consequently, equally prone to responsibility voids due to misunderstanding. However, what the agents do are no longer stand alone actions, and they do not merely exchange some background information.

Instead, the different actions highly depend on each other to the extent that they achieve nothing alone, or even counter-act the purpose of the group activity. In individual agency, the different stages towards execution of actions are linked by various cognitive features. When we plan some action, for example, we draw on a wealth of experience and knowledge about the specifics of our action performance. We know how we do something, how reliable we are, how fast we adapt to sudden changes and so on and so forth. Clearly, the information flow between the different agents in group activity can carry only a small fraction of its internal counterpart. Thus, the agents can only share the most relevant information, but must rely on assumptions that fit each other's role in the group activity.

The procedural split of tasks, thus, runs into trouble that goes beyond misunderstanding. Corresponding to a portion of the group activity, the procedural split establishes roles for the different agents. The introduction of more or less defined roles allows the agents to properly link their actions, but they are prone to misconception. The forewoman, for example, naturally assumes that the carriers carry the pieces of construction material essentially the way she would carry them, or, at least, that the different carriers carry the pieces roughly the same way. To her surprise, however, one of the carriers lets her piece drop onto the assigned spot, instead of putting it down slowly–maybe she is tired or her back hurts. Unfortunately, the forewoman did not expect such an unusual performance in her decision making and the unfinished pile collapses from the impact. There was at no point a misunderstanding or a failure of information flow. The different activities–deliberating about where to put the piece and actually putting down the piece–simply presupposed sensible facts: the forewoman assumed the carrier puts down the piece of material normally with no effect on the yet unstable pile. The carrier, not aware of temporary instabilities in the unfinished pile, assumed it would not matter how she puts down her piece as long as she puts it down in the right place. Both, the forewoman and the carrier fell victim to a misconception of each others' roles–a reasonable misconception which they must make to efficiently work together.

Splitting a task procedurally is a great idea to get the best out of the abilities of the involved agents, but it comes with a greater need for information flows, and it requires agents to trust that the other agents perform their roles based on reasonable conceptions. If the externally defined roles are insufficient or display unexpected features, the link between the different action stages fail and create, even in cases with proper information flow, responsibility voids grounded in a misconception of the other agents' roles. In these cases, too, the agency of the individuals is disrupted in the sense that they give up control not only of the other stages of action to other agents, but also rely on externally defined roles and their specifics.

2.2.2.3 Rules

The external realization of agential features is not obvious when the only method of coordination is a split of tasks. A more explicit case, which is equally common, is the introduction of rules. Rules can be restrictive or prescriptive and often both elements come together in a set of rules. A work-contract, for example, often specifies broadly what the employee and the employer are expected to do—it is prescriptive—but it also specifies what the employee and the employer are not allowed to do, which is clearly restrictive.

Restrictive rules are usually not used for coordination, but avoidance or mediation of conflicts by restricting the range of allowed actions or behavior in general. The playful version of this is found in most competitive games. A set of rules defines what the players are allowed to do in proving their superiority. Nonetheless, there are also cases in which restrictive rules are used for coordination, e.g., when a restrictive rule prevents double work.

Prescriptive rules, on the other hand, prescribe a particular course of action to individual agents in specific circumstances. The course of action suggested by a rule, ideally, draws from knowledge and experience, which makes it superior to what the agent herself would come up with. Such rules relieve the agent from asking for advice or going through the thought process herself. Prescriptive rules can also be used by individuals to control their own behavior on future occasions. More commonly, however, they are used in group activity as a powerful tool for coordination. A group that relies on rules reduces the need for constant communication and increases reliability and quality at the same time. Rules even enable the coordination of actions of agents who are not aware of each other's existence, or have not interacted personally, but only with the person providing them with the rule.

Rules enable agents to act without giving it another thought. From a pragmatic perspective, this is very useful. In games, restrictive rules allow us to test our limits in a relatively safe, recreational environment. It allows us to fight our friendly or hostile disputes. In more serious circumstances, rules allow for predictability and reliability in high pressure situations, where erratic behavior would otherwise dominate. Whenever people are overwhelmed, unable or simply unreasonable, rules are of greatest importance and value. Even if you are not overwhelmed, unable or simply unreasonable, it usually is a good idea to thoroughly verify your own reasoning before breaking a well-established rule. This implies that the decision control of an agent is weakened substantially by rules, if not completely by-passed. Rules are externally realized reasoning principles, which quite literally over-rule the agents other reasoning principles.

In conclusion, the introduction of rules into group activity allows for coordinated group activity without a need of active interaction in specific situations. This is a great, often indispensable advantage. At the same time, rules prescribe specific actions or types of actions such that agents are relieved from making decisions, especially in demanding situations. Following the rules is usually the right thing to do, and it usually improves the agents' performance. Yet, rules fail to fit all situations. Eventually, the application of rules will in some situations lead to results that were neither intended by the designers of the rules, nor the applicants.

Compared to the information flows and role conception of the previous examples, rules introduce a very easily observable external mechanism of coordination. Furthermore, the feature that is externalized is more substantial with regard to agency. Rules codify reasoning of the form, e.g., 'If situation S arises, do A', which ideally draws from expert knowledge and experience. Note, how this changes how an individual acts. Instead of deliberating different action options, or acting from the agent's own experience or habituation, the agent acts on an externally provided rule possibly against better personal judgment. As a consequence, decision control of the individual agents is diminished. Clearly, this is a significant disruption of an individual's agency, which is exactly why responsibility voids occur.

2.2.2.4 Disruption of agency in simple group activity

The discussion of three of the simplest methods of coordination shows that even in rudimentary group activity the interaction of the agents can lead to responsibility voids. Misinformation due to corrupt information flows, misconception of the individuals' roles and misapplication of rules are the reasons the voids occur. In all cases, some feature required for successful agency is externally realized in order to allow the agents to coordinate their actions. This enables them to achieve what neither of them could achieve alone, but it also disrupts their individual agency such that the results of their activity cannot be explained entirely by way of the individual agents' agency, i.e. the agent responsibility of the individuals does not cover the results of the group activity.

Notably, I have discussed only group activity failing to produce a desired result. The reason was that a failure can usually be traced back to a very specific source, thereby teaching us something about agency in group activity. However, we need to consider how the results of the discussion of responsibility voids in cases of failure transfer to cases of success. If the agents are not necessarily responsible for the failure, are they also not responsible in case of success? The answer to this question depends on how deeply the individuals' agency is disrupted. Either the externalized agential feature *itself* takes away a crucial aspect of the individual's agency, or it is only *a failure* in the externalized agential features disrupting the individual's agency. If the responsibility void is only due to a failure, it does not transfer to cases of successful group activity. The failure is simply an external influence disrupting the individual agents' agency. This is identical to external disruptions when an agent is acting alone. In contrast, if responsibility voids occur because the agents give up a crucial feature of their own agency in order to empower agent interaction, then they are likely to transfer to cases of success as well.

Regarding the three methods of coordination discussed above, only rules have the potential to disrupt individual agency in such a fundamental way. If the agents in a group create an information flow to coordinate the individual actions, this is merely helpful for the individuals to perform well together. If they are successful, this clearly goes back to their performance as agents. This was the first case that I discussed. The second coordination method was based on implicit or explicit definitions of roles. This allows a procedural split of a task, but relies on how the individual's conceive the roles. This, too, does not take a way an important aspect of agency from the individuals, but merely allows the different agents to perform the task of the group activity best fitting their skill set. When a group introduces rules, the third example of simple coordination methods discussed above, the agency of individuals is potentially affected in a more substantial way. Rules provide reasoning principles that may override the agent's own considerations. If something goes wrong, the agent may claim she only (and rightly) followed the agreed upon rule. If everything goes according to plan, however, it is also possible that the agent merely applies the rule and is not responsible for the outcome by way of her agency. She may not know what the outcome of applying the rule is supposed to be, but merely applies it because the conditions obtain. Surely, she is responsible for applying the rule, but she may not be responsible for the outcome. The outcry 'I just followed the rules' has to be critically evaluated in each case, but it is a valid excuse in at least some cases.

In cases of simple group activity, however, rules will rarely have such a strong impact on the agents. It is hard to conceive how a handful of agents may agree upon rules disrupting their agency in such a fundamental manner. Instead, rules, as with the other simple coordination methods, allow the agents to efficiently exercise their agency towards a specific result. The external realization of agential features enables them to combine their potency as agents and multiply it. The binding element of external agential features gives a sense of collectivity, while the important aspects of agency remain with the individual agents. In this sense, I use the term *collective agency* to capture the character of simple group activity:

(CollAg) Collective agency is a broad term for group activity characterized by external realizations of agential features such that the agents interact in a meaningful sense, yet, are fully responsible for the results of the group activity by way of their individual agency as long as the external agential features function properly.

2.2.3 Complex coordination and corporate agency

Up to now, I implicitly referred to small-scale cases of doing something together. More elaborate forms of coordination are usually found in large-scale cases of working together. Starting from where I left off, I discuss the next level of rule-based coordination, namely, standardization, automation and, potentially, computerization in group activity. This already has great impact on how we perceive group activity, but two further phenomena turn out to completely reshape the way we act together. *Diffusion* is the term I use to describe the practice that agential features central to agency are divided and distributed over the involved agents such that no single person owns or even oversees the entire structure. I discuss diffusion of means-goal structures as a particularly common and important method in group activity. *Alienation* is the term I use to describe the practice that agential features relevant for group activity are smartly linked to agential features on the individual level. Again, I discuss alienation of the means-goal structure in group activity.

With diffusion and alienation, individual agency in group activity is disrupted in a way that responsibility voids not only come up when something in the external agential feature goes wrong, but even when everything works as it is supposed to, i.e. even in successful group activity the individuals are not responsible for the results by way of their agency. This is what generally characterizes *corporate activity*.

2.2.3.1 Standardization, Automation, Computerization
In the previous section, I discussed coordination by simple rules. Rules can be evolved into, for example, standard working procedures, automation and computerization. These rule-based methods are often used to support effective splitting of tasks, but they also do more.

Standard working procedures are not merely prescriptive rules for individual agents; they are detailed execution guidelines, which not only specify what to do but also how to do it. Every important aspect of the action is spelled out and the agent merely becomes the body that executes the action. The agent does not even need to know what she is doing, but merely needs to follow the instructions. In fact, the agent need not know anything about the overall activity in order to follow the procedures. Standard working procedures externalize execution plans, something that usually the individual agent comes up with, when she thinks about how to do something. Standard working procedures also reduce the need for communication between agents drastically. Consequently, failures of information flow are less likely to occur, and so are responsibility voids due to misunderstanding. At the same time, working procedures are often defined in such a detailed way that the risk of misconception, too, is reduced significantly in comparison to simple rules.

In an automated process, this goes even one step further. The individual becomes a part in a process, a body that moves. After a short while, the agents need not even actively control their actions, and this is exactly what automation is aimed at: the elimination of any influence of the individual traits of the executing agent. The individual agents can be replaced by any other individual with the same, usually not very demanding motor skills. The paradigmatic example is, of course, the industrial assembly line worker in mass production. Automation guarantees that a task is done exactly as it is supposed to be done. Responsibility voids due to misconception are virtually impossible in an established automated process. Since the environment is controlled as well, misapplication is also almost always a fault of the executing agent and responsibility voids are unlikely to occur.

At this point, coordination has reached a form, in which the individual agents are interchangeable. As we have seen, this has the advantage of reducing the occurrence of responsibility voids by reducing the possibility of error. But it also opens up a possibility that was not present before. Agents in an automated or standardized environment get along without knowing much about the overall activity. They also get along without thinking much about what they do or what they are part of. This allows for significantly larger groups to work together for two reasons. First, the need for communication is greatly reduced so that more agents can participate, while still being efficient. Second, the cognitive requirements for participation are lowered drastically and, consequently, allow agents to participate without understanding or even knowing about the overall activity. At the same time, those forms of coordination systematically make it unlikely for the agents to fulfill the requirements for agent responsibility. They have no decision control, even their execution control is reduced to controlling their body movements according to the automated work steps, and they may know nothing or little of the results of their actions.

In fact, in some cases so little is required of the agents that they are replaced by robots or software or other technological solutions. Even the physical control itself, so to say, is externalized. This step is a consequent continuation of the previous practices, but it also fundamentally changes the view on agency. Suddenly, it is not actions of agents that are coordinated, but the tasks executed by machines and the agents vanish altogether. Obviously, we still require agents. Most machines and software need to be developed, operated, supervised and repaired. But it is not clear that those agents are responsible for what the machines do, it is not clear that, e.g., software is a simple extension of the programmer's agency.

In "The Responsibility Gap" (2004), Andreas Matthias points at several technological advances that imply, first, that "the programmer role changes from *coder* to *creator* of software organisms" (p.182) and, second, that *"errors are unavoidable features of any reinforcement learning system* [...] and not merely a product flaw" (p.179). The impact on agency from these paradigmatic changes in our technological progress can hardly be overstated. For self-learning software implemented on neural networks, for example, it is unknown how information can be extracted or directly manipulated in order to achieve a specific result. Evolutionary algorithms solve complex problems by adapting themselves over and over again, which eventually results in code that is often superior to what any human programmer could have written directly in comparable time spans. The programmer really does change from coder to creator of such software organisms. At the same time the programmer loses control not only about the execution, but also simple decision making.

The power of neural networks and evolutionary algorithms lies in their learning capabilities. To harvest this power, however, they are to be trained in the target environment–the robots or software have to learn by trial and error. Errors, thus, are a necessary element of the process, much like it is for human learning. The programmers are not responsible for these kinds of errors in the sense that they are a result of their agency. Instead, if we want to use powerful software in robots or computers to help us, we have to accept that they produce results that cannot be traced back to the programmers.

Operators or engineers are also not responsible in those cases. Many software products are autonomous nowadays; they do not even need an operator. At best, a human agent may supervise them, but the software may have a large advantage in information quantity and processing. Matthias gives navigation computers and radar-based flight control as examples. Indeed, it seems supervision may be reduced to powering up and shutting down the software. Additionally, the software needs engineers or programmers, who fix broken parts, if they can be fixed. Matthias gives convincing support for all of this and rightly concludes that we are faced by ever increasing responsibility voids.

While this technology-based responsibility void is not specific to group activity, the reason for its occurrence is of the same nature: agential features are externalized to machines and software and the agents lose control about these features eventually. With regard to group activity and agent interaction, two types of uses are particularly relevant. First, technology can be used just as it is used outside group activity, i.e. to externalize the actual action execution and immediate decision-making around action execution. Given that execution control and basic decision making are central features of agency, this is a substantial disruption of agency in group activity as pointed out above. Second, however, technology can also be used to coordinate agents in group activity. Modern postal services, for example, rely mainly on intelligent software to coordinate the deliverymen[3]. More and more maintenance services employ complex software to manage efficient assignment of engineers[4]. Since these are highly computational problems, the software results are usually superior to what a human would come up with. In other words, technology takes over complex problem solving and decision making about what human agents are supposed to do in the group activity. The results–faster delivery of service, minimal down-time of work-force, fewer errors–are not results of an agent exercising her agency, unless, of course, one is willing to view software organisms as agents.

Use of technology, as a consistent continuation of standardization and automation, thus, produces responsibility voids that not only apply to failed activity, but to successful activity as well. The externally realized agential features are central to agency, but no longer belong to an agent. This is a deep disruption of agency. Even when we set aside technology and only consider group activity that uses standardization and automation of human actions, agency is impacted in a similar way. While the individual agents are responsible for their particular actions, it will often be the case that they are not responsible for the overall results of the group activity by way of their agency. Thinking of the classical assembly line worker, whose actions within the group activity are completely dictated by standards and automation, it is even problematic to identify how exactly she still is a part of the group activity, rather than just an executing agent for others.

2.2.3.2 Diffusion

What is the deeper insight behind the intuition that the assembly line worker is contributing to a greater activity, yet, is not viewed as a part of the overall activity? One reason is the interchangeability due to a meticulous split into standardized or automated sub-tasks, which evolved from a rule-based approach to coordination through splitting tasks. Clearly, such elaborate coordination requires supervision. In fact, it quickly takes an entire agent's time and effort to coordinate or supervise the coordination of the actions of all involved agents. We observe this in essentially

---

3 Accenture, for example, published a report about the post and parcel industry highlighting AI solutions that augment labor and optimize the delivery network (Accenture, 2016).
4 An impressive example is the AI-based coordination of more than 10,000 maintenance workers in the Hong Kong subway system. The network has a near perfect on time record compared to human-organized networks (Hodson, 2014).

every modern large-scale group activity, e.g., within companies. However, the need for coordination or supervision of large scale group activity inevitably leads to a serious problem: eventually, no single person can coordinate all the actions. More so, no single person can even oversee or supervise the entire structure. Distinct divisions are created, departments within divisions, units within departments, projects across many of these and so on and so forth. It is easy to see how such a structure becomes unmanageable for a single person. How are, for example, companies still functional despite this problem?

Clearly, the overall activity has to be split into manageable units. This is the very idea of creating an organizational structure. More importantly, the units have to be linked such that their work properly contributes the overall activity. To achieve this, it is not enough to have an organizational structure, but an additional structure linking the units within the organizational structure is required. In most cases, this simply is a means-goal structure. Means-goal structures are well known from individual agency. We usually start out with goals, figure out how to achieve them by creating a chain of sub-goals and means. In group activity, this structure needs to be made explicit and cut into over-lapping means-goal units that can be managed by the agents. That means different means-goal units govern different agents' actions within the group activity. The means-goal structure is *diffused* over the group in the form of means-goal units.

The *diffusion* of the means-goal structure can then be mirrored by a company structure as indicated above, e.g., different departments for development, production, marketing, sales and so on. A sales officer is only concerned with everything around the sale of a product and need not be concerned with the company's strategy to gain market share or the actual production of the product. The overall goals of the company are split into manageable units and the different agents are assigned to the various units. The employees concerned with a particular unit of this means-goal structure need not share, or even know, the overall goals or the goals of different units.

In fact, different units within such a structure might have competing goals and conflicts erupt. The marketing department might fight the development department over resources within the company. This is simply a consequence of the insight that distinct means-end units are created such that every agent only has one or few in sight. This is true vertically within an organizational structure, i.e. the top-manager only oversees the means-end structures down to some depth, and the low-tier manager or employee only oversees the means-end structure up to some level. It is also true horizontally, i.e. the manager of one department may have a completely different means-end unit from another. Aside from conflicts with each other, diffusion can also lead to conflicts and incoherence in execution. Imagine Wonderland University is in fiscal trouble. In order to earn more money, the WU leadership focuses on the attraction of more students. The different departments receive a memo to actively promote their disciplines. The economics department immediately starts a campaign highlighting the efficiency of fast-track programs and well-structured study plans at WU. At the same time, the literature department starts an equally well-executed campaign highlighting the flexibility in course choice and absence of streamlined education at the WU. Clearly, the means chosen by the different departments send conflicting messages to potential students and may even make the WU less attractive for students.

I identified external realization of agential features to be the general principle allowing efficient group activity. At the same time, externalization leads to responsibility voids as discussed above. Diffusion of means-goal structures also externalizes an agential feature, viz. the structure that connects means to goals. Usually, we find a unity of means and goals within one agent, which respects rather strict rationality constraints so as to avoid, e.g., contradicting means. In diffused groups, the unity is broken, and the only way to avoid conflicts, like the one at Wonderland University, is to communicate. It does not suffice to have a single individual oversee the communication to assure unity, however, because the assumption was that it is not possible for a single individual to oversee all levels of activity. Consequently, failures can be minimized by effective communication, but this communication cannot compensate flawed means-goal diffusion.

I discussed diffusion using the example of means-goals structures and large-scale groups, but both restrictions can be lifted and the concept of diffusion easily generalized. Next to the means-goal structure, there are many other agential features that can be divided into overlapping, self-sufficient units and spread over various agents such that the individual agents are only involved in one or a few of the units. Complex decision making, for example, can be easily diffused into a group of agents by splitting up, e.g., information gathering, analysis, interpretation, solution generation and definition of decision criteria. All of these parts of decision making can be structured through self-sufficient units that require the full attention of one or more individuals, e.g., an entire team's only purpose may very well be the acquisition of certain information, and that is all they are doing from their perspective. The structure that ties the different units together may partly be overseen by individual agents, but it might also be controlled by fixed procedures, which are only supervised or changed if a need arises to do so. Diffusion, therefore, is a coordination principle not tied to a particular agential feature but it is applicable quite generally.

The second restriction to large-scale activity is not required either. Large-scale activity only makes diffusion indispensable, but it may also be viable in cases that could do without it. The practical advantages will often outweigh the practical disadvantages. Diffusion is even imaginable in three person cases: the three agents may know that all of them are somehow involved in the overall activity, but each agent only knows about the specific connection of her part of the overall activity to the other's parts. What none of them know is how the two others are connected and how this figures into the entire group activity. Clearly, with only 3 agents involved, we have to assume a certain ignorance on the agents' part, but maybe they are busy with other things or they simply dislike each other very much and minimize communication as much as possible. Typically, however, diffusion is employed whenever it is easy to lose oversight and self-sufficient units are required to coordinate effectively. For later reference, I summarize:

> (Diff) Diffusion is a coordination method splitting up an agential feature into over-lapping, but independent units. Individual agents may only operate with one or few such units to contribute to the overall activity.

While the practical advantages of diffusion are obvious, it has a deep issue. Consider diffusion of means-end structures. We can think of a large group with a diffused means-end structure as a group of sub-groups. The goals of lower-tier sub-groups are given by the means for the goals of higher-tier sub-groups. On the group-level, they form a connected structure. The individuals within the sub-groups, however, may only care about the goals and means of their sub-group. This was exactly the purpose of the diffusion mechanism. For individual agents, consequently, the connection to the group as a whole may remain abstract. The goals from an agent's everyday experience do not sufficiently connect to a larger purpose. This explains how an agent still is part of the group as a whole, but in a much different sense than she would be in a non-diffused group. She may fail to identify with the purpose of the group activity on any other level than her own. This down-side of diffusion is almost inevitable for agents like the assembly line worker, but I will discuss now that the deep challenge for group activity results in an even more fundamental disruption of agency that affects agents on all tiers.

2.2.3.3 Alienation
The downside of diffusion is a loss of identification of the individuals' activity with the group activity. For the case of a diffused means-goal structure, a loss of purpose is particularly plausible, especially for employees at the lower end of the structure like the automobile assembly line worker. Individuals will distance themselves from what they are doing due to the lack of purpose or a failure to identify with what they do in general. Consequently, they need additional motivation different from the purpose of the overall activity. In companies, the lack of purpose is often compensated for by providing personal benefits connected to the goals of the

group activity. The assembly line worker may be motivated by the money at each end of the month. The boss of the assembly line worker may be motivated by the money and the pleasure of ordering people around. The manager of the factory may be motivated by the respect she earns in her community from her job. The manager's protégé may be motivated by the outlook of being in the manager's position. None of them is motivated at their job to actually motorize the country, earn the shareholders profits or build the best cars in the world; all of which could be viable goals of an automobile manufacturer. The mechanism of mirroring a group's goals and means with individual goals or benefits is what I call *alienation*.

Alienation is not necessarily a bad thing. The often inevitable lack of purpose, which eventually arises in sufficiently fine-grained diffuse group activity, needs to be addressed in order to sustain the overall activity. Yet, the consequences of alienation are somewhat disturbing. Next to a structure of overlapping but independent means-goals units, a shadow structure of individual goals and the translation from the former into the latter must be added. Indeed, a main task of implementing a business strategy is to find proper incentives for the employees to actually support the company's course. From the employee's perspective, what they do is a means to their individual goals, which is intelligently arranged to also be a means to the group's goals. They do not share the overall goals anymore; there is no common motivating root whatsoever. This is exactly what is disturbing about the assembly line worker.

Alienation, however, does not only affect the assembly line worker, as already pointed out. It works at every level of a group structure. It is easily imaginable that a large part or even an entire group consists only of alienated agents. The alienated individuals interact with each other, but not in pursuit of some common goal. They are instead individual agents within the environment given by the group. Yet, they still are part of the overall activity. Quite literally, two layers of agency are created, or at least a central feature of agency is split into two layers; a purely individual layer that takes place within a group layer. The idea of agency within agency is a first indication that the disruption of agency is not merely destructive towards individual agency, but potentially creates a new form of agency that goes beyond individual agency.

To better understand the surfacing of different layers of agency, it helps to understand what alienation does in terms of externalization of agential features. On the one hand, goals and corresponding means are externalized and not just the structure that connects them. It is not required anymore that the members of a group share overall goals, or that they work towards a means for the group goal as means to *those* goals, but rather to individual goals. One can also view alienation as an externalization of motivation. The group structure provides motivation for individual agents to act so as to fulfill their role properly. A failure of the motivational goal-system is always possible and allows for all sorts of negative outcomes. The view on agent responsibility (AR) in this case seems to be analogous to the case of coordination through rules. Neither the individuals nor the designers of the motivational goal-system are responsible for the results of the group activity by way of their agency. Consequently, we will find responsibility voids in groups with alienation.

Alienation, in conclusion, is an advanced coordination method that to some extent makes the group activity independent from the individuals' agency. Agential features central to the group activity are smartly linked to agential features used in the exercise of individual agency. The individual agent, thus, by acting on her own accord, also contributes to the group activity. I discussed how this works for the goals of the group activity, but it can also be used for other agential features in much the same way. Agents in a group may not only have incentives to achieve a particular goal by performing a particular action, but also to solve a complex problem, to make a strategic decision, to come up with optimized action procedures, or to improve a groups knowledge pool, and so on and so forth. At the same time, the idea that the individual agents are responsible for the results of the group activity by way of their agency is deeply challenged. For later reference, I summarize:

> (Ali) Alienation is a coordination method linking agential features on the individual level to externally realized agential features on the group level such that the individual agents contribute to the group activity without them explicitly acting for the group.

2.2.3.4 Disruption of agency in complex group activity

Diffusion and alienation with respect to the goals of the group activity lead to an important question: to whom do the goals belong? The alienated agent might only know her personal goals and the means to achieve them, which is offered to her by the means-goal structure. The goal from the group's perspective cannot belong to the alienated agent. Then to whom does it belong? Two answers come to mind. First, one may claim that higher tier members of the group, e.g. top-managers in companies, own the goals, but diffusion and alienation affects them just as any other agent within the company. They, too, only know and possibly own goals on their respective level of management. They, too, may only work towards a group goal because they have proper incentives to do so. The popular discussion of manager bonuses is just one example of this. The idea that high tier group members own the group's goals, thus, does not carry far.

The second answer is more original in claiming that the goals belong genuinely to the group as an agent in its own right. I used the picture of layers of agency before, which has the potential to give solid meaning to groups as agents. However,

for the suggestion to be convincing, it seems the group needs to fulfill some requirements. Above, I only characterized the relevant cases as being large-scale. As I
pointed out, however, large-scale activity only makes it necessary to employ a more
complex coordination mechanism. The same mechanism may be used in simpler
group activity to the same effect. Characterizing the group by being large-scale,
thus, will not help. Fortunately, the coordination principles themselves suggest a
characterization. The important insight about the impact of coordination methods
like standardization and automation, diffusion and alienation is that they disrupt
agency in such a fundamental way that the involved agents are not responsible for
the result of the group activity by way of their agency. The reason for this disruption
of agency is the external realization of agential features that are crucial to agency.
The requirements that groups need to meet to even consider them to be agents,
thus, is that all agential features that are at the core of agency must be externally
realized.

The theoretical padding required for this preliminary definition of group
agents, however, is quite daunting. We would have to agree on what agential
features make up the core of agency. This topic alone has been an ongoing focus
of philosophical theory since the beginning, but has not culminated in a position majority of philosophers agree upon. Additionally, we would have to specify
those features in a way that is compatible with both individual agents and group
agents. Even if we had done this, we would need to provide at least a reasonable
perspective on how groups are entities with their own identity over and above
the individuals who make up the group. I will, in fact, tackle some of these issues
later on, but I will not do so in pursuit of proving that groups can be agents. I
concede that the theoretical barriers for such a claim may be too high. Neither,
however, will I claim that the goals belong to the individual agents the way we
know it from individual agency. In answering the question to whom the goals
belong in a diffused and alienated group, so I claim, we have a third option next to
the individual agents or the group as an agent.

I propose, as a third option, to pick up on the notion that different layers
of agency are created and conclude that such group activity sprouts a new form
agency. This proposal carefully considers the disruption of individual agency that
comes with the externalization of fundamental agential features in complex group
activity, but refrains from introducing new types of agents. The owner of the goals
in a group with a diffused means-goal structure and alienated agents is not the
group as an agent, but the group as a collection of agents who are bound together
by the respective externally realized agential features. I take this to be the basic
character of *corporate agency*.

If I summarize the coordination methods I discussed above, the notion of corporate agency becomes clearer: alienation externalizes goals that motivate action,

diffusion externalizes the corresponding means-goal structure, standardization externalizes execution plans, automation is a way to externalize direct control over the execution and even the execution itself may be partly externalized by use of robots or computers. The very nature of these methods make the group activity independent of the individual agent's agency in a fundamental way. For example, the results of group activity cannot be described as a result of the individual agents' agency anymore. Consequently, the individual agents are not responsible for the results of group activity by way of their agency. In conclusion:

> (CorpAg) Corporate agency is the agency displayed in group activity characterized by external realizations of agential features such that the agents interact in a meaningful sense, but are not responsible for the results of the group activity by way of their individual agency.

2.3 Insights from the disruption of agency in group activity

The leading question of the second chapter was how we should understand statements of the form (GA), Group G did action A, in terms of agency. I argued that such statements themselves are too suggestive. Instead, we should think about whether or not the results of group activity are proper results of the individual agents' agency, i.e. whether or not the individual agents are responsible for the results of the group activity by way of their agency. If this is not the case, group activity leads to *responsibility voids*. The advantage of thinking about responsibility voids in group activity is that they lead us to specific *disruptions of agency*, which help understand how group activity affects individual agency. The discussion showed that the disruption of agency in group activity is rooted in *external realizations of agential features*. This principle simply means that required features for successful agency are created on the group level to coordinate the interaction of the agents within the group activity. As a result, the agents form powerful groups, but they also give up parts of their agency. I identified two forms of group activity by the depth of disruption. On the one hand, if agential features are externally realized such that the individual agents are still fully responsible for the result of group activity by way of their agency, I propose to talk of *collective agency*. Responsibility voids in collective agency only occur when external agential features are in some way dysfunctional. Individual agency is then not disrupted in a fundamental way. However, if agential features are externally realized such that the agents are not properly responsible for the results of the group activity, I propose to talk of *corporate agency*. Responsibility voids in corporate agency occur systematically. Individual agency is fundamentally disrupted. As a consequence, we describe the results of group activity not in terms of individual agency, but use statements of the form (GA).

The concept of corporate agency does not imply that the groups themselves are agents, but we have to concede that a new type of agency is created that cannot rely on the idea of individual agency alone. The coordination methods I discussed in the last part provide specific examples of how corporate agency might emerge and how this goes beyond individual agency. I explained the principle of *diffusion* that splits an agential feature into several overlapping units and assigns them to different agents or groups of agents. In particular, I analyzed diffusion of means-goal structures. Single means-goal units of a diffused means-goal structure may still belong to an individual agent in the sense that their actions are directed at the goals by realizing the respective means, but the overall structure cannot be properly said to belong to any of the individual agents—it belongs to the group of agents and empowers their corporate agency. Diffusion allows for complex and large scale groups to work effectively and efficiently. This, however, also prevents a satisfactory ascription of responsibility on the individual level when various units are involved. Furthermore, individuals in diffused groups may only identify with their particular part of the group activity and fail to recognize the larger goal, which may lead to a serious lack of meaning and motivation.

The down-side of diffusion directly leads into *alienation*. Alienation pushes the external realization of agential features even further. Agential features relevant for the group activity are smartly linked to agential features of individual agency such that individual action and group activity are executed at the same time. In the case of means and goals, incentive systems are a paradigmatic example of this: individual agents are provided with personal goals in terms of money, promotions or social status. The individual agent may achieve her personal goals only by also achieving the group's goals. Again, the major practical advantage of alienation is the independence of the group from individuals' motivation to participate in the group activity—the corporation simply provides an effective motivation for the individuals to do their part. Clearly, the ascription of responsibility becomes even more difficult on the individual level. For alienated agents, the results of their actions on a group level become mere side-effects to their personal goals, and in many cases we do not even expect them to know about it.

I also discussed automation, standardization and computerization as a way to effectively take away execution control from individual agents by meticulously prescribing the tasks or outright replace the human agent by robots and software. Additionally, standard procedures are usually used to run various processes and administrative tasks. The practical advantages, again, come with the disadvantage that responsibility can no longer be ascribed to individuals. The agency of the individual agents is disrupted fundamentally on the execution level.

With diffusion and alienation of the means-goal structure, and execution control through standardization and automation, individual agency is stripped of its core features with respect to the group activity. The agents, to a large extent, become interchangeable. The classical assembly line work-station typically displays all these features. This is not to say that assembly line workers are not passionate about the overall group activity–but they could be without significant impact on the group activity. In particular, they could be completely ignorant of the context of their work in the group activity, while being strongly passionate about what they are doing from their individual perspective. Once these principles are accepted, it is easy to see that they apply just as well to higher tier members in a group. Top managers, for example, are also tied to internal regulations and procedures, act on personal motivation, and only oversee a small part of the group activity.

Corporate agency, as I characterized it here, presents a major challenge for action theory. The explanation of corporate agency cannot rely only on individual agency, but needs to account for the different layers of agency seen in particular forms of group activity. While this seems like a tough challenge at first, I want to draw attention to a helpful fact about external realizations of agential features: they are *external*. Information flows, for example transfer information from one agent to another. The agents interpret them, react to them, change them and so on and so forth. You can write a meeting protocol to manifest the external information flow on a physical medium for everyone to read. The big advantage is, of course, that you can literally observe how the information flow impacts the group activity. The same is not true for individual agency. As of yet, we cannot look into an agent's information management and observe how it affects her agency. In fact, we know very little about the information management within human agents. The same is true for more substantial agential features: we have very little idea how 'having a goal' is realized within a human agent and how exactly it affects her agency. In group activity, the externally realized agential features are much more accessible. The big challenge posed to action theory by corporate agency, thus, also comes with an at least equally big opportunity for a fresh approach to action theory by taking group activity as a guide.

As a first step, I need a better understanding of this guide. In the next chapter, I discuss group activity apart from coordination methods. There are different forms of group activity. My goal is to make sure we can clearly distinguish them and reap the benefits of existing philosophical research. Indeed, the literature provides a great number of approaches to group activity. While they are largely unconnected, similar themes and concepts are developed or used repeatedly. The discussion here will help put the insights of the disruption of agency in group activity into perspective and specify the respective challenge this poses for action theory.

3 Characteristics of group activity

In the previous chapter, I have argued that group activity can disrupt individual agency in fundamental ways. I showed this by looking at various coordination methods used to enable powerful agent interaction. Group activity, however, has a wider scope than coordinated interaction and much philosophical research has been done to discover the principles of agency in group activity.

In this chapter, I discuss the most prominent positions as well as insightful alternative positions on agency in group activity. When going through the literature, however, it quickly becomes apparent there is no systematic body of research with a coherent vocabulary. I decided, therefore, to analyze the object of research. First, I provide an explorative analysis of what it means to do something 'together'. This analysis yields a research map containing basic types of group activity that must be explained by action theory. In the second part, I turn to the literature on agency in group activity. The review highlights the coverage of the research map. More importantly, I point to recurring concepts in the theories key to understanding group activity. I observe that 'collective intentionality' is central to the discussion. While the accounts differ greatly in what exactly this means, virtually all of them take the notion of 'having a common goal' as a crucial part of collective intentionality. This prompts an investigation into both, intentionality and goals, in the next chapter.

3.1 Acting together

Group activity ranges from quite dull small-scale activities like two people sunbathing together to astoundingly complex large-scale activities like developing, producing and selling cars world-wide as seen in a company like Toyota. Given this great range, identifying the object of analysis is not trivial in group activity. The analysis of the disruption of agency in the second chapter suggests there are genuinely different types of group activity. A sensible and helpful categorization is required to anchor the analysis of group activity, interpret existing theories of group activity and understand how potentially different forms of group activity are related. Indeed, I propose a research map of group activity to use as a basis for these purposes. To make this proposal as generic as possible, I start with a basic exploratory analysis of what it means to do something together without introducing new concepts.

https://doi.org/10.1515/9783110628623-003

3.1.1 The meanings of 'together'

So far, I have used group activity as an overarching term for all activity, which is done by more than one agent in some meaning. In our everyday language, we use 'together' to characterize such situations. I will analyze the different meanings of 'together' to provide a starting vocabulary for a theory of group activity. The philosophical literature provides several concepts about what it means to do something together. There are theories of acting together referring to sharing (Bratman, 1992) and/or cooperation (Bratman, 1992; French, 1995) and/or collectivity (Miller, 2006) and/or forms of jointness (Gilbert, 2006), all of which are either used to describe the general phenomenon of people somehow acting together, or already appeal to some intuitive notion of doing something together. I do not defend any of these theories. Instead, I use basic concepts to discover what 'doing something together' means.

At first glance, 'together' merely seems to mean 'not alone' or 'with somebody or something else'. Examples like playing tennis or fighting with somebody show this is not enough: doing something together not only means doing it with somebody else, but also not doing it against someone. Still, the translation of 'together' into 'not alone and not against' seems too simple for a term that is rarely used stand-alone, but embedded in a rich context.

The context of 'together' involves at least two subjects and usually something that is done:

(T) P and Q do X together

The appearance of 'together' in (T) suggests that there is a particular relation between the subjects and what is done. This is exactly the context defining the different meanings of 'together'. Notably, the statement (T) is sensible when P and Q are not agents and X is not an action: flowers 'make up' a bouquet together, a proton and an electron 'form' a hydrogen atom together and so on. 'Together' is used to indicate that two objects *constitute* an object or structure. This, too, is possible with agents, e.g., 'Muslims constitute a minority in the U.K.' Clearly, the constitutive meaning of 'together' has nothing to do with agency.

We might also say wind and rain, taken together, eroded the landscape or, together, the drought and the heat caused a giant bush-fire. The fact that the drought and the heat cause a bush-fire is merely *incidental*. For the incidental use of together, the subjects need to be independent of each other. We would, for example, not use 'together' if the two subjects were necessarily connected, e.g., in a causal chain: the iceberg ramming the Titanic did not sink the ship together with the massive leakage–the iceberg caused the leakage and, through this, sank the ship. 'Together' indicates a relation between otherwise independent subjects. Agents, of course, may also do something together incidentally, and we have to take care not to mix this up with more substantial meanings. A characteristic of the incidental meaning of 'together' is that we can replace it by 'taken together' or separate it by commata. More substantial uses of 'together' cannot be treated the same way. It is right that, taken together, my wife and I drank all the coffee, but it is wrong that my wife and I, taken together, had breakfast. The breakfast that we had together was not incidental.

When agents do something together in a more substantial sense, i.e. when agents act together, they do more than merely bringing about something. Imagine Robert, who is trapped under a heap of rubble. Monica comes by, sees Robert and decides to lift the rocks and move them away. Maria also comes by, sees Robert and equally decides to move away the rocks. It does not sound off to say that Monica and Maria moved away the rocks together, but the reason why it does not sound off is not obvious.

Monica's and Maria's actions are purposeful, i.e. they move away the rocks to save Robert, but this is not enough to allow for a more profound meaning of moving the rocks together. Imagine that Monica and Maria are, in fact, fairly advanced robots M IV and M VI capable of recognizing rocks and people, moving in unknown terrain, and designed to lift rocks from people in order to rescue them. The robots' actions are purposeful, and they do what every agent would do–move the rocks away from Robert. However, they do not do it together in any other sense than the incidental sense. They do not recognize each other, let alone the fact that they are bringing about the same result. They just happen to be at the same place at the same time and just happen to have the same goal. Monica and Maria, on the other hand, do recognize each other. Without need of any communication, they identify each other as working towards the same goal, and they adjust their actions correspondingly, e.g., Monica does not grab the same rock as Maria, and Maria moves out of the way when Monica crosses her path.

Recognition alone, obviously, is not enough either. Margaret may walk by, recognize Monica and Maria as agents purposefully moving the rocks. She then even takes care to move out of the way, but she continues her walk. There is nothing Monica, Maria and Margaret do together in that scenario. As it seems, then, a common purpose *and* recognition in combination allow a more substantial use of 'together'. Indeed, if the M-robots were even more advanced and recognized each other, then it is sensible to say that they are moving the rocks together not only in the incidental sense. This also indicates the meaning of 'together' employed here is still quite *primitive*.

Doing something together primitively is rather rare when agents like Monica and Maria are involved. The interaction between them is restricted to individually adjusting their respective actions to what they see is going on. This is realistic in cases where the tasks are simple, where time is of the essence or other limitations prevent more complex interaction. In the second chapter, however, I have discussed that the interaction between agents like Monica and Maria usually is of a fundamentally different breed. Agents start to coordinate themselves interpersonally based on mutually dependent action considerations. I also pointed out that coordination methods enable agents to participate in group activity without actually sharing a common goal. Doing something together by way of coordination, accordingly, is independent of doing something together primitively.

Indeed, we often do something together without a common goal. In fact, many if not most instances of doing something together lack a common goal, but the individual agents pursue personal goals. Me and my colleague may read and discuss McCann's marvelous paper "Settled Objectives And Rationality Constraints" (1991) together, yet, I do it to better understand settled objectives, while my colleague does it to better understand rationality constraints. We do it together *opportunistically* to achieve our personal goals. While we do not pursue a common goal, there still needs to be something we do together. Coordination alone is not enough to establish a meaning of 'together'. When Margaret walked by Monica and Maria, they may coordinate each other to avoid collision, but they did not 'evade each other's pathways together'. There need not be a common goal, but some common benefit is required, which happens to help achieve the personal goals of the agents.

Yet, some activities we do together do not even have common benefit, or feature coordination. Sometimes we do something together and bring about nothing. The previous example featured Margaret, who was taking a walk. 'Taking a walk' is something we often do for its own sake and not to bring anything about. The same is true for many recreational activities. Clearly, Margaret may also take a walk together with Michael. In most cases, taking a walk together serves no purpose at all but simply to enjoy each other's company, have a nice chat, share the experience of walking with somebody else. Obviously, the agents taking a walk together also recognize each other in doing so, but this seems secondary. What is more important is the fact that the agents want to do something *together* regardless of what it is they are doing. The group activity so characterized displays an *inclusiveness* not present in the other types of group activity discussed so far. It is not clear that inclusiveness comes from a basic sense of 'togetherness' or 'sociality' in general, but there at least seems to be such a distinctive type of group activity that needs to be explained.

Up to this point, I have come across five meanings of doing something together. Two of those are irrelevant for agency, which are the *constitutive* meaning and the *incidental* meaning of bringing something about with no relation of the agents whatsoever. We only need to keep those in mind to avoid confusion. The other three meanings of together are, indeed, relevant for agency. First, agents can act together *primitively*, which requires that they recognize each other as agents that pursue a common goal. Beyond this, action theory needs to account for acting together *opportunistically*, i.e. the individual agents do not act together in pursuit of a common goal, but coordinate themselves in order to achieve personal goals. Last but not least, agents may act together simply because they enjoy the togetherness. This *inclusive* type of acting together does not require common goals or coordination; it does not even require personal goals. In summary:

> (ATP) Agents act together in a primitive sense if they pursue a common goal and recognize each other in doings so.

> (ATO) Agents act together in an opportunistic sense if they coordinate themselves in pursuit of some common benefit for their distinct personal goals.

> (ATI) Agents act together in an inclusive sense if they do something together because they prefer doing it together rather than alone.

These types of acting together are prototypes, which can, but rarely do, occur in these pure forms. Clearly, agents can have a common goal *and* coordinate themselves to achieve this goal. This type of group activity certainly is not primitive any longer, and it is not merely opportunistic. Instead, I propose to use the term 'cooperative' to describe this way of acting together:

> (ATC) Agents act together cooperatively if they coordinate themselves in pursuit of a common goal.

Additionally, agents may also act together inclusively *and* pursue a common goal. While taking a walk together usually does not entail a particular goal, climbing a mountain together would be a good example for this. Just like a purely primitive form of acting together, this combined type seems to be a rather rare type in reality. Most of the time, if two agents inclusively act together towards a common goal, they also coordinate themselves, i.e. all three features come together. This *fully-integrated* sense of acting together is the most common and most discussed type of doing something together:

> (ATF) Agents act together fully-integrated if they coordinate themselves in pursuit of a common goal and prefer doing it together rather than alone.

From this, I can start to draw a research map (figure 3.1) that contains three relevant prototypical types of group activity that give rise to at least 2 more relevant cases of group activity. The prototypical types are primitive group activity mediated by a common goal and mutual recognition, opportunistic group activity established by coordination of the individuals in order to achieve personal goals and inclusive group activity just for the sake of doing it together. Relevant combinations of these types are cooperative group activity featuring a common goal and coordination as well as fully-integrated group activity merging all three types together.

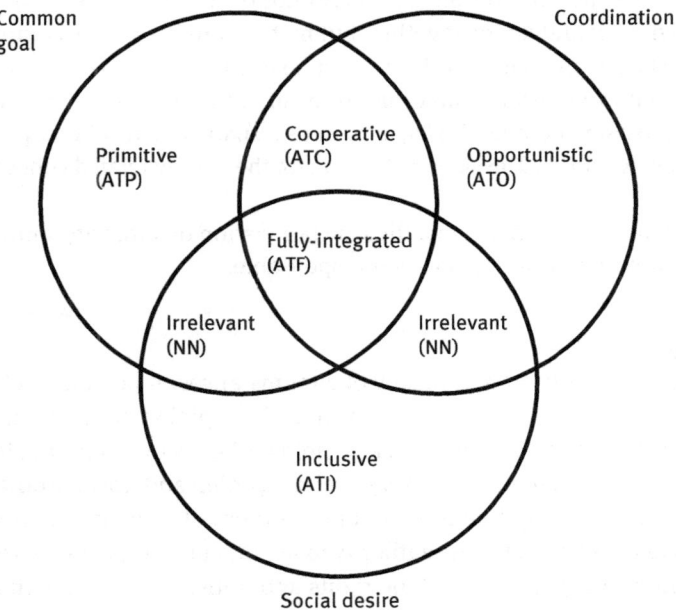

Fig. 3.1: Visualization of most relevant types of group activity described as agents 'acting to-gether' based on common goals, coordination and/or a social desire to do something together. The three prototypical forms are acting together primitively (ATP) towards common goals and mutual recognition of doing so, acting together opportunistically (ATO) using some method of coordination towards some common benefit for personal goals and acting together inclusively (ATI) based purely on a desire to do something together. More commonly observed are the two combinations of acting together cooperatively (ATC) in a coordinated manner towards a common goal and acting together fully-integrated (ATF) where a social desire to act together is also present. The remaining two combinations are practically irrelevant.

3.1.2 Acting together beyond acting together

In the first chapter I discussed statements of the form (GA), 'Group G did action A', and concluded that they indicate a new form of corporate agency. In particular, in some cases (GA) can neither be replaced by action statements about individual agents nor can it be replaced by statements about agents 'acting together'. Undoubtedly, however, (GA) requires that various agents are somehow involved in a group activity. This implies that there are forms of group activity going beyond acting together.

Corporate agency is not the only such form. Authority and authorization also enable group activity beyond acting together, but matters are even more complicated with them. On the one hand, authority can be used as a method for coordination in a straight forward way, but other forms of authority deviate in both directions–as an extension of individual agency or as a characteristic of group activity beyond 'acting together'. The same holds true for the closely related concept of authorization.

For a research map of group activity, thus, a clarification of authority, authorization and, of course, corporate agency is indispensable.

3.1.2.1 Authority

The concept of authority is used in a variety of circumstances. A person can be an authority in a scientific field, for example, meaning her opinion has particular weight in scientific discourse. A person can also hold authority over a particular area or sphere. I have, for example, authority over my garden and how I arrange the flowers in it. It is mainly up to me what happens there. If someone entered my garden unwanted, I would have the authority to tell him to leave, because the garden is regarded my property with all the rights and duties that come with it. The authority over my garden, thus, implies that I also have authority over other agents and their actions to some extent.

In the second chapter, we already encountered a case of group activity that resembles authority. I discussed coordination of agents by splitting a task into sub-tasks. I introduced the notion of procedurally splitting a task. When we think back to Robert who is lying injured under a heap of rubble. Maria and Monica may apply a procedural split for the rescue. If the heap is unstable, the weaker but smarter Maria carefully chooses the rocks that can be lifted without collapsing the heap and tells Monica which rock to lift next. Monica does the heavy lifting without making any decisions about which rock to lift next. It looks like Maria has authority over Monica, because she tells her what to do, but this is not enough for authority.

Maria may point at a rock and say 'That one.', but this is not necessarily an act of authority. Instead, Monica may understand it as conveying important information to her, namely, that it is safe to pick up this particular rock. So, she picks up this rock rather than another one. Monica's reason to lift the rock is not given by Maria's telling her to do so, but Monica has her own reasons, e.g. rescuing Robert who is trapped under the rocks. Maria's telling her to lift this particular rock only gives her relevant information. Said differently, Maria's telling Monica to lift this rock is not sufficient for Monica to do so, but the content of what Maria tells Monica is helpful. Another way to see that Maria does not necessarily hold authority over Monica's lifting the rocks is the possibility of Monica holding authority over Maria without changing the scenario otherwise: Monica may order Maria to tell her which rock to lift. Clearly, Maria does not hold authority over Monica–but still tells her what to do.

Eventually, however, the split of tasks gives rise to a new quality of interaction. When the ambulance arrives, for example, the emergency doctor tells Monica to hold up Robert's legs. She complies. If she is asked why she is holding up Robert's legs, then the answer will most likely be that the emergency doctor told her to do so. We can even imagine that Monica actually does not want to hold up Robert's legs. Maybe she thinks holding up Robert's legs is the wrong thing to do according to what she saw on a medical TV show. With this in mind, it is clear that Monica does not hold up Robert's legs because of some important information conveyed to her by the doctor. Rather, Monica holds up his legs because the doctor told her to do so.

In a first approach, thus, authority over other agents can be generally characterized as:

(GenAy) An agent A has authority over another agent B, if agent A's telling agent B to do some action X is sufficient for agent B to do X.

The general characterization of authority (GenAy), however, is too broad to tell apart different types of authority. It is helpful to look at the genesis of typical authority structures to do so.

First, authority can be the result of coordination efforts. I argued above that Maria does not necessarily have authority over Monica's actions in the example of lifting the rocks, but she might. In such situations, a person is explicitly or implicitly put into authority. In the case of Monica and Maria, the authority is given to Maria because of certain skills. But the reason for giving somebody authority can be much simpler. In "Prediction, Authority, and Entitlement in Shared Activity" (2014), Abraham Sesshu Roth points at the familiar example of going to dinner together. One person simply lets the other decide where to go to because it is her birthday or because she could not decide last time and it is her turn now (p.640). In these cases, authority is generated by informal implicit or explicit consent, and it is usually restricted to small area of interaction:

> (ConAy) Agent A has consent-based authority over an agent B of the form (GenAy) on a restricted domain D as long as agents A and B implicitly or explicitly agree that agent A decides what to do in the domain D.

Second, authority may also have normative roots. Whenever work contracts are signed, the employee implicitly or explicitly agrees to take her place within the authority structure of her employer. She is normatively bound to the agreement by the contract. This case, too, is based on consent, but it is not a personal consent and it cannot be as easily retracted as the first type of authority. Instead, the consent has a normative character. The authority of the emergency doctor in the previous case is also an example for normative authority. The normative roots are expressed by the title or status given to the doctor upon thorough training and proper ceremonies. The uniform and the ambulance are associated with extraordinary rights. Furthermore, the authority of an emergency doctor cannot be easily rejected: imagine that Monica refuses to hold up Robert's legs because she does not think this is a good idea. As a consequence, unfortunately, Robert dies. Monica is responsible for the death of Robert because she did not do what the doctor told her to. In contrast, if the emergency doctor had not arrived yet, and Maria told Monica to hold up Robert's legs, Monica is free to reject this order, if she thinks that holding Robert's legs is harmful or some other action is called for to save Robert. If Robert dies, she will not be responsible for it on the grounds that she did not do what Maria told her. Normative authority can be characterized as:

> (NormAy) Agent A has normative authority over agent B the form (GenAy) on restricted domain D if agent A is entitled so by some normative agreement.

The pressure that comes with normative authority can easily transition into a third form of authority not justified by any normative or personal agreement. Roth cites a passage from Velleman's paper "How to share an intention" (1997) in which Velleman characterizes authority by the idea that "you will do whatever I tell you to do" (p.34). Roth calls this a "dictatorial authority" (Roth, 2014, p.642), Bratman the "mafia sense" of acting together (Bratman, 1992, p.334). Indeed, the relationship between employer and employee, for example, often develops this type of authority beyond the normative authority given by the work contract. A manager might abuse her normative power to extend her authority to a domain not covered by the normative agreement, e.g., she makes personal demands or even abuses her subordinates.

Thus, third, authority may also be forced upon the weaker by the stronger. Stronger and weaker here simply means the stronger has substantial power over the weaker. In the most extreme case, one person has full control over another person's actions. A far-fetched example would be a hypnotized person doing as the hypnotizer wishes. I would like to exclude pathological cases of this kind. More commonly, a mother, for example, can usually simply order her child to do something with an appropriate tone. Police officers or a prison warden can use physical force to bring people in line. In less extreme cases, the weaker still have choices, but the choices are dictated by the stronger to benefit her will. If the choice is to die from a shot by a gun pointed at your head or to fulfill the wishes of the one holding the gun, the latter choice usually prevails. Dictatorial authority can only be rejected with grave consequences, it is obviously not based on any sort of consent, and it is only restricted by the power of the agent in authority:

> (DicAy) Agent A has dictatorial authority of agent B of the form (GenAy) in the domain D if agent A has power over agent B in the domain D such that agent B cannot reject the demands of agent A without grave consequences.

When it comes to agency and acting together, the different types of authority invite different conclusions. Beginning with dictatorial authority (DicAY), it seems wrong to describe two agents as acting 'together' when, e.g., agent B does something for agent A because she points a gun at her head. Instead, agent B is described as an individual agent forced to act in a certain way by agent A. Imagine a cashier in a small bank who is forced by a robber to empty the cash deposit boxes into a bag. The robber is robbing the bank, and the cashier is forced to help her by emptying the cash deposit boxes. Clearly, the robber and the cashier are not robbing the bank together, despite the fact that they both contribute to robbing the bank. The robber robs the bank; the cashier is forced to help her by emptying the cash deposit boxes.

Dictatorial authority (DicAy), however, can be used to coordinate agents' actions. Imagine the robber forces the cashier and a customer to empty the cash deposits. She throws a bag to the customer and tells her to hold it open. She tells the cashier to empty the cash deposits into the bag. In this scenario, it is still not the case that the three of them empty the cash deposits together, however, it is the case that the cashier and the customer empty the cash deposits together. The reason is not in the authority of the robber, but in the fact that they coordinate towards a common benefit in order improve their chances of survival. They act together opportunistically (ATC) when they empty the cash deposit boxes.

Finally, the robber herself could play the role of the customer in emptying the cash deposits, i.e. she holds open the bag and tells the cashier to empty the cash deposits into the bag. With what I have said before, it makes sense to say they empty the cash deposits together opportunistically, i.e. for different personal reasons, but they still do not rob the bank together. As before, the reason for saying they empty the cash deposits together is not the authority relation itself, but the fact that they coordinate their actions, which is enforced by authority. The robber might even say something like 'Look, we are going to empty these deposits together, then we are going to leave in my car together, and once the police is off our tail, you can go free. Now move!'

Still, when only the robber and the cashier empty the deposits, we might hesitate to describe them as doing it together. The reason for this, I believe, is twofold. First, the decision between getting shot and emptying the cash depositsis forced upon the cashier by the robber. The decision is a very limited expression the agency of the cashier. This is in line with the second reason. Following the conditions for agent responsibility (CAR), the cashier is not responsible for emptying the cash deposits together with the robber, but the robber is responsible. Agent responsibility and action execution fall apart. The robber orders the cashier to execute whatever she wants. The cashier empties the deposit boxes *for* the robber and not *with* the robber, and it is the robber who is responsible for the empty cash deposit boxes.

I have previously discovered a dissociation of agent responsibility and action execution in group activity. The reason for this were external realizations of agential features. Indeed, the principle in the case of authority is the same, except the agential features are not realized on a group level, but the robber uses the features of another agent for the action execution. The cashier empties the cash deposits, yet, this is not a result of her agency in a proper way, but her agential capabilities are used by the robber. The robber, on the other hand, does not empty the cash deposits herself, but it is clear that she is responsible for it by way of her agency. Dictatorial authority (DicAy), thus, empowers *individual* agency even though multiple agents are involved.

Normative authority (NormAy) often displays the same pattern. Recall Monica and the emergency doctor. Should Robert die because Monica holds up his legs as ordered by the doctor. Monica is not responsible for Robert's death even though her action killed him. The doctor is responsible because she used her authority to extend her agency onto Monica. In contrast to dictatorial authority, however, it is not clear that it empowers individual agency. Indeed, the major advantage is to empower particularly capable agents, but the introduction of a normative element is to empower her given that other agents may also contribute. Normative authority is ambiguous with respect to agency and group activity. The employee-manager relation based on a work-contract shows this ambiguity: sometimes it is appropriate to say the employee does something *for* the manager, but other times it is appropriate to say they achieved something together partly because of healthy authority.

With authority solely based on personal consent (ConAy), the case is less ambiguous. When Monica and Maria lift up the rocks together, Monica may give Maria authority to tell her what to do next. If Maria makes a wrong decision and orders Monica to lift up the wrong rock and the pile of rocks collapses, they are both responsible for the collapse by way of their agency. The reason is quite simple. Monica freely accepts the authority of Maria; it is neither forced upon her nor normatively required of her. They merely establish the authority relation in order to optimize their interaction.

In summary, I characterized authority over other agents and their actions by the fact that if the agent under authority is being told to do something by the person in authority, then this is sufficient reason for her to do so (GenAy). This characterization, however, is compatible with different types of authority. First, so I argued, authority can develop from coordination efforts and is based on personal consent, either implicitly or explicitly (ConAy). This type of authority does not undermine the fact that the involved agents act together. In fact, the reason why we say they act together is mainly because they use authority as a coordination principle. Secondly, authority may have normative roots (NormAy). Especially in work relations, authority of this kind often still serves the purpose of coordinating the involved agents and, thus, explains why we talk of them working together. However, authority with normative roots need not necessarily serve the coordination of agents, but can also be used to empower individual agents with extraordinary skills. Emergency doctors or police men, for example, are given extraordinary rights allowing them to fulfill their assigned roles using their acquired skills. Authority used like this does not necessarily result in agents acting together. Rather, it often enables individual agents to use the agential features of other agents for their own agency, usually the actual execution of an action. The same is true for almost all instances of dictatorial authority (DicAy). As a consequence, action execution and agent responsibility fall apart. While the agent under authority acts, the agent in authority is responsible for the action and its consequences. The general insight behind this is that externalizations of agential features can also be used by individuals to extend their agency to other agents, but this extension of an individuals' agency onto other agents cannot be properly described as them acting together despite the fact they are involved in the activity.

Thus, while authority can be the basis for acting together, it can also reach beyond acting together. I have shown how authority relates to the meanings of 'together' and explained how the concept of externalization of agential features may account for the different types of authority, but it remains a challenge for action theory to incorporate authority.

3.1.2.2 Authorisation

Some instances of authority, so I have discussed above, enable agents to extend their agency through other agents, i.e. one agent executes an action, but that action is a result of the agency of the agent in authority. Authority is quite invasive in terms of agency, but there is another option for individual agents to extend their agency onto other agents. David Copp uses an example featuring Jones, who "gives someone power of attorney and orders him to purchase a certain building for him" and Copp argues that "then, if the attorney buys it for Jones, Jones has bought it" (Copp, 1979, p.177). At first, this looks like an example for authority since Jones "orders" the lawyer to buy a building for him. There is, however, a second aspect expressed by the idea that Jones gives his lawyer "power of attorney". When we replace the order with a mere request it is still true that the lawyer buys something for Jones. How is this possible?

Usually, only Jones is entitled to buy something himself. Surely, others can buy things for Jones, and then gift Jones with the item, but then Jones will not have bought the item. Even if I steal money from Jones, then buy something and give it to him, Jones will not have bought the item. Buying something is not just an exchange of goods, but it comes with a personal agreement, which is usually achieved by the buyer and seller in person. Otherwise, it is not an act of trade between these two persons. This normative component of 'buying' gives Jones a special position or a special power with respect to acts of 'Jones buying something'. As the example suggests, however, this power can be given to other persons like lawyers, which is called *authorization*.

Authorization comes in at least two variants. First, I can authorize a person to do something she wants to do, but cannot unless I allow it. For this to be true, I may indeed have authority over her, or authority over something else, e.g. my property, and I might allow her to use it for whatever she needs. The principle is still the same: the authorized person can do something that usually only the authorizing person can do herself. This variant of authorization essentially equates with permission. The authorized person acts within her own agency and the agency of the authorizing person is not affected and vice versa. Permissive authorization, thus, is quite uninteresting with respect to agency.

Second, and this is exemplified by Jones and his lawyer, I can authorize a person to do something in my name, something *I* want to do. The authorized person acts, and this act constitutes another act ascribed to the authorizing person, which is essentially the model that Copp develops[1]. The lawyer's act of buying a building for Jones really constitutes Jones' buying a building:

(ConAz) Agent A can authorize agent B such that the actions of B constitute the respective actions of A.

To explain how constitutive authorization (ConAz) is possible, however, we must go beyond Copp's model of constitution. Constitutive authorization, so I argue, is a particularly intriguing case of externalization of agential features used by an individual. When I discussed dictatorial authority, I already pointed out that the agent in authority outsources the execution of some action to her subordinate. In case of constitutive authorization, the execution of an action also often is externalized, but this only accompanies authorization. Rather, with authorization, the normative power of an agent is externalized, e.g. part of her status and rights. Usually, it requires an actual physical document signed by the authorizing agent literally carrying the normative power for the authorized agent to do something in the name of that agent. Only as a second step is the execution externalized by way of her authority, a request for help or a business proposal.

By using constitutive authorization, agents like Jones can literally act by way of another agent's action, like the lawyer buying a building for Jones. So far, this has nothing to do with acting together, despite the fact that multiple agents are involved in one and the same action. But is easy to see how authorization can play a vital role in acting together: the normative power of agents may be shared so that agents can physically replace one another in interactions with others. This obviously greatly simplifies acting together. Suppose, for example, that two agents prepare holidays together. One of them takes the task of organizing the passport and visa arrangements. To do so, the other agent signs a piece of paper authorizing her to do most of the administrative paperwork in her name. Furthermore, it is also possible that many agents authorize one person, or a group of persons, to act in their name. Thomas Hobbes used this idea to explain the creation of a commonwealth in his classic book "Leviathan" (1651, 1909). He describes what must be true of every person in a common wealth: *"I authorise and give up my Right of Governing my selfe, to this Man, or to this Assembly of men, on this condition, that thou give up thy Right to him, and Authorise all his Actions in like manner.* This done, the Multitude so united in one Person, is called a COMMON-WEALTH" (p.132).

---

1 Copp defines 'secondary actions' as being constituted by 'primary actions' in a certain way making them actions in there own right while still being dependent on other actions (Copp, 1979, p.182).

Authorization, like authority, walks the line between acting together and only acting with multiple agents involved, which is why I discussed it as a second case of acting together beyond acting together. The discussion revealed a very potent mechanism, i.e externalization of normative power, which needs to be incorporated into a complete action theory. I will now turn to the last case of 'acting together beyond acting together'.

3.1.2.3 Corporate agency

In the second chapter, I introduced the notion of corporate agency. I will now argue that corporate agency, too, goes beyond acting together in any of the usual meanings. Two elaborate coordination principles led to the notion of corporate agency. First, alienation (Ali) means that an agential feature of an individual and the respective agential feature on the group level fall apart. I used the example of how personal goals may be smartly linked to the goals of the group activity such that achieving the individual goals also achieves different means or goals within the means-goals structure of the overall activity. Second, diffusion (Diff) means that externally realized agential features are distributed over various agents. I used the example of complex means-goal structures that are divided into smaller, overlapping means-goals units, each belonging to different agents. Individuals may work within one or more of these units, but they need not or cannot work within all of them.

Alienated agents in a diffused means-goal structure need not share the overall goals, and what they do may only be a means to their individual goals. The idea of acting together based on a common goal, thus, can be immediately excluded. In fact, individual agents may even oppose the overarching goals, sabotage others in the overall means-goal structure and, thereby, effectively work against the group's interest. Yet, they still contribute to the achievement of the group's goals, if they are successful within their means-goal unit. Diffusion and alienation still leaves us with agents whose actions are coordinated and, in a sense, what they are coordinated towards is at least beneficial to them. Yet, it is not clear that such agents act together opportunistically–most certainly inclusiveness is not required.

Indeed, diffusion and alienation has taken us to a version of doing something together not mirrored in our everyday language. When Microsoft releases a new operating system, it is challenging to find a group of people of which we are comfortable saying they did it together. The help desk employee contributed by keeping Microsoft operations running, but she did not release the new operating system together with all other employees of Microsoft. Maybe she did not even know about the system due to diffusion, or she did not care about it due to alienation. The team actually managing the release–did they release the operating system together? They certainly contributed a large part to it, but they did not do it alone. Research and development build the operating system, the employees in the call center helped fund it by keeping Microsoft running as well as the investors. It is possible all agents only acted within their restricted means-goal unit not even caring about the company goals, but only the attached personal goals. This would lead to the odd conclusion that Microsoft released its new operating system, but the agents, who constitute Microsoft, did not do it together. One might be tempted to reject this conclusion on grounds of intuition, but we must admit the entire means-goal structure can only be ascribed to Microsoft as a whole. The same is true for the alienated goals structure containing the individual goals linked to the company's goals.

The alternative to rejecting the conclusion is to explain it by recourse to a new form of agency–which is exactly what led me to the notion of corporate agency in the first place. The tension between acting together and corporate agency is the last of the three cases of 'acting together beyond acting together' I discuss. Corporate agency completes the research map.

3.1.3 Research map for action theory of group activity

With the discussion of group activity described as 'acting together' and types of group activity that go beyond acting together, I can now draw a more complete research map for group activity as shown in figure 3.2.

First, I looked at the different notions of doing something together. I found three basic meanings of 'together' corresponding to three basic types of group activity and at least two relevant combinations. First, agents may act together primitively in pursuit of some common goal while recognizing each other in doing so (ATP). Action theory needs to develop a clear cut concept of having a common goal to account for this type of group activity. Second, even if the agents only have personal goals, they might still act together in an opportunistic sense (ATO). The only reliable feature of this type of doing something together seems to be that the agents coordinate themselves. A thorough understanding of coordination, thus, is essential to understand group activity. Indeed, in my discussion of coordination in the second chapter, coordination turned out to heavily rely on the externalization of agential features, which is fundamental to understanding group activity. Third, acting together might not involve any purposeful activity or coordination whatsoever. Agents might simply do something together inclusively for the sake of doing it together (ATI), e.g. sharing an experience or enjoying company.

The three relevant meanings of 'together' are mirrored by respective types of group activity, but they can also be combined. Very rarely we find group activity

Types of group activity described as...

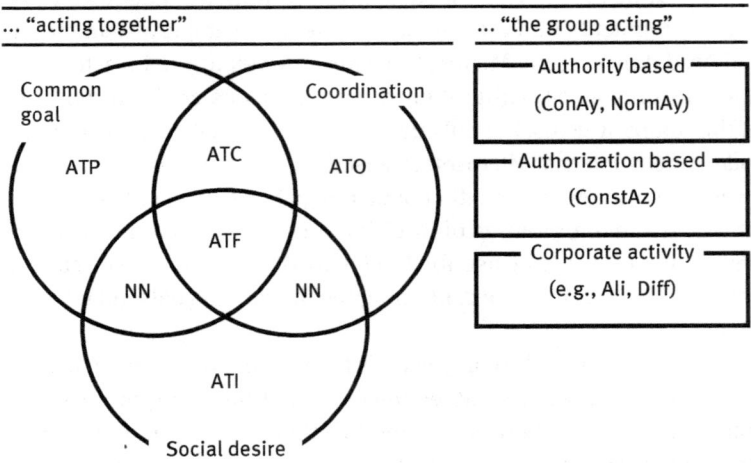

Fig. 3.2: Visualization of the research map for action theory of group activity. The left hand side shows group activity described as agents "acting together" based on common goals, coordination and/or a social desire to do something together, in particular: "Acting together opportunistically" (ATO), "acting together inclusively" (ATI), "acting together cooperatively" (ATC), "acting together fully-integrated" (ATF) (comp. 3.1 for details). The right hand side shows types of group activity not properly described as agents "acting together," but as agents acting on behalf of a group or simply "the group acting" based on consental or normative authority structures (ConAy, NormAy), constitutive authorization (ConstAz) or external realization of fundamental features of agency in corporate activity, e.g., using coordination methods like diffusion (Diff) and alienation (Ali).

characterized by a common goal, coordination, or inclusiveness. Often, agents co-ordinate themselves towards a common goal (ATC). They cooperate without being inclusive. In many cases, the three types come together and we have fully-integrated group activity characterized by agents that coordinate themselves towards a common goal and do so, in part, because they want to do it together, rather than alone (ATF).

Beyond acting together, I looked at three more cases of activity involving multiple agents, in which the agents cannot properly be described as doing something together. First, certain types of authority may not serve the purpose of coordination, but empower the agency of the agent in authority at the expense of the agency of the agents under authority (DicAy, NormAy). I described this in terms of externalization of agential features. Authority allows an agent to outsource the execution of an action to other agents. Despite the activity being literally spread over multiple agents in a non-incidental way, ordinary language does not describe them as doing something together. Other forms of authority, in contrast, clearly are used to mediate group activity (NormAy, ConAy).

Second, the same is also true for authorization. In cases of constitutive authorization (ConstAz), normative power is transferred from one agent to another, such that the latter may perform actions in the name of the former. The actions of the authorized agent constitute the action of the authorizing agent, which can be used to empower individual agency or enable instances of group activity. However, it may also be relevant for corporate agency, which is the third type of group activity that goes beyond acting together. In corporate group activity, the externalization of agential features can reach a level where it seems incorrect to describe the involved agents as acting together. Specifically, I discussed how diffusion and alienation create what can best be identified with corporate agency, which goes beyond acting together.

Now that I have outlined the explanatory quest of action theory with regard to actions involving multiple agents, I will review the literature on agency in group activity to show which parts of the maps are already covered, and which are not. Not surprisingly, many of the aspects have been covered in philosophical discussion, but they are largely disconnected, and often it is not clear whether or not they can be connected. Also, not surprisingly, most positions heavily rely on action theory for individuals. I have pointed out that this focus is not necessarily justified given that external realization of agential features in group activity are a viable starting point for thinking about agency themselves. Indeed, the literature on collective agency is forced to discuss concepts of agency without reference to agency as we experience it individually.

3.2 Philosophical research on group activity

In the discussion of the disruption of agency in group activity, I have shown the importance of external realizations of agential features and their role in group activity; however, it remained unclear what exactly is meant by 'group activity'. In order to clarify this notion, I provided an analysis-based research map of group activity in the last section. I argued for five modes of doing something together, three fundamental types and two combined types, and three further forms of group activity usually not described as doing something 'together', but understood as an extension of another individual's agency or, indeed, an activity of a group as a whole.

Clearly, not all types of group activity display a new form of agency. In fact, most of them certainly do not. Nonetheless, it is important to account for all of them to properly distinguish them and recognize the relevant aspects ultimately creating the bridge from group activity to group agency.

In this last section of the third chapter, I will review the existing literature to help with this task. The philosophy of group agency is young within action theory, and modern action theory itself is young compared to other topics of philosophical research. The field was mainly developed and still is shaped by Michael Bratman, John Searle, Margaret Gilbert and Raimo Tuomela beginning in the 1980's. They are sometimes referred to as the 'Big Four' (Chant et al., 2014). Important contributions were also made by Philipp Pettit/Christian List, the psychologist Michael Tomasello and, more recently, James Butterfill and Elisabeth Pacherie. The philosophical research struggles with two issues at the moment.

First, the focus of the discussion up to recently is rather narrow: of main interest is the question of how to construct a solid notion of intentionality on the group level and how this relates to individual intentionality. The focus on intentionality is, of course, due to the outstanding position of 'intentionality' in action theory. Since Anscombe's famous monograph "Intention" (1957) and Davidson's ground breaking paper "Actions, causes and reason" (1963), intentions are usually thought to be the very mark of agency opposed to other forms of behavior. A successful extension of the notion of intentionality to group activity, ideally by reducing it to individual intentionality, would warrant a continuous action theory. Bratman's account, for example, "is broadly individualistic in spirit [...]. It aims at a noncircular account of [shared cooperative activity]; one that is reductive in spirit and that emphasizes an important kind of interdependence of intention" (Bratman, 1992, p.341). Indeed, Bratman himself often stresses that his account shows nothing new is needed to explain group activity, or at least one form of shared agency. Unfortunately, the variety of group activities fails to be recognized with such a focus. Over the last decade or so, psychological research about the development of infants by, e.g., Tomasello et al. (Tomasello et al., 2005) has widened that focus and triggered a vivid philosophical debate about forms of 'shared intention lite', as it is called by Elisabeth Pacherie (Pacherie, 2013). This leads directly to the second concern.

There is no clear structure of what exactly is discussed, and the respective positions are still rather unconnected, both, in terms of the object of analysis as well as terminology. As far as I know, David Schweikard's "Der Mythos des Singulären"[2] from 2011 is essentially the first book providing an in-depth overview of the main positions culminating in an attempt to bring them together. Bratman's

---

2 The German title "Der Mythos des Singulären" roughly translates to "The myth of singularism" (my translation).

book "Shared Agency" from 2014 consolidates at least his own papers on the topic. Equally, Phillip Pettit's and Christian List's book "Group agency" from 2013 is a well-rounded theory developed from their previous papers with attempts to accommodate other approaches, or at least show compatibility.

Given these two deficits, I decided to provide a research map on my own, which can be used as a helpful structure in researching this topic. At the same time, I used as little conceptual assumptions as possible in my analysis to allow for the wide focus adequate for the phenomenon. I use the research map to discuss the major positions on group agency and a selection of alternatives. I will provide a brief summary of the respective positions, show their explanatory reach with respect to the research, discuss their relation to other positions and point at possible weaknesses or limitations. Most importantly, I will pick up recurring ideas of outstanding importance to action theory for groups.

Two themes are of particular relevance. First, as already pointed out above, there is a focus on collective or group intentionality. Much of the discussion revolves around how a particular form of individual intentionality, or a particular relation between the individual's intentions constitutes collective intentionality, or whether or not there may be a completely new form of intentionality on a group level. To support their respective views, most accounts explicitly define what intentionality in agency means, e.g. functional specifications, but also other seemingly simpler concepts like goals, plans, decision procedures, and so on. This way, the construction of intentionality on a group level refers to more basic features of agency.

One of these features, and this is the second theme, is the idea that individual agents in group activity share a goal, or have a common goal, or a joint goal. The notion of a common goal in some form is considered necessary for group intentionality and, thus, group agency. The specification of what it takes for agents in group activity to share a goal, however, is surprisingly incoherent across the different positions. Worse even, the concept of a goal in general is unclear and the implicit and explicit characterizations outright contradictory. Given the outstanding importance of goals according to most accounts, this is a serious research gap.

3.2.1 Most influential accounts for group activity

Michael Bratman, John Searle, Raimo Tuomela and Kaarlo Miller, Margaret Gilbert, and Philipp Pettit and Christian List created five distinct accounts for particular types of group activity, respectively. Their accounts shaped and keep shaping the philosophical debate and are referred to in essentially every work concerned with group activity. Summaries of their positions are easy to come by, e.g., (Roth, 2017). However, as mentioned above, there is no common terminology, and even the objects of analysis are often different. Consequently, I provide a brief summary of the accounts with a focus on what exactly they are aiming to explain and what the key concepts are to do so.

3.2.1.1 Bratman's shared agency

The presumably most prominent position was developed by Michael Bratman, who started to think about group activity in the 1980's. In one of his first papers on the topic, Bratman presents basic principles for "Shared Cooperative Activity" (1992). His "account is broadly individualistic in spirit [...]. It aims at a noncircular account of SCA, one that is reductive in spirit" (p.341). Two ideas expressed in this statement drive Bratman's research program. First, the individualistic and reductive spirit is owed to Bratman's preference for a parsimonious theory of group activity, i.e. a theory that does not introduce any new phenomena, but makes use only of concepts known from individual action theory. Besides theoretical elegance, this would mean a construction of a social phenomenon without using any inherently social concepts, i.e. 'sociality' would be explained in a non-circular way. The second idea is to provide a set of sufficient conditions for a specific type of group activity respecting exactly this parsimony condition. If this is possible for one specific type of group activity, so the rationale, it should be possible to extend the strategy to other types of group activity. The defense of the non-circularity and sufficiency of his account have become central elements in his most recent book "Shared Agency: A Planning Theory of Acting Together" (2014), which summarizes his theory developed over the past decades.

At the heart of Bratman's account for shared cooperative activity is the construction of "Shared Intention" (1993). Bratman proposes to "understand shared intention, in the basic case [two agents engaging in shared cooperative activity], as a state of affairs consisting primarily of appropriate attitudes of each individual participant and their interrelations" (p.99). The appropriate attitudes are, on the one hand, intentions of the form "I intend that we J" (Bratman, 1997a), where J is the shared cooperative activity. On the other hand, the agents need to have certain beliefs about the other agent's attitudes including knowledge that the other agent also intends that we J and that they both do so partly because the other is intending that we J. 'Intending' something, thus, is the basic individual concept in Bratman's theory for group activity. Bratman draws on his own theory of intention to explain what this exactly means.

According to Bratman, "[d]esires, beliefs and intentions are basic elements" (Bratman, 1984, p.399) contrary to views that intentions are reducible to desires and beliefs. This strongly suggests intentions are mental entities just like desires and beliefs. Bratman explains "Intentions [...] are normally stable elements of partial plans [...] subject to demands for coherence and consistency, demands which help structure further planning" (Bratman, 1993, p.101). Thus, 'intending' something means rationally 'planning something'.

When Bratman characterizes planning agency, he distinguishes between what he calls mere 'goal-directed' behavior, which can be seen in simple machines and animals, and planning agency in which intentions serve to achieve "complex goals" (Bratman, 1984, p.380). Plans seem forged to achieve goals of a certain complexity as compared to 'mere' goals. From his rather implicit remarks on this, I conclude a 'complex goal' is different from a 'mere goal' by how far in the future the goal is and, presumably, how many actions are involved in achieving the goal. Confirming this interpretation, Bratman notes that "[a]n individual planning agent needs to be able to conceive of her agency as extending both into the future and backwards, into the past. She needs to be able to see herself as an agent whose present conduct is part of larger planned activity" in "Responsibility and Planning"(Bratman, 1997b, p.38/40).

Bratman's model of shared cooperative activity includes more than intentions of the individuals that are elements of a larger plan in order to achieve a complex goal. To be truly cooperative, the individual attitudes must also be properly related. Bratman usually uses the metaphor of 'meshing' to account for this interdependence. The "individual sub-plans concerning our J-ing [, i.e. the individual intending that we J',] *mesh* just in case there is some way we could J, which would not violate either of our sub-plans but would, rather, involve the successful execution of those sub-plans," describes this metaphor more precisely (Bratman, 1992, p.332). Clearly, successful meshing is closely related to successful coordination.

There are many more important and insightful details to Bratman's account of shared agency, but I will move on to discuss its explanatory reach, its limitations and the key concepts that need further investigation.

The qualifications 'shared' and 'cooperative' can be read as the group sharing a plan with the corresponding goal and cooperating with each other using some coordination method in order to ensure proper 'meshing' of the plans, respectively. The scope of Bratman's account, thus, is rather narrow, which is exactly in line with Bratman's approach. Bratman wants to provide a reductive analysis of one specific type of group activity, and he chooses a rich type of group activity in order to make the reasonable claim that such a construction will be possible for other types of group activity as well. Indeed, he excludes all the other forms of group activity shown by the research map.

Bratman wants to "keep things simple" and only looks at "cooperative activities that involve only a pair of participating agents". Furthermore, he explicitly excludes "activities of *complex institutions with structures of authority*" (Bratman, 1992, p.327). Thus, we cannot expect explanations for corporate activity, group activity shaped by authority structures and authorization is also excluded.

Since Bratman aims at a reductive set of sufficient conditions for shared cooperative activity, Bratman appeals only to "intentions in favor of joint activities *characterized in cooperatively neutral ways* (p.339). I take this to exclude the inclusive sense of acting together that relies exactly on the agents doing something together for the sake of doing it together, rather than alone.

With regard to the research map, thus, Bratman's account explains group activity characterized by a common goal and coordination and explicitly excludes all other types of group activity (see figure 3.3). Accordingly, he called the group activity in his account shared cooperative activity, and I chose the same term in the research map.

Types of group activity described as...

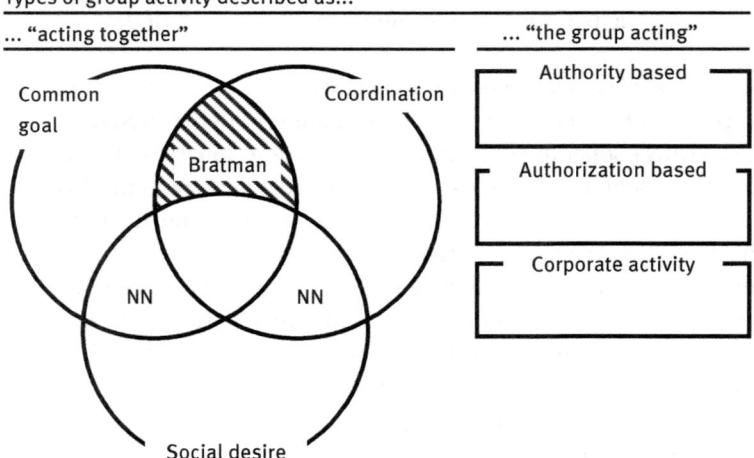

Fig. 3.3: Visualization of the research map of action theory for group activity (comp. figure 3.2 for details) with the added account of Bratman's "shared cooperative agency" covering group activity described as "acting together cooperatively" based on common goals and use of coordination.

Bratman's account, while being a milestone in the philosophical discussion of group activity, has at least two shortcomings. First, as pointed out in the beginning, Bratman aims at showing that a sense of sociality can be created using only individual concepts from action theory, but he shows this only for specific types of group activity. There may be a way to extend his account to all other types of group activity, but the chances of that seem small. It is unclear, for example, how his account can be extended to inclusive group activity, which does not require common goals, coordination or plans. At the same time, the restriction to two persons makes the account inapplicable to group activities characterized by phenomena that only appear when more agents are involved. Arnold offered an extended account of Bratman's theory in (Arnold, 2006). However, with three agents already, structures are possible challenging the idea of reducible group activity, as I will review hereafter. Furthermore, I already argued, e.g. in corporate activity, agents do not share intentions in the way Bratman proposes.

The second concern is about one of his key concepts. According to Bratman, intentions are elements of plans, and they set apart planning agency from lower forms of agency. This somehow involves the appeal to 'complex goals' guiding the group activity; yet, Bratman does not provide an explicit concept of 'goals' or 'having goals'. Instead, the notion of complexity seems to invoke the time span of the goal realization and amount of involved actions. Both parameters, however, are gradual. Therefore, the distinction between goals known from goal-directed behavior and complex goals relevant for planning agency seems to be only gradual as well. If it is only gradual, however, who is to say at which point a qualitative difference arises? I have found no answer in Bratman's works on this topic.

Overall, Bratman's approach confirms the importance of goals and coordination in group activity, but it does so under the umbrella of the concept of intentionality, which is explained with recourse to the idea of planning agency. At the same time, the explanatory reach of his theory is rather limited by the explicitly excluded types of group activity displayed in the research map. It is not clear that an extension of his account is possible not only to more than two agents, but to other forms of group activity as well. This doubt is further nourished when looking at the next currently well recognized position developed by Pettit and List.

3.2.1.2 Pettit and List on corporate agency

The monograph "group agency - the possibility, design, and status of corporate agents" (2011) by Pettit and List approaches the topic of group agency from a different angle than Bratman and with a completely different outcome. In contrast to Bratman's reductive analysis, List and Pettit's view "asserts that group agency exists but that it materializes superveniently on the contributions of the group members" (p.75). This is quite a claim, but they readily substantiate it.

The starting point of their discussion is the observation of the so-called "discursive dilemma" (Pettit, 2001, 2003) when it comes to "the aggregation of intentional attitudes" and decision making in particular (List and Pettit, 2013, p.42ff.). The 'paradox' or 'dilemma' for collective decision making is, essentially, that an aggregation of individual, rationally consistent attitudes may lead to an aggregated set of attitudes that is rationally inconsistent.

The dilemma is far from being a pathological construction, but was observed across various disciplines with practical relevance in numerous fields of society. A simpler version is the 'doctrinal paradox' in law decision making described by, e.g., Kornhauser and Sager, who rightly remark "how poorly we understand the collective nature of judging and of how troublesome that failure of understanding can be" (Kornhauser and Sager, 1993, p.2). The same kind of paradox is also known from political theory as the 'voting paradox' or 'Condorcet's paradox', first described by Condorcet (Condorcet, 1785) for a simple majority voting system. The social choice theorist Arrow extended the voting paradox to the 'Impossibility theorem', which holds for all types of voting systems as long as they satisfy some reasonable conditions[3]. The phenomenon picked up by Pettit and List, thus, is real and deserves thorough treatment.

For the dilemma to occur, the group needs to have at least three members, and the attitudes in question, e.g. decisions, preferences, judgments and so on, have to be logically linked. List and Pettit provide several examples in their book; here is one of them: "The legislature seeks to form preferences on the following propositions". The first proposition is that taxes are increased, the second that spending is reduced and the third that there is no budget deficit. In order to avoid a budget deficit, i.e. the last proposition to be true, at least one of the first two propositions must be true. Given that there are three rational legislators, the preferences may be as shown in table 3.1, similarly found in List and Pettit's book(List and Pettit, 2013, p.46). The dilemma now becomes clear. While all the individuals have a rational combination of preferences respecting the logical dependence of the propositions, a simple aggregation by majority of the individual preferences for each of the propositions results in an irrational set of propositions. This becomes particularly relevant when the choices are made one after another.

---

3 Arrow formulated two axioms and five conditions in his original work and altered them himself in the 1963's 2nd edition (Arrow, 1963). Since then various reformulations have been developed. One established version features four conditions: 'unrestricted domain' (all logically possible combinations of individual preferences can be aggregated to a single social preference), 'social ordering' (every aggregated social preference on a set of alternatives is a ranked list, not just a pairwise preference), 'weak pareto' (if all individuals prefer a certain alternative, the alternative should also be preferred after aggregation) and 'non-dictatorship' (the social preference is not determined by a single individual) (Morreau, 2016).

Tab. 3.1: Aggregation of preferences leading to the discursive dilemma as discussed by List and Pettit in (List and Pettit, 2013, p.46)

	Increase tax?	Reduce spending?	Budget deficit?
Agent 1	Yes	No	Yes
Agent 2	Yes	Yes	No
Agent 3	No	Yes	Yes
Group	Yes	Yes	Yes

While the principle of the discursive dilemma is easy to understand when we take a majority vote for the aggregation of the individual attitudes, other methods of aggregation are possible for which this is not so easy to say. However, List and Pettit assure us that no system for the aggregation of votes on a logically connected set of options overcomes the dilemma as can be shown based on Arrow's impossibility theorem (Arrow, 1963; List and Pettit, 2013).

The discursive dilemma, thus, is a deep challenge to the idea of attitude aggregation. Three possible reactions are immediately relevant to group activity. First, one could enforce only individual attitudes that do not result in a dilemma. Individuals would need to change their attitudes after group discussion in order to produce a coherent group attitude. Weirich claims this is one way to rationally defuse the discursive dilemma (Weirich, 2014, p.204). Obviously, however, this significantly restricts the freedom of choice for the individuals, and List and Pettit rightly note that this is only "compelling if the aggregation of attitudes is preceded by a period of group deliberation" (List and Pettit, 2013, p.52). I share List's and Pettit's doubts that this solution is generally applicable, but it is a solution for some groups.

A second solution, also proposed by Paul Weirich, is that a "committee's members are committed to majoritarian methods and are willing to tolerate occasional inconsistencies [...as...] a cost the committee pays to achieve its other goals" (Weirich, 2014, p.204). The idea of this second proposal is, essentially, to (rationally) abandon collective rationality. List and Pettit quickly reject dropping rational consistency, since this leads to unacceptable practical outcomes. Instead, they propose to drop rational completeness, i.e. the group should simply refrain from a position on the affected propositions. As an example, they point at the UN Security Council, which follow a strongly consensual aggregation principle in order to respect national interests. As is well known, this leads the UN Security Council to "frequently [...] suspend attitude" (List and Pettit, 2013, p.53), which most certainly is not a solution for other groups.

Finally, and this is the option preferred by List and Pettit, a group could implement procedures to form collective attitudes from already existing collective attitudes and neglect the respective individuals' attitudes. Looking at legislators, this would mean a vote for staying within budget and a vote to not increase the taxes already fixes the decision about reducing spending without consulting individual votes on this very decision. The legislators agree on a "premise-based procedure" as suggested by List and Pettit, and, consequently, they reduce the spending despite the fact that the majority of them would not have so decided.

The upshot of the entire discussion is that there are, in fact, some groups that display collective attitudes towards some specific propositions which cannot be properly reduced to individual attitudes on this proposition. In fact, the individuals do not even need to form an attitude toward these propositions. Rather, the group has implemented an aggregation procedure ensuring a rational set of attitudes.

In a second step, not necessarily related to the discursive dilemma, List and Pettit note that "many different possible combinations of individual attitudes [...] can give rise to the same group attitude," i.e. the group attitude displays 'multiple realizability'. At the same time, the group attitudes also influence the individual attitudes and not just the other way around (p.77). Consequently, List and Pettit identify the relation between group attitudes and individual attitudes to be a supervenience relation and open a far reaching analogy: "consciousness exists but [...] it is supervenient on the contributions of the neurons. In almost exact parallel, [...] group agency exists." (p.75). Given that the attitudes in question usually belong to the domain of the mind on the individual level, this explains Pettit's catch phrase "Groups with minds of their own" (Pettit, 2003). As a consequence, groups displaying these features are considered group agents by List and Pettit and "we can interact with them, criticize them, and make demands on them, in a manner not possible with non-agential systems" (List and Pettit, 2013, p.76).

The notion of an 'agential system' is taken from their functional understanding of agency. They take three features to be crucial. An agent needs to have "representational states that depict how things are in the environment [...,] motivational states that specify how it requires things to be [...and] the capacity to process its representational and motivational states leading it to intervene suitably" (p.20). This is possible for simple machines, but also for humans whose "minds have a reach in space, time, and modality that the simple robot's mind does not" and they refer to Bratman's planning theory as a sign of this reach (ibd.) In particular, "the precise physical nature of intentional states [...] may be of a wide variety of kinds [,...] electronic or neural configurations of the agent, for example" (p.21). Whether or not an entity has intentional states, consequently, is not so much a matter of their physical constitution, but their functional and explanatory role in the agent's behavior.

List and Pettit discuss how their three features of agency may be realized in groups using the aggregation procedures as proposed. In particular, they show that groups can form and track the truth of beliefs even better than their individual members, if organized accordingly (p.82ff). Additionally, they discuss that a group can pursue their goals even though its members have competing self-interests as long as they have proper incentives. Towards their third feature of agency, they take it as given that well organized groups are particularly potent; so potent in fact, that they discuss principles to protect the members of the group from its power.

Overall, List and Pettit's approach is less theoretically motivated than Bratman's approach. Where Bratman drives for theoretical parsimony and a theoretical show-case for a reductive account of group agency on an equally parsimonious level of group activity, List and Pettit start from a pragmatic issue that is not even possible in Bratman's two-person show-case, the discursive dilemma, and observe how group activity goes beyond individual activity in a comprehensible way. Following this, they identify agential features realized through an organizational design in groups that allows groups to fulfill general agency conditions.

List and Pettit, thus, account for a thick notion of group activity. The title of their book refers to "the possibility, design, and status of corporate agents". I assume, therefore, the groups that have employed the aggregation procedures to realize the three agential features listed by List and Pettit are meant to be corporate agents. Unfortunately, they say very little about corporate entities. They seem to adopt the notion of corporations known from economics and law when they say "corporations [...] pursue the financial welfare of their shareholders as their ultimate purpose [...] and exhibit the characteristics of agency in full dress" (p.40), but this does not match their use of, e.g., corporate responsibility later in their book.

Given the insufficient characterization of what exactly their account is trying to explain, I will simply take my notion of corporate agency which happens to fit well with their line of thought. I characterized corporate agency by the idea that the externally realized agential features are fundamental to agency such that the group activity cannot be interpreted as individuals acting together anymore, i.e. it is not an expression of the individual's agency, but a new layer of agency on group level emerges. As examples of how this is possible, I described the phenomena of diffusion and alienation. List and Pettit follow exactly this strategy, even though they do not make it explicit, and describe how decision making can be realized on the group level.

It is now easy to see that Bratman's account and the account of List and Pettit are not competing, but target different types of group activity (see figure 3.4). However, the two accounts differ significantly in their action theoretic assumptions. Where Bratman links his account of group activity neatly with a well-developed theory on individual agency, List and Pettit only propose a broad idea of agency that also includes robots, whose only purpose is putting cylinders upright (p.19). This is a little surprising given the powerful concepts they have uncovered.

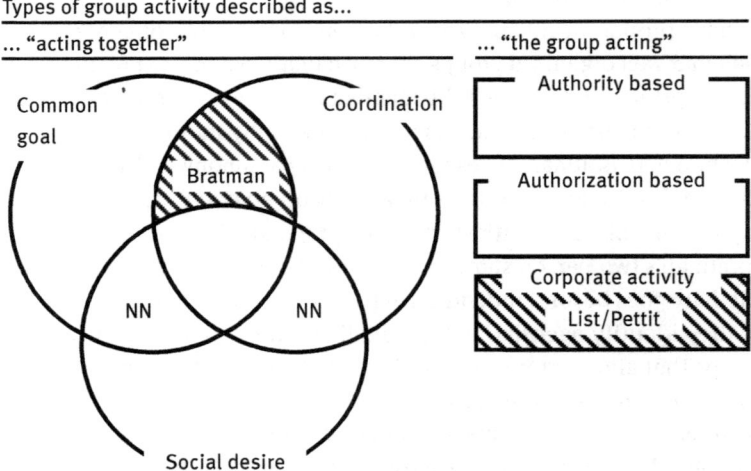

Fig. 3.4: Visualization of the research map of action theory for group activity (comp. figure 3.2 for details) with the added account of List's/Pettit's "group agency" covering corporate activity described as "the group acting" based on external realization of fundamental features of agency.

Overall, List and Pettit deliver a very insightful discussion of corporate activity, in which they compellingly explain how corporations may display agency beyond individual agency. Notably, they do not fall back on the idea of collective intentionality and do not even use it in their broad definition of individual agency. At the same time, however, their idea of agency also renders simple machines agents, which weakens their claim of group agency.

3.2.1.3 Tuomela and Searle on we-intentions

Like Bratman, Tuomela and Searle put intentionality at the core of their accounts for group activity but, unlike to Bratman, they favor the introduction of concepts which do not exist in individual action theory. Nonetheless, both accounts are reductive in the sense that they do not open a new layer of agency on a group level.

Raimo Tuoemela together with Kaarlo Miller introduced the notion of "We-Intentions" in their equally titled 1988 paper that draws much from Tuomela's monograph "A Theory of Social Action" from four years before. Usually, Tuomela and Miller are associated with the idea that group activity can be explained by the members of a group doing their parts of the group activity and corresponding participatory intentions. I have always been confused about this interpretation for it seems to miss the core idea of their proposal. The reason for this is, I believe, that in their most influential paper the core idea is not as prominently placed as it could be. The key concept of their account is what they later called the "we-mode," e.g., in (Tuomela, 2006).

The idea of the 'we-mode' is seeing "my being one of the members of the group [...] as a partial, other-regarding reason for my doing one or more other actions". This results in a conception of 'I' not in the sense of me as an individual, but an 'I' "in this sense is concerned with 'one of us' and thus with what it is to be a member of *our* group". Consequently, "I do what I do at least in part *because* I, a member of G, have the intention expressed by [We will do X]"(Tuomela and Miller, 1988, p.368). The view of myself as a member of the group generates a 'we-mode' in reasoning about what to do and intentions derived using this 'we-mode' are genuine 'we-intentions'.

The specific form of the resulting 'we-intentions' is, indeed, captured by participatory intentions, i.e. the agents of a group have an intention to do their parts of a group activity X (ibd.) Formally, 'we-intentions' look even more reductive than Bratman's shared intentions. Bratman introduces the idea of 'I intend that *we* J', while Tuomela and Miller do not even grant this kind of 'we' in the personal attitudes. However, they explain that "a central feature of we-intentions [is] that they are based on *social* motivation" (p.377). Thus, 'we-intentions' have implicitly defined a basic social attitude later called the 'we-mode'.

The social nature of 'we-intentions' becomes clearer, when Tuomela and Miller explain how the 'we-mode' leads to the participatory 'we-intentions'. In "Collective Goals Analyzed" (2014), they propose that the 'we-mode' attitude of the individuals enables them to collectively accept and commit to a common goal. By way of collective acceptance and commitment the collective goal becomes "equivalent to full-blown collective intentions" (p.34) These collective intentions, which they call 'joint intentions' in another paper (Tuomela, 2006), provide a 'we-mode reason' for the individuals to deliberate and form participatory 'we-intentions' to realize the collective goal/'joint intention'. The participatory 'we-intentions' in their account, thus, only appear after everything interesting about group activity has happened.

Evidently, Tuomela and Miller see sharing a common goal as necessary for a substantial case of group activity. The idea of participatory 'we-intentions' results in coordinated group activity. The core idea of the 'we-mode', I take it, can be viewed as an account for inclusiveness as displayed in the research map. Thus, the account aims at explaining what I called 'fully-integrated' group activity.

Given the tight connection between 'we-mode', collective goals and participatory intentions, it is hard to see how this theory accounts for group activity which is not fully-integrated, e.g. cases were the relation between the individuals is not simply captured by the idea that they share a goal. Furthermore, the notions of 'joint intentions' and 'we-intentions' hardly resemble their individual version but become mere headers for a collection of the truly important concepts. This suggests a continuity between individual action theory and collective theory, where, in reality, a strong conceptual break should attract attention.

One way to approach this conceptual break is shown by John Searle. For Searle, "[w]e-intentions cannot be analyzed into sets of I-intentions, even I-intentions supplemented with beliefs, including mutual beliefs, about the intentions of other members of the group" (Searle, 1990). To solve this problem, Searle suggests "[w]e simply have to recognize that there are intentions whose form is: We intend that we perform act A; and such an intention can exist in the mind of each individual agent who is acting as part of the collective" (p.408). Searle's 'we-intentions', thus, are original, i.e. non-reducible attitudes hold by individuals.

To make the idea of such we-intentions plausible, Searle, first, links his account for collective intentions to his account of individual intentions to explain how they lead to actual action. Secondly, he discusses how it is possible for humans to have such intentions. The first aspect is achieved by interpreting we-intentions as means-goal intentions, where the goal part contains the collective goal and the means part contains the individual contribution to that goal (p.412). Allowing such complexity in the individual's attitudes, 'we-intentions' can be spelled out in the same formalism used for individual intentions in Searle's theory[4](Searle, 1979). This is very similar to Tuomela's and Miller's characterization of 'joint intentions' and the corresponding individual participatory inventions.

The second aspect addresses the possibility of such distinct 'we-intentions' and Searle suggests a "biological primitive sense of the other person as a candidate for shared intentionality" (Searle, 1990, p.415). This primitive sense enables

---

4 Searle's formal analysis of successful intentional action takes the form 'i.a. (this i.a causes: physical event A) CAUSES: PHYSICAL EVENT A'. This is to be read as: A successful intentional action requires an 'intention in action' (i.a.) to cause a physical event (described in capital letters) with the condition of satisfaction that this very intention comes with a mental representation that it causes the respective event (small letters in brackets). Searle then allows nestings of the 'causes:' relation and he allows 'intentions in action' to include a 'by means of' relation to account for means-goal descriptions of intentional action, i.e. 'i.a. A by means of M (this i.a. causes: means M, causes: physical event A)'. His version of collective intentionality, then, can be expressed by intentions in actions of the individuals as 'i.a. collective A by means of singular M (this i.a. causes: means M, causes: physical event A) CAUSES: MEANS M, CAUSES: PHYSICAL EVENT A' (Searle, 1979, 1990).

human beings to have 'we-intentions' and, consequently, act together. Searle, thus, does not propose a 'we-mode' meaning that an agent views himself as part of a group, but rather the "primitive sense" refers to a perspective of an agent onto others. Essentially, however, the account of Tuomela and Miller and the account of Searle show strong conceptual similarities, while they differ in the idea how 'we-intentions' are psychologically realized.

From this brief review, it is easy to see that Searle, as well as Tuomela and Miller, aim at explaining fully integrated group activity, which is characterized by having a common goal, coordination and inclusiveness at the same time (see figure 3.5). Inclusiveness, however, is at the core of what needs to be explained from their perspective and they are not shy to suggest that human beings have a special ability to form 'we-intentions' by way of some human-specific psychological feature, be it a 'we-mode' understanding of oneself or a 'primitive sense' of others as agents. While either proposal is intuitively appealing, both solutions are speculative with respect to human psychology. Neither account provides solid empirical evidence that human beings have such a 'primitive sense' or a 'we-mode' perspective onto themselves. In fact, they do not even propose how such a psychological phenomenon could be observed or tested for.

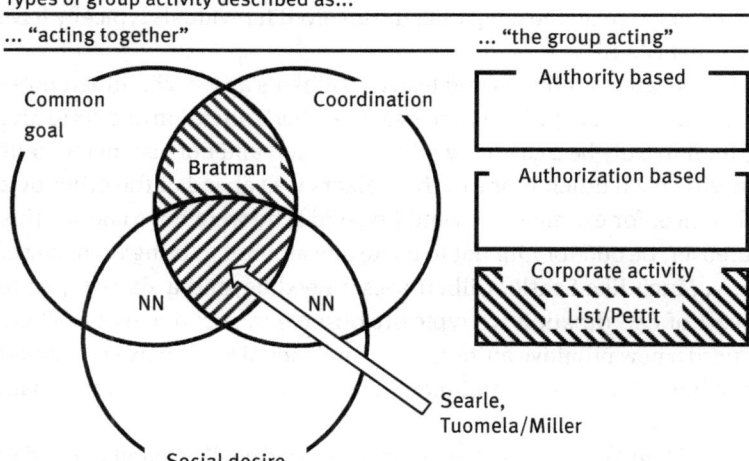

Fig. 3.5: Visualization of the research map of action theory for group activity (comp. figure 3.2 for details) with the added accounts of Searle's "we-intentions" and Tuomela's/Miller's "we-mode/we-intentions" covering group activity described as "acting together fully-integrated" based on common goals, coordination and a social desire to do something together.

3.2.1.4 Gilbert's joint commitment

In the last part of the most influential accounts of group activity, I look at Margaret Gilbert's position. Margaret Gilbert became popular for her idea of 'plural subjects', i.e. seemingly supra-individual entities acting much like individuals do. Her discussion of group activity, however, starts a lot more modest. In "Walking Together: A Paradigmatic Social Phenomenon" (1990) she starts with "[t]he idea [..] that we can discover the nature of social groups in general by investigating such small-scale temporary phenomena as going for a walk together" (p.2). Notably, Gilbert does not set out to develop an action theory for groups, but merely to understand the 'nature of social groups'. Clearly, one of the most important aspects of social groups is that members do things together and so Gilbert starts her investigation at the most simple case of doing something together she can think of.

Gilbert approaches the topic from two directions. First, she notes when people do something together they somehow pursue a shared goal, and she offers two interpretations. The "weak shared goal" reading means the individuals have the same personal goal, but do not know it. Clearly, this does not provide the sociality seen in taking a walk together. The "strong shared goal" goes a step further by requiring the individuals know of each other's identical personal goal possibly through communicating it (p.3). This is essentially the characterization of what I called primitive group activity in the research map. Still, per Gilbert, even a strong shared goal does not explain the obligation the involved individuals typically have towards each other (p.4).

The role of obligations is the second focus of Gilbert's approach. Gilbert notes even when walking together "each has a right to the other's attention and corrective action" (p.4) for it to truly be a case of 'walking together' and not just incidentally walking alongside each other. If one of the walkers was ahead of the other by a significant distance, for example, "it would be odd if he were not to notice this. It would, moreover, be odd for him not to make any attempt to bring them closer together" (p.3). Much like Searle, Gilbert sees a need beyond a shared goal to explain the sort of coordination we typically observe in social activity. Where Searle introduced a new primitive attitude on the individual level, however, Gilbert introduces the idea of a 'joint commitment' on a collective level to satisfy said need.

The notions of 'joint commitment' and 'strong shared goal' go hand in hand in Gilbert's original approach. The form of the 'joint commitment' is "a special form of *conditional commitment* such that [...] only when *everyone* has done similarly is *anyone* committed" (p.7), and the content to which everyone is committed is exactly the shared goal: " I have said very generally that the pool of wills is dedicated, as one, to the relevant goal. This, though vague perhaps, is the guiding idea" (p.9). In

Gilbert's own work, it remains vague indeed how this 'pooling of wills' is supposed to work. Bratman reads it as, essentially, a contractual concept (Bratman, 2006a), while Velleman sees it as a gap in her account he gladly closes[5] (Velleman, 1997). This shows Gilbert's idea can be easily adapted for individualistic as well as non-individualistic accounts of group activity. Gilbert herself seems to follow the latter when she writes, e.g., a "joint commitment, [...] is a commitment of two or more people. It is not a conjunction of a personal commitment of one and separate commitments of others. Rather, it is the commitment of them all." (Gilbert, 2006, p. 100).

Gilbert then uses 'joint commitment' to lift the concepts of individual agency onto the group level in a one-to-one fashion. First, she introduces the idea of a 'plural subject', which is constituted by the people who are jointly committed towards a shared goal. This plural subject may then have, in the technical sense advocated by Gilbert herself, 'joint intentions' by way of its members being 'jointly committed' to intend and 'joint beliefs' by way of its member being jointly committed to believe (Gilbert, 2006).

The account developed by Gilbert explains inclusiveness in group activity, but she also claims that group activity necessarily comes with a goal. The idea of coordinated group activity is explained insofar as the 'joint commitment' results in a social pressure on the individuals to coordinate towards achieving the common goal. Thus, Gilbert's model accounts for fully-integrated group activity. Gilbert's account, therefore, is in direct competition with the accounts of Searle and Tuomela/Miller (comp. figure 3.6). The main difference in her account is that she does not refer to an individual psychological phenomenon, but to a social phenomenon based on social obligation that she calls 'joint commitment'.

The discussion of Gilbert's work has gone in every direction. Some outright reject her account because they "find Gilbert's core notion of a plural subject somewhat opaque" (Miller and Makela, 2005, p.638) or they think the notion of joint commitment "is stipulative: a brute conceptual connection that does no explanatory work" (Fagan, 2014, p.180). Others, like Bratman, pick up on the notion of obligation and provide an alternative model. Still, others again embrace ideas like the 'pooling of wills' and extend the theory accordingly as was done by Velleman (Velleman, 1997).

---

5 Velleman takes Searle's formalism of 'intentions in action' but allows the representation required for such intentions to be carried by, e.g., speech acts rather than individual mental states. This way individuals can 'pool their wills' as suggested by Gilbert by using speech acts that represent the individuals as doing something together. These 'stories' function as collective 'intention in action' giving rise to common individual intentions as described by Searle.

Types of group activity described as...

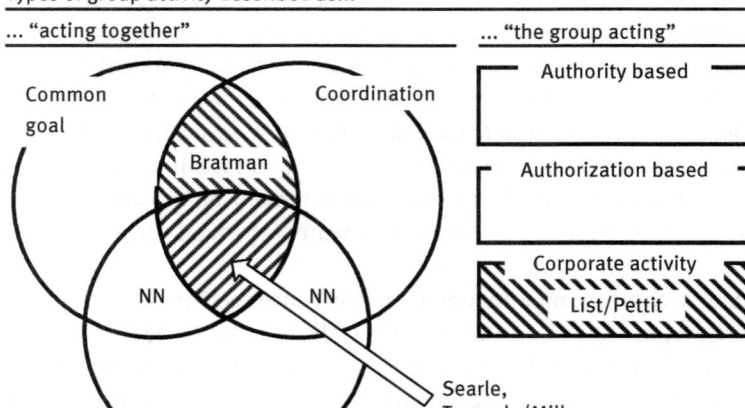

Fig. 3.6: Visualization of the research map of action theory for group activity (comp. figure 3.2 for details) with the added account of Gilbert's "joint intentions" covering group activity described as "acting together fully-integrated" based on common goals, coordination and a social desire to do something together.

I, too, have reservations concerning the somewhat stipulative introduction of 'joint commitment', but even if follow this, the rest of the account has at least two further flaws. First, Gilbert claims the joint commitment is a commitment towards a common goal. In taking a walk together, her prime example, however, it is not at all clear there is a common goal. Additionally, I already showed there is group activity that explicitly excludes common goals, but the agents only act together opportunistically. The relation between goals and 'joint commitments' in Gilbert's account, thus, needs reconsideration. Second, her shift to action theory is unsatisfactory for she simply transfers all agential features to the group level using the 'joint commitment'. Given that I have already discussed several ways of how this is possible without anything like a joint commitment, this strategy is not needed.

Overall, thus, Gilbert claims there is an obligation-based phenomenon in group activity called 'joint commitment' towards a common goal. This allows her to explain agency of 'plural subjects' with reference to 'joint intentions' and 'joint beliefs' mediated by the 'joint commitment'. Central to this approach is the notion of shared goals and mutual obligations.

3.2.1.5 Conclusions from the most influential positions on group activity

The discussion of the five most influential accounts by Bratman, List and Pettit, Tuomela and Miller, Searle, and Gilbert shows the broad range of philosophical analysis of group activity. The coverage of the research map, however, illustrates that agency in group activity is not fully addressed (see figure 3.6). Further review of alternative accounts is required to extend the coverage.

At the same time, it has become evident that the most influential accounts do not necessarily compete, but possibly complement each other. Indeed, the accounts are partly compatible, but they also are based on fundamentally different assumptions either on individual action theory or on how the sociality of human beings is created. Instead of dwelling on the differences, it is insightful to point at the themes they agree on for these themes are more likely to be the foundation of agency in group activity.

First, essentially all of them see the idea of sharing goals as crucial for a rich type of group activity often characterized as being jointly intentional, or as displaying shared intentionality and so on. It is surprising they put only little effort in the philosophical analysis of this idea with the exception of Tuomela and Miller. Their analysis, however, draws heavily on their original concept of the 'we-mode'. Independent analysis is required.

Second, all but List and Pettit attempt to merge intentionality from individual agency into their accounts of group activity. This is often motivated by conceptual continuity and the fact that intentionality is taken to mark actions over less sophisticated behavior in individual action theory. For the construction of a similar concept on the group level, the positions offer solutions ranging from completely reductive constructions through introductions of new individual attitudes to supra-individual explanations. Unfortunately, the positions do not share one and the same understanding of intentionality in action theory for individuals, which prevents an easy comparison of the different approaches.

Third, there is also a strong focus on understanding how group activity goes beyond agents merely doing something in parallel–be it meshing sub-plans, decision procedures, participatory intentions or simple means-goal relations. All of them propose a way how the actual execution is coordinated.

The three recurring themes are, thus, goals, intentionality and coordination. I now discuss alternative approaches in order extend the coverage of the research map and learn more about the key concepts for agency in group activity.

3.2.2 Alternative accounts for group activity

Next to the most discussed accounts, there is a wealth of literature on agency in group activity, group responsibility, or both. Many of them refer to one or more of the above positions and either expand them or attempt to merge them together, but there are also original contributions offering completely new ways to think about group activity. I focus on a few positions I feel are most inspiring. As before, I focus on what exactly the scope of the positions is and what the key concepts are.

3.2.2.1 French's corporate internal decision structure

Peter A. French polarized with his 1979 thesis of "The Corporation as a Moral Person" before the accounts discussed above even appeared. However, in his refined account presented in, e.g., "Corporate Ethics" (1995) he noted "it has become clear to me [...], that calling corporations moral persons creates more confusion and mis-understanding than clarity" (p.10). Consequently, he concedes "that actors and not persons are the primary units of the moral community" (ibd.) While he ultimately aims at understanding the moral role of corporations, he first focuses on their status as agents. As a basic understanding of agency, French essentially takes over Bratman's theory of planning agency.

French addresses the issue from two directions. From the one side, he thinks about corporations from a metaphysical perspective. From the other side, he explores the functional capabilities of corporations and how they match capabilities required for acting.

The key to understand the metaphysical status of corporations is the observation that people in corporations usually hold more or less well-defined positions giving them certain tasks and power within the corporation. These positions are usually defined independently from the particular individual chosen to fill the position and so it is possible that "People come and go. The positions endure" (p.17). They endure a change of who is filling the positions and they potentially endure time spans larger than any individual's life-span. Given that persons can be changed almost arbitrarily into the various positions and the extra-ordinary durability of positions, it is possible to say the identity of a corporation does not depend on the individuals making it up, but that corporations have an identity of their own much like Theseus' ship has an identity independently of its wooden planks[6]. Naturally, the relation between individuals and the respective corporation is more complex.

This leads into the second question about functional capabilities of corporations. A corporation needs a way to "subordinate[] and synthesize[] the intentions and actions of various human persons (and even the behavior of machines) into corporate action" (p.25). French describes a way to do this by pointing at defined procedures and standing policies in corporations. Procedures may govern specific processes that run between various positions in the corporation; they describe what should be done in particular situations. This could include, for example, the decision making procedures described in the account of List and Pettit. Policies are less specific. They may only provide high level orientation for the general purpose and behavior. Nonetheless, procedures and policies guide the individuals filling the different positions in the corporation to achieve coherent group activity. Equally important, procedures and policies draw a line between individual agents acting out of personal interest compared to acting out the position they are holding.

The combination of these two corporate designs, an organizational chart of positions on the one hand and procedural rules and policies on the other hand, are what French calls a "corporate internal decision structure" or "CID structure" (p.27). A corporation with a functioning CID structure, according to French, can fulfill all requirements needed for moral agency. Moreover, the "CID structure accounts for the personality of the corporation" (p.35).

The scope of French's position is clearly tailored to corporate group activity. The position, thus, does not add to the coverage of the research map, but complements the position of List and Pettit on corporate group activity from an even more practical perspective. The key concept of his account is the 'corporate internal decision structure'. While this structure is internal to the corporation, it is external to the individuals making up the corporation. In fact, the individuals live large parts of their lives in this structure and shape it doing so. French's account fits neatly with the idea of external realization of agential features, and it carries much practical insight. From an action theoretic point of view, however, it is rather slim. French rejects the view that acting requires beliefs or desires mainly because this would exclude any entity that cannot have desires and beliefs. Instead, he points at Bratman's planning agency that essentially equates intentions and plans or elements thereof. As discussed above, however, Bratman's planning theory

---

6 "The ship wherein Theseus [...] returned [...] was preserved by the Athenians [...] for they took away the old planks as they decayed, putting in new and stronger timber in their place, [...] this ship became a standing example among the philosophers, for the logical question of things that grow; one side holding that the ship remained the same, and the other contending that it was not the same (Plutarch, 75).

understands intentions not reducible but on par with beliefs and desires: "Desires, beliefs and intentions are basic elements" (Bratman, 1984, p.399). Thus, if French rejects desires and beliefs as suitable for describing agency not restricted to human beings, then so he should do with Bratman's intentions.

As with List and Pettit, the action theoretic assumptions of French do not match the otherwise insightful and comprehensible theory for corporate agency. Intentionality, in particular, seems to be at the center of this problem.

3.2.2.2 Schweikard's practical integrity

David P. Schweikard takes the problem of intentionality in group activity head on in his 2011 monograph "Der Mythos des Singulären". Schweikard's approach strictly adheres to his understanding of action theory, and he follows this up by an analysis of the most discussed positions on group activity. He then offers an intelligent symbiosis under the header of 'practical integrity'.

Schweikard favors an externalist understanding of intentional actions described by Harry Frankfurt, according to which acting intentionally is about guidance of one's actions in a sophisticated sense. Following this proposal, intentions are not characterized by being particular states of mind, but 'practical attitudes' which may be realized in many ways (p.161). Accordingly, intentions can be quite complex in form, and Schweikard determines that intentions might differ in their subject (who is intending), their content (what is intended) but also their mode (who is supposed to bring about the content of the intention) (p.173). Bratman's 'I intend that we J', for example, has 'I' as its subject, 'J' as its content, and it is in the 'we-mode'. Tuomela's participatory intentions, on the face of it, are in an I-mode with an I-subject, but the content refers to a relation to a greater collective act. Searle's we-intentions have a 'we' as their subject, and they are in a we-mode with a common content.

Schweikard's insight into the discussion of intentionality in group activity is very revealing. It shows how the different accounts of group activity found different ways to alter the notion of a common individual intention in order to apply it to group activity. One cannot help but notice, however, a certain arbitrariness in the discussion about where a 'we' needs to be put in the expressions of intentions in group activity. This is particular astounding given that the various accounts present distinct, fundamental concepts for agency, which should be the focus instead of intentionality. The same holds for Schweikard's account.

Schweikard analyzes the accounts of Bratman, List and Pettit, Tuomela and Miller, Searle and Gilbert and merges the best of each together to provide what he calls the model of 'practical integrity'. Practical integrity is a 'cluster of structural properties' (comp. page 404) that enables a group to control actions in the way demanded by Frankfurt's account for agency. It does so by proper integration of its members. The list of properties contains 14 items, and only one of them is directly concerned with intentions. It starts with having a common goal, it picks up Tuomela's idea of collective acceptance, Gilbert's idea of collective commitment in an altered, more precise form, Pettit's ideas on how decisions are made in a collectively rational manner and he adds some criteria himself that describe, e.g. membership and how execution of decisions is supervised. Among the 14 items, he demands the intentions that refer to the common goal must be in the mode of 'we', rather than 'I'.

Schweikard's account is one of the first attempts to bring together the main contenders for an explanation of group activity. He himself notes the existing works are only minimally connected and are largely disparate in their basic premises, examples and terminology (p.198). My review supports this view. With his discussion of intentionality in group activity, Schweikard provides a framework to compare and discuss these positions on an equal footing, and he directly addresses the action theoretic assumption of the different accounts. This in itself is a much needed discussion in the field.

Surprisingly, despite the insight that the dominant accounts are largely disparate, Schweikard attempts to merge the different ideas into one account of group activity. This, I believe, leads to a slightly paradoxical situation. His idea certainly is to *widen* the reach by merging the different accounts. However, the accounts contain elements that exclude particular types of group activity. If these elements are merged, it is equally possible the explanatory scope is *reduced* instead. Tuomela's collective acceptance of a common goal, for example, effectively excludes group activity where the means-goal structure is diffused over various stages. At the same time, elaborate forms of membership and decision-making procedures exclude more primitive forms of group activity.

With a list of 14 properties, the question arises how many groups can fulfill the demands and be proper collective agents having 'practical integrity'. Schweikard seems to be aware of this problem and explicitly restricts his model to medium-sized groups in which it is possible for the members to directly discuss their common goals and how to pursue them as well as their internal organization (p.319). This is a strong restriction. It excludes any larger companies shaping today's world and, at the same time, simpler forms of group activity not relying on elaborate internal organization.

Furthermore, Schweikard claims the attitudes and actions of the group are irreducible to their individual counterparts. Instead, the collective versions are *constituted* by the individual versions together with structural elements of the group organization. The resulting model is a hybrid. It aims at a new level of agency grounded in its irreducibility claims, but it also restricts itself to group activity in which the members remain accountable for important features like goals and supervision of execution. As such, the kind of group activity described by Schweikard hovers somewhere between elaborate versions of fully-integrate group activity and light corporate group activity.

Not only does this reduce the applicability of the idea of 'practical integrity' to a minority of groups and group activity in reality, but it also prevents a clear perspective on how group activity displays a qualitatively new type of agency. This result of what I found to be the best attempt of merging the different accounts of group activity, thus, is unsatisfactory. Another conclusion needs to be drawn from the observation of the distinctiveness of the different accounts. Still, Schweikard's discussion once more highlights the most important concepts found in the literature, and he provides a model for a very specific and elaborate type of group activity.

3.2.2.3 Tomasello, Butterfill and Pacherie's conclusions from child development

Most of the group activities in reality are not very. In fact, small children seem to engage in group activity before they even develop a full understanding of another person's mental capabilities including intentionality.

Pacherie gives a summary of what children are capable of with increasing age according to psychological research in her paper "Intentional Joint Action: Shared Intention Lite" (2013). Surprisingly, even before the age of 15 months, children already have some sort of social instinct. Vaish et al. have shown that small children avoid helping others with harmful intention (Vaish et al., 2010). Hamlin, Dunfield and Kuhlmeier observed preferences for persons based on past helpful behavior, and Kinzler observed a preference based on common language (Hamlin et al., 2007; Dunfield and Kuhlmeier, 2010). From age 14 months to 18 months, children already help others to attain their goals independent from a reward according to research by Warneken (Warneken and Tomasello, 2007). Brownell observed skillful coordination in novel situations in 2 year old infants (Brownell, 2011). Around the same time, between a child's second and third year, Gräfenheim, Hamann, Rakoczy and Warneken found that children understand normative aspects of cooperation like rules, agreements, commitments and so on (Gräfenhain et al., 2009; Hamann et al., 2012; Rakoczy et al., 2008; Warneken et al., 2006). All of this happens before children pass Perner's false belief test[7], which happens around 4 years of age,

---

7 Wimmer and Perner designed experiments so that "subjects observed how a protagonist put an object into a location x and then witnessed that in the absence of the protagonist the object was transferred from x to location y". They found that when asked to show which location the

i.e. before they ascribe beliefs to other persons independent of their own beliefs (Wimmer and Perner, 1983, p.103).

These observations make elaborate accounts of group activity inapplicable. Mutual knowledge conditions found in most of the above accounts require beliefs about other persons' beliefs. Thus, they exclude very young infants despite the fact they engage in joint activity. Furthermore, normative elements are only understood by infants after they first engage in joint activity which excludes any obligation based approaches á la Margaret Gilbert.

Tomasello's origin of cultural cognition. In " Understanding and sharing intention: The origins of cultural cognition" (2005), Tomasello et al., consequently, reject the idea that the basis for human agents to act together lies in their capabilities to read each other's minds alone. While they agree "[h]uman beings are the world's experts at mind reading" and "that the crucial difference between human cognition and that of other species is the ability to participate with others in collaborative activities with shared goals and intentions" (p.675), they contend that mind-reading alone is insufficient to explain such activities. Two observations lead them to this conclusion. First, small children possess only a reduced set of mind-reading capabilities and still engage in joint activities rendering elaborate forms of mind-reading not necessary. Second, some great apes and autistic human beings are capable of basic mind reading capabilities but do *not* engage in comparable joint activities, thus rendering mind-reading not sufficient for joint activity.

A little understanding of other agents, however, is required. Tomasello et al. present three basic capabilities in early development that seem relevant. First, we learn to "distinguish[.] animate *self-produced* action from inanimate, caused motion" (p.678). Second, we "understand[.] that the actor has a goal and behaves with *persistence* until reality matches the goal". Third, we "perceive[.] and understand[.] that the actor considers action plans and *chooses* which of them to enact in intenticnal action" (p.678).

The concepts in these statements have very specific meaning. Tomasello et al. "distinguish the external goal–a certain state of the environment such as an open box–and the internal goal–an internal entity that guides the person's behavior." An intention, on the other hand, "includes both a means (action plan) as well as a goal" (p.676), i.e. it is literally the specific action plan of bodily movements that change the world so as to match the world represented by the goal that an agent has.

---

protagonist will look for the object "[n]one of the 3–4-year old, 57% of 4–6-year old, and 86% of 6–9-year old children pointed correctly to location x.

The three basic abilities, understanding animate behavior, understanding goal-directed behavior and understanding behavior in terms of means and goals, result in different forms of joint activity of increasing complexity. They only do so, however, if another ingredient is added. Tomasello et al. claim that human beings have "a special motivation and capacity to share emotions with each other," which is observed as early as 3 months of age in the interaction of newborns and their parents (p.682). From the emotion-based motivation, a general "motivation to share psychological states" develops that enables other forms of interaction as well (p.681), so they claim.

The model is intriguing in its simplicity and convincing with its psychological evidence. It explains inclusive group activity (ATI) by pointing at a basic, empirically observable desire to share emotions. Tomasello's account, thus, truly extends the coverage of the research map (compare figure 3.7). If a basic desire to share emotions is, indeed, confirmed by scientific research, I am happy to embrace the idea. I am, however, skeptic about the explanatory reach. In particular, the generalization to a 'motivation to share psychological states' needs thorough examination and, with it, the extension of this model to goal-directed group activity and cooperative group activity. It is not clear that group activity solely involving a common goal should rely on a motivation to share this goal. It is not uncommon, for example, that the agents have a motivation *not* to share anything with the other, but are forced to by circumstance.

It is a reasonable assumption that a basic desire to share emotions helps us in our development to engage with others in the first place. But once we do, we should consider that group activity stops to rely on this basic desire much like we do not need to like someone in order to make mutually beneficial trades. Instead of postulating a somewhat counter-intuitive 'motivation to share a goal' or 'motivation to share an intention', we must make sense of the more sophisticated forms of group activity in a different way. After all, we do not explain agriculture by our new-born instinct to latch onto our mother's breast either.

Notably, however, prominent psychological research, too, acknowledges the importance of goals and intentionality in group activity.

Butterfill's plural activities. Stephen Butterfill takes a different route to explain simple types of group activity. Instead of introducing a new basic phenomenon, he describes how multiple agents may engage in joint actions without the need of complex mind-reading. The keys to his account are, on the one hand, a simplified notion of shared goals and, on the other hand, a sufficiently connected set of expectations.

A goal, as Stephen Butterfill uses the term, "refers to an outcome, actual or possible, and not a state. [He] makes[s] no direct use of the notion that agents can have goals." Goals, in this sense, are purely external to an agent's mind and do not

Types of group activity described as...

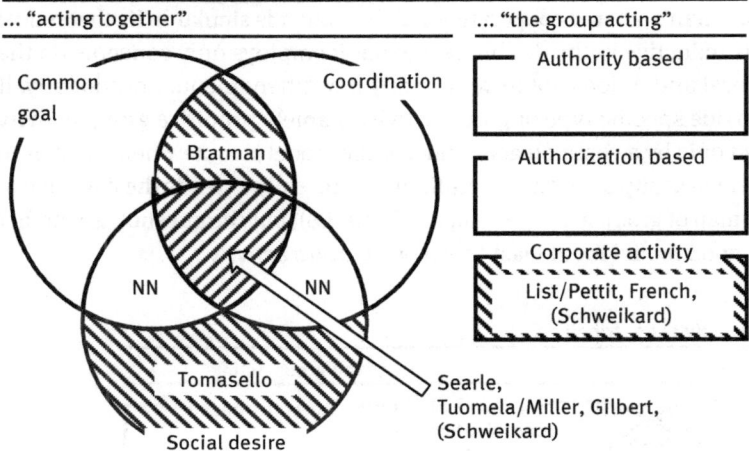

Fig. 3.7: Visualization of the research map of action theory for group activity (comp. figure 3.2 for details) with added accounts of French's "corporate internal decision structure" covering corporate activity, Schweikard's "practical integrity" covering corporate activity and group activity described as "acting together fully-integrated," as well as Tomasello's "cultural cognition" covering group activity described as "acting together inclusively" based on a social desire to do something together.

require any sort of mind-reading in order to be understood. The idea of 'sharing a goal', similarly, is a descriptive notion given by the fact that "each agent's activities are individually organized around a single outcome"(Butterfill, 2012, p.35).

The structure that Butterfill proposes is presumably inspired by Bratman's account, but instead of interlocking intentions and mutual beliefs, it makes do only with the external understanding of goals and individual expectations. Each agent must direct her actions towards a single goal, which requires no interaction whatsoever. Doing so, the individuals must identify each other as agents–this can be compared to understanding the other as 'animate' as discussed in Tomasello's et al. position. Additionally, each agent must expect each other agent to perform an action towards the goal, and they must expect the goal to occur as a common effect of the individual contributions. The idea of expectations suggests that the agents view each other merely in relation to the goal, but not in relation to each other. In particular, the individual expectations do not interlock in a more elaborate sense, i.e. there are no expectations of what the others expect, and the expectations do not depend on each other. If a group of agents fulfills these conditions, they are said to engage in 'plural activity' (p.10ff.)

'Plural activity' is, indeed, a much less demanding form of group activity than, e.g., Bratman's 'shared cooperative activity', but it is similar in its theoretical features. It is reductive in the double sense that it employs only concepts on the individual level and it does not introduce any new phenomena. Additionally, it is tailored to one specific type of group activity, namely primitive group activity characterized only by a common goal. Indeed, the model is mute when it comes to any other form of group activity. Butterfill, therefore, truly extends the coverage of the research map of group activity (compare figure 3.8), but the question is whether or not it is a good model for at least this type of group activity.

Types of group activity described as...

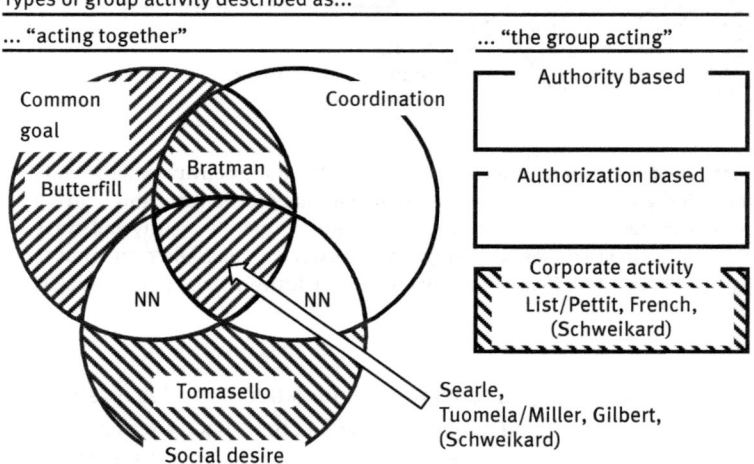

Fig. 3.8: Visualization of the research map of action theory for group activity (comp. figure 3.2 for details) with the added account of Butterfill's "plural activities" covering group activity described as "acting together primitively" based a common goal.

The answer to this question hinges on the plausibility of the concept of a goal introduced here. The attempt to make group activity independent of mind-reading capabilities relies mainly on a purely external understanding of goals. Butterfill characterizes goals as 'outcomes' of some sort, but he does not specify what they are outcomes of. I assume they are meant to be outcomes of behavior, but this is insufficient to specify a goal simply because there are many outcomes of an agent's activity. In order to identify one of those outcomes as a 'goal', further input is required. Butterfill gives no clue as to what this input might be. Without it, we do not have the means to say whether or not the factual requirement that each individual must direct its actions towards a single goal is fulfilled or not.

Similarly, the convergence of the different agent's expectations to involve exactly the same goal seems ambitious. If there is a shared experience of some repeatedly achieved goal, e.g. the building of one and the same tower from blocks several times, then it is reasonable to assume that the different agents form corresponding expectations. In any novel situation, or in case one of the agents slightly changes his goal, e.g. building a tower with a different top, the model does not capture what is happening appropriately.

It turns out, as with many of the previous models as well, that Butterfill's account does not go into sufficient detail on the concept of a 'goal' and he explicitly excludes the notion of 'having a goal'. A proper action theory for group activity, consequently, has to address this topic that appears over and over again, but with completely different, often contradictory definitions. If, indeed, the concept can be explicated purely in external terms, Butterfill's account may well be the solution for group activity mediated only by a common goal.

Pacherie's shared intention lite. Elisabeth Pacherie explores how to simplify the notion of *intentionally* acting together in her 2013 paper "Intentional joint agency: shared intention light" in order to account for simple forms of group activity. She acknowledges Butterfill's account of 'plural activity' but notes there is "a stronger notion of intentional joint action" that is "not just as bringing about outcome *O*, but as bringing about outcome O *together*" (p.1821). This excludes cases where "agents can have, and act on [..] a shared goal without understanding their actions as comprising anything more than a plural activity" (Butterfill, 2012, p.18), which is possible in Butterfill's account.

Her first change compared to Butterfill's account is a more complex understanding of goals. She "introduce[s] a distinction between agent unmarked specifications of goals–e.g., *to move the table*–and agent marked specifications of goals–e.g., *I move the table* or *we move the table*" (Pacherie, 2013, p.1821). In other words, "the joint-ness of [intentional joint action...] is part of the goal itself" (p.1822).

To explain how a 'we' could potentially enter the specification of an individual's goal, Pacherie builds on an unfinished theory of team reasoning by Bacharach (Bacharach, 1999, 2006). Reasoning, according to Bacharach is done within a frame, i.e. "a set of descriptors used when thinking about a situation" (Pacherie, 2013, p.1831). Combined with the equally well established phenomenon of group identification (Brewer and Gardner, 1996), Pacherie offers a 'shared intention lite' account: Individuals may identify themselves with the group, i.e. "each has a self-conception as a member of the team" (Pacherie, 2013, p.1833). Naturally, others are also believed to be members of the team. This sets an appropriate frame for each individual not only to specify a goal attached to the group, but also to reason what the best course of action for the team is and, consequently, to intend whatever is the individuals part in this course of action.

Pacherie's account is similar in structure to Miller's and Tuomela's account, and to Searle's account as well. All of them introduce some basic social phenomenon–the 'we-mode', the 'we-intentions' or, here, a type of group identification. The crucial difference is, however, that what binds the group together in Pacherie's account is a psychological mechanism triggered by external clues. This mechanism is not an ad-hoc postulation like, e.g., Searle's 'we-intentions' but taken from psychological research, which makes her account compatible with empirical research results by design. Additionally, for an individual to appropriately group identify and team reason, she does not need to consider the other members' beliefs, reasoning or intentions, she simply expects them to act as members of the group and "forming expectations about others' actions is not the same thing as ascribing intentions to them and does not require the kind of cognitive and conceptual skills intention ascriptions requires" (p.1835), which was equally claimed by Butterfill.

Pacherie's account can be applied to persons engaged in group activity who do not have the capacity of elaborate mind reading or who cannot use them due to, e.g., limited communication. The scope of this account, I believe is identical to the scope of Butterfill's account, i.e. restricted to group activity characterized by a common goal. One might be tempted to also apply it to inclusive group activity by focusing on group identification, but the model of group identification does not necessarily imply inclusiveness. I might identify with a group while I have no desire whatsoever to engage with the members of the group beyond what is necessary to achieve common or personal goals. I might even plan my actions such that I do them on my own and hand over the results to be used in the group. Equally, her account cannot be easily extended to more complex types of group activity. Coordination in her account is done by the individuals based on what they expect the others to do, i.e. the individuals only influence each other's actions passively. This, of course, is a very weak notion of coordination for it would imply that I also coordinate my actions with inanimate entities in my environment. Coordination, as I introduced it, requires that the individuals influence not only each other's actions, but also their considerations that eventually lead to action. Coordination, thus, requires high level cognitive skills, and that is exactly what the agents in Pacherie's model do not have.

It is unclear, however, how her model of group activity transitions into cognitively more demanding activities. Much like Tomasello and Butterfill, Pacherie aims at explaining how it is possible for human beings to engage in group activity in the first place and what the minimal capabilities are. This, however, is compatible with completely different mechanisms for group activity once the agents are more developed. This is the same problem of Tomasello's account and a quite general issue with accounts of group activity that focus on psychological features: knowing what capabilities are required on a psychological level is certainly interesting and might provide conceptual insight as well, but we may miss the wood for the trees with such a focus. An instinct to grab things only goes so far in explaining tool-use, and an instinct to do things with others only goes so far in explaining fully-integrated group activity, let alone corporate activity.

As matter of fact, the more psychologically motivated accounts add only little to the conceptual framework of group activity. As before, goals play a central role, and a construction of some sort of intentionality remains to be the dominant focus. What stands out in these accounts is the external understanding of the relations between the individuals. The relations need not be constituted within the content of individual attitudes. Rather, the individual attitudes are linked by being directed at the same (external) goal, and the individuals form expectations what the other one will do to achieve this goal *independently* of what the other wants, expects or intends. Indeed, children as young as 1 year seem to employ efficiency rationales as is implied by studies of Csibra and Gergely (Csibra et al., 2003; Csibra and Gergely, 2006) to form appropriate expectations. Thus, the different actions interlock only because the individuals more or less incidentally identify the same goal as the common goal, and they interlock efficiently only when the expectations more or less incidentally add up in an efficient manner. This obviously leaves room for all sorts of failure in group activity, especially in novel situations. When talking about young children, this is acceptable, and, from what I have experienced in my life, quite accurate. More capable agents, however, usually succeed in proper engagement in group activity. That does not exclude the approach from being correct, but additions need to be made.

3.2.2.4 Roth and Copp on authority and authorization

I have now reviewed models that account for almost all types of group activity. Group activity characterized by authority and authorization, however, is still uncovered. Given that authority structures and closely related authorization processes are presumably one of the most used mechanisms to establish successful group activity, the neglect of this aspect is surprising, to say the least. More often than not, authority is explicitly excluded and authorization is not even mentioned. The reason lies, I believe, in the different types of authority and authorization discussed in my analysis above. Both phenomena walk the lines between group activity properly described as multiple agents acting together, group activity that involves multiple agents but cannot be so described, or even individual agency.

I briefly discuss two convincing positions that can be applied to authority and authorization, respectively, which link these phenomena to the problem of agency in group activity.

Copp's primary and secondary actions. In his 1979 paper "Collective actions and secondary actions," Copp agrees that a group "can only have impact "through" the actions of persons," but he rejects the conclusion that groups, therefore, do not act at all. He also concedes that "it is not possible for a collection to have an intention," but he regards it "a sufficient condition of an agent's performing an action intentionally [...] that it perform it for a reason" and claims that "it is possible for a collective to have an objective and to do something in order to achieve that objective" (p.178). By having a goal and bringing it about, thus, collectives have reasons and act. The more interesting question for Copp is exactly how collectives act 'through' their members.

Copp's central claim is "that the actions of a collective are constituted by actions of persons" (p.183) the same way actions of individuals may be constituted by actions of other individuals. In this view, persons are capable of 'primary actions', which are stand-alone actions we know from everyday human agency. However, an agent may also do something by 'secondary actions': "An agent's action is a secondary action if, and only if, it is correctly attributable to this agent on the basis of [..] an action of some other agent," i.e. secondary action of one agent is 'constituted' by primary actions of other agents (p.177). The constitution relation between primary and secondary actions is not a causal relation. Copp spells it out in terms of specific sufficiency conditions involving the circumstances under which an action is done and the agents and actions themselves (p.182).

While the idea of 'primary action' and 'secondary actions' in this sense is intuitive, it remains unclear how one action can sufficiently constitute another action. After all, 'sufficiency' is merely a logical notion while actions have substantial influence on reality. Since a causal relation is excluded by Copp, he must have in mind some other relation between the actions. While he does not give a general principle of what this relation looks like, his examples feature authorized agents acting in the name of other agents or groups. In my analysis, I described authorization as a transfer of a normatively defined power of one agent to another. Therefore, authorization indeed links the actions of one agent to another in a non-causal way and opens up a sensible way in which the actions of one agent can be sufficient for an action of another agent in the way described by Copp.

The application to collectives is straight forward with these instruments. Actions of the group and actions of its members may be normatively linked, i.e. individuals are acting 'in the name of the group' and these individual actions constitute the group's action. Unfortunately, this interpretation of Copp's model limits its explanatory reach significantly. Copp certainly wants to provide a model for how the action of individual agents constitute a group's action *in general*, and not only for groups with explicitly authorized agents. Instead of using authorization to establish a sufficiency relation between individual actions and group actions, one could flesh out Copp's proposal that groups have goals and, therefore, act for a reason as Copp suggests. The sufficiency relation would then be based on a link between the individual actions and the group's goal. Obviously, it is not enough that individual actions directly bring about the goal, but they would have to bring it about in the 'right' way, e.g. being guided by the group's goal.

Copp's idea of primary and secondary actions, thus, can be taken in two directions. First, it is a compelling model for group agency in groups with established authorization mechanisms. If groups can have goals in a meaningful way, and if this gives rise to an acceptable degree of agency, then Copp's model explains how the group acts. Secondly, the analysis of group goals required for the first interpretation could also be used to describe group agency independent of authorization, if the resulting concept of a group goal yields a solid connection between individual actions and group goals.

Roth's entitlement in authority relations. Lastly, I want to discuss a promising account of authority in group activity. Authority is one of the most common methods of coordination in group activity. Yet, many prominent accounts neglect it. In contrast, Abraham Sesshu Roth claims that "[f]ar from evading the matter of authority in an account of shared activity, we must figure out how to best embrace it" (Roth, 2014, p.648). The embrace must account for the coordinative power of consent-based authority (ConAy), while excluding dictatorial authority (DicAy) used by individuals to get others to do their bidding. Roth is quite aware of the challenge and he takes it head on.

Roth's core idea is that it is possible for an agent to act "*directly* on another's intention" (p.640ff.) The agent does so just like she acts on her own intentions for future actions: "I can act directly on your intention [means] that your intention figures in my practical thought in the way that my own prior intentions do" (p.642). For the proposal to work, however, individuals need to have "some sort of authority over other participants in shared activity" (ibd.) This is how authority enters Roth's account of group activity.

To characterize authority as it is used in acting 'directly' on another person's intention, Roth observes that authority structures in group activity often come with an "*entitlement* to the reason and the deliberation that went into [...] issuing the intention" (p.643). Entitlement is exactly what sets apart dictatorial authority (DicAy) from forms of authority used for coordination (ConAy, NormAy). If I am under your authority and something seems off, I am entitled to the reasons for your intention rather than blindly following your order. If the reasons are, indeed, counter-acting our activity in some obvious manner, the authority relation breaks down just like my own intention would break down in light of new reasons relevant for action. Entitlement ensures that the autonomy and agency of agents under authority is not simply overridden as is the case in dictatorial authority (DicAy).

Entitlement also ensures that the authority is limited to the coordinative function in group activity. If the agent under authority asks for the reason behind an order and finds out that it was issued only for personal benefits, she is free to reject. Indeed, this is what we expect from, e.g. authority relations in a proper employee-employer relation. You are not expected to fulfill personal wishes for your superior, and you may simply rebut any such orders. In reality, the authority of the superior in relation to the work often also results in dictatorial authority, but this requires some degree of abuse from the superior's side. Entitlement succeeds in capturing the coordinative power of authority in group activity while excluding stronger forms of authority used by individuals for individual gains.

The only concern I have with Roth's account has to do with the reference to intentions. Authority, so I conclude from his discussion, is given if one agent somehow expresses his intention to another agent, who then acts directly on that intention. The point of being in authority, however, is that one can order others to do the things one does not intend to do oneself. The intention that Roth needs here cannot be the intention to do a particular action. Intentions for the future, however, to which he compares the intentions relevant in authority relations, are usually intentions to perform particular actions.

The discussion of group activity based on authority and authorization leaves us with a largely covered research map (compare figure 3.9). Notably, the different position each cover only specific types of group activity. Furthermore, opportunistic group activity (ATO), which is solely characterized by coordination towards some common benefit, is not explicitly covered. I reflect on those two observations and the insights gained in this chapter in the concluding section.

3.3 Insights of the analysis of what we do together

In the second chapter, I argued that agency is fundamentally disrupted in group activity. At least for some cases, a solution is the introduction of a new form of agency, corporate agency. For this to be viable, however, group activity needs to display agential features on a group level. In order to discuss group agency, a proper understanding of group activity in general is required. In this chapter, thus, I explored different types of group activity and ordered them into a research map (see figure 3.2). In a second step, I reviewed the literature on group activity in search for inspiration in explaining the different types of group activity.

Types of group activity described as...

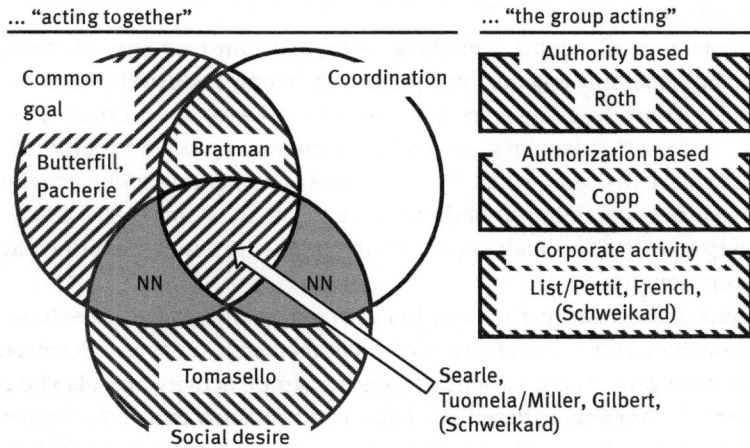

Fig. 3.9: Visualization of the research map of action theory for group activity (comp. figure 3.2 for details) with added accounts of Pacherie's "shared intentions lite" covering group activity described as "acting together primitively" based on a common goal, Copp's "collective and secondary actions" covering authorization-based group activity and Roth's "entitlement" covering authority-based group activity. The resulting research map is largely covered by the most prominent positions of Bratman, List/Pettit, Searle, Tuomela/Miller and Gilbert as well as selected alternative accounts of French, Schweikard, Tomasello, Butterfill, Patcherie, Copp and Roth, but shows little overlap of the positions. The type of group activity described as "acting together opportunistically" based solely on coordination is not covered.

The literature offers various accounts of group activity, but usually introduces contestable concepts to explain its nature. I chose to explore group activity without introducing any new concepts, and only then discuss explanatory approaches.

I started by exploring why we say of two or more agents that they 'do something together'. When agents are involved in bringing something about, I discovered three relevant meanings of 'together'. First, 'together' draws its meaning from the fact that agents have a common goal and recognize each other in bringing it about. I called the type of group activity associated with this meaning of together *primitive*, because it does not require actual coordination between the agents. Second, whenever agents do coordinate themselves, we usually also describe them as doing something together, even though they might not have a common goal, but only work together *opportunistically* to achieve their personal, distinct goals. Third, we sometimes talk about doing something together just for the sake of doing it together rather than alone. There need not be a common goal or coordination, e.g. some people rather travel in company than alone. I coined this the *inclusive* meaning of together.

While opportunistically doing something together is quite common, we rarely find agents doing something together only primitively or only inclusively. Rather, a combination of the three types are more common, which suggests two further types of group activity. In particular, agents often have a common goal and coordinate themselves to achieve that goal, which I called a case of *cooperative* group activity. When all three aspects of doing something come together, we may talk of *fully-integrated* group activity. The remaining two combinations are possible in principle, but uncommon enough to ignore them.

The analysis of the meanings of 'together', in conclusion, reveals three basic types of group activity and at least two more important composite types. However, beyond the idea of agents doing something together, group activity may also take forms that cannot be properly so described. I discussed *authority* and *authorization* as two cases of activity that involve multiple agents, but cannot be described as these agents doing something together. The notion of agential features and the possibility to externally realize them helped understand these concepts.

Authority, in this view, virtually enables the agent in authority to outsource the execution of an action to an agent under authority. It would be very unusual to say the two agents acted together. Instead, we say, for example, the agent under authority did something *for* the agent in authority. However, it is obvious authority is not restricted to individual agency, but plays an important role in many group activities as well. Authority, thus, not only walks the line between individual agency and group activity, but also goes beyond acting together in a meaningful way.

Authorization is a different concept that also enables the authorizing agent to outsource the execution of an agent, but it does not require an authority relation. Instead, the authorizing agent transfers normative power to the authorized agents so the latter may act in the name of the former. Authorization, too, is often used by individuals to improve the reach of their agency, but it is also well known from more complex group activity. Spokesmen are authorized to talk to the press in the name of a group, for example. Like authority, thus, authorization is in between different levels of agency.

Finally, I discussed *corporate* group activity by picking up the discussion from the second chapter. The reason why corporate activity cannot be properly described as agents doing something together is that the agential features required for the group activity cannot be properly ascribed to any set of individual agents any longer. Rather, the entire group, or a large part of the group has the respective agential feature.

With the resulting research map for group activity, I then turned to the literature. I looked at the most influential philosophical positions on group activity as well as selected alternative positions. It turns out the research map is well covered by the different positions (compare figure 3.9), but most of them cover only one specific type of group activity. In itself, this is not a problem but the different positions are not linked to each other and it is not likely or at least unclear how they may be connected. Some of them even outright contradict each other and they do so on various levels.

For one, there is no consensus on what phenomena need to be explained in order to unravel the complexities of group activity. Philosophers like Bratman and Gilbert take as a starting point two-person activities and seem to imply that the results of their analyses can be somehow extended to other cases as well. Clearly, however, this is not a trivial task given the fundamentally different issues in more complex group activity, as shown by, e.g. Pettit and List. At the same time, the discussions of two-person activities are already too elaborate to account for less sophisticated group activity. Small children engage in such activities, and adults do so as well. I discussed works by Tomasello, Butterfill and Pacherie that show very different explanations are needed to account for this. The research map and the fragmented coverage display these discrepancies well. This is an important insight because, on the surface, the terminology used in the different accounts is quite similar.

Indeed, most philosophers take 'intentionality' to be central to understanding group activity. This assumption is clearly inspired by the outstanding position of intentionality in action theory for individual agents. However, a closer look reveals that the action theoretic assumptions in the accounts vary greatly. Bratman provides his own rather elaborate concept of intentionality in agency, while Pettit and List, for example, make do with a very simple functional understanding. Searle, like Bratman, has his own theory of intentionality on which he builds his account and others like Gilbert simply gloss over the topic or presume some intuitive understanding. The colorful spectrum when it comes to intentionality in agency is, however, not a sign of a research gap. Rather, there simply are many different proposals for how to understand intentionality in agency, none of which as dominant as to provide a commonly accepted basis for further research.

Notably, almost everyone agrees that groups do not literally have intentions like human agents have. Schweikard's analysis reveals how the different positions account for group intentionality nonetheless. He provides a structured concept of 'intentions' and shows how the different positions introduce a 'we-ness' through different docking points in this concept. I argue that this reveals a concerning arbitrariness in the discussion of whether a 'we' enters the subject, mode or content of intentions. In particular, group intentionality becomes more of a technical term than anything else. On the positive side, however, the constructions attempt to capture the functionality of intentionality in agency on a group level by using more basic concepts of agency. Naturally, we should consider whether or not this strategy is valid for agency *in general*.

One of the basic concepts that recurs in essentially every account is 'goals' or 'having goals'. Either by themselves, or as basis for the construction of group intentionality, 'common' or 'shared' goals seem to be the most important feature of group activity. So important, in fact, that group activity without a common goal is poorly covered. In particular, neither the most influential accounts nor the selected alternative accounts provide a model for acting together purely opportunistically (ATO), i.e. acting together coordinated without a common goal and without a particular desire to to act together. The reason for this, I believe, lies in a profound confusion about what it means to 'have a goal' or 'having a common' goal in case of group activity.

Indeed, a detailed analysis of goals is lacking in most accounts. The ad-hoc characterizations, on the other hand, range from goals as mere states of world to goals as mental entities guiding planning and reasoning. The only detailed analysis of collective goals by Tuomela and Miller makes heavy use of their original concepts. Surprisingly, they arrive at the conclusion that collective goals essentially *are* collective intentions (Tuomela and Miller, 2014).

In contrast with intentionality in agency, the remarkable variety in the understanding of 'goals' does not trace back to a similar variety in philosophical proposals. In fact, the idea of 'goals' and their role in agency is surprisingly neglected. I assume the neglect is owed to the strong focus on intentionality, but the discussion of group activity so far has shown that a solid understanding of goals may be even more important than the discussion of a technical construction of intentionality on a group level.

In conclusion, I take away two closely related research tasks from the review of the positions on agency in group activity. First, I follow up on the idea that intentionality in agency can be substituted by more basic concepts relevant for agency. This is the prevalent strategy for accounts of group activity, and it is worth looking at how compatible this strategy is with action theory for individual agents. An investigation into individual intentionality, thus, is the first topic of the next chapter. Second, I will close the research gap on goals. This is important in its own right, but it is particularly fruitful in combination with the discussion on intentionality. 'Goals' are a major part of the idea of intentionality in agency– or so the research on group activity suggests. Thus, if I successfully provide an understanding of 'goals' and their role in both, individual and group activity, we have a proper show-case for how we can theorize about agency without a strong focus on intentionality in agency.

4 The cutlery of agency

In the previous chapter, the review of the literature on group activity showed a strong focus on intentionality across almost all accounts. This is not surprising because intentionality is often considered the single mark of action in individual action theory. It only makes sense to assume the same when more than one agent is involved. The concept of intentionality in agency, however, is challenging for individual agency already. Making sense of it in group activity seems to be a cunning undertaking, but it also has an important advantage. Interactions of agents are mostly out in the open for everyone to understand because agential features, i.e. features that enable agency, are externally realized in group activity (ERAF). Accordingly, most accounts for group activity construct concepts of group intentionality from more basic features. The central elements in the construction of group intentionality are 'goals' and the idea that a group as a whole or the individual agents 'share a goal' or 'have a common goal'. It is not clear, however, how exactly goals, as an agential feature, help constitute intentionality in agency.

In this chapter, I follow the path which I just outlined. I start by looking at the phenomenon of intentionality in agency from a traditional, individual perspective and find there are at least six different notions associated with it. Consequently, the idea that intentions are the single mark of action can only retain its elegance, if those notions are unified under one concept. The unification, so I argue, is futile given the involved concepts are fundamentally distinct. Rather, so I continue, the different concepts associated to intentionality in agency are themselves sufficient to understand agency, which is supported by the explicit constructions of intentionality in theories for group agency. Instead of aiming at a single, unified mark of agency, thus, we are more successful with a diversified understanding of agency.

As a showcase, I provide an analysis of 'goals' and 'having a goal'. On the one hand, such an analysis is important in its own right because there is very little explicit philosophical discussion in action theory. On the other hand, a solid concept of 'goals' and 'having goals', which is potent enough to explain crucial aspects of agency, sets an example for a diversified understanding of agency without reference to the overarching notion of intentionality.

4.1 Intentionality in agency

Intentionality in agency seems to play an outstanding role in our lives according to most philosophical theories. Not only is it commonly used to set apart actions from mere behavior, but it also explains our actions. It is generally conceived

https://doi.org/10.1515/9783110628623-004

among philosophers that intentionality in agency comes in three flavors, viz. acting intentionally, having an intention with which one acts and having an intention to act at a future point in time. This is usually associated with the intriguing analysis done by G.E.M. Anscombe in her book "Intention" (Anscombe, 1957). One of the central tasks of philosophy of intention, then, is to unify these three seemingly different features of intentionality in agency into one concept, or so it is claimed by Kieran Setyia in the Stanford Encyclopedia of Philosophy (2011). Indeed, the most popular standard conception of action developed by Donald Davidson in several of his essays is inspired by this question(Davidson, 1985). Newer approaches by, e.g., Michael Bratman, also try to understand the facets of action by understanding intentionality in agency in a certain way.

The appeal of such an approach certainly comes from introspection. Intuitively, there are many things we do, and among them are the things we do intentionally. These intentional doings are the central elements of our lives practically, ethically and personally. In a first step, I explore the introspection and show there are, in fact, not three but at least six agential features associated with intentionality in our everyday experience of agency. This leads into the thesis, that intentionality in agency has become a mere header for various distinct concepts even in individual agency, and that the idea of unification into one concept is theoretical at best and futile at worst.

4.1.1 Six features of intentionality in agency

Elizabeth Anscombe studied intentional action by analyzing the senses with which we can sensibly ask the question 'Why?' I follow in her footsteps, but allow a wider range of questions, including those questions that directly refer to the idea of intentionality in our everyday language about it. In particular, a set of closed questions strikes me as more resourceful to determine the nature of intentionality in agency, rather than the utterly open question 'Why?', which allows for so much confusion. The first question that comes to mind in the form 'Did the agent do the action intentionally?' is demonstrated in the example: the spiller spills his coffee by quickly twisting his wrist (and, thus, tilts the cup). The quizzer may ask a question to find out whether the spiller was surprised by this, i.e. whether the twisting of his wrist merely happened to him, or whether the spiller actually twisted his wrist much like you would push a door handle when opening a door or chew on your food when eating. The question in this sense often comes with an air of astonishment: 'Did you really just tilt that cup?' or 'That looked odd, did you do that?' or it might indeed be 'Did you do this intentionally?' with a puzzled tone. In this first sense, intentionality is merely a concept tied to the qualitative experience of the agent while doing something. Searle calls it 'the experience of acting' in his 1980 essay "The Intentionality of Intention and Action" (p.55). He compares it to the experience you have when you do something but remove the actual movement from it, e.g., the experience of raising the arm when you remove the fact that the arm goes up. This is of course a famous example of Wittgenstein who, most likely, would not share Searle's conclusions[1] (Wittgenstein, 1953, §621). At least it seems to be clear there is such an experience often described as 'voluntariness'.

Anscombe rejects the idea to use 'voluntariness' to explain intentionality for the danger of circularity. She concedes that some physiological involuntary doings like jerking and peristaltic movement are to be excluded from the realm of intentional action, but 'voluntary' and 'involuntary' have additional richer meanings. Austin shows in "A Plea for Excuses" (1956) that the voluntarily and the involuntarily "are fish from very different kettles" where the " 'opposites', of 'voluntarily' might be 'under constraint' of some sort, duress or obligation; the opposite of 'involuntarily' might be 'deliberately' or 'on purpose' or the like" (p.9/10). In light of this insight, it is wise to follow Anscombe and restrict the meaning of voluntariness in this context to physical voluntariness. Consequently, I will leave it at the fact that often enough we talk about actions being intentional and mean that the movements constituting the action did not merely happen to the agent, but that her performance was under voluntary control in a physiologic sense. This is the first agential feature associated with intentionality in agency:

(VolI) Intentionality in agency sometimes refers to a voluntary physiological control of actions, which can be distinguished by a particular agential experience that lacks when our body moves involuntarily.

The second notion associated with intentionality is epistemic in nature. The things an agent does can be re-described in many ways. As a consequence, it is sensible to say an agent intentionally does something under one description, but not under another. Anscombe presents an example featuring an agent sawing a plank. The plank may happen to be Frank's plank. Clearly, sawing the plank is intentional in

---

1 Wittgenstein explicitely states that he does "not want to say that in the case of the expression of intention "I am going to take two powders" the prediction is a cause—and its fulfilment the effect" (Wittgenstein, 1953, §632). This is not immediately in contradiction to Searle's causally effective 'intention in action' because of the different time frames. However, Wittgenstein continues to argue against an understanding of intention as a representation of a particular experience or state of mind, but rather understands expressions of intentions as parts of language-games telling someone something about the agent "which goes beyond what happened at that time" (Wittgenstein, 1953, §659).

the first sense, i.e. it most certainly is voluntary physiologically. It is still sensible to ask, however, whether the sawer intentionally saws *Frank's* plank and not just any plank. The reference to 'intentionally' in this sense can be replaced by the notions of awareness or knowledge. Indeed, we may ask the sawer, 'Are you aware that you are sawing Frank's plank?' The term 'awareness' alone, though, does not seem to be enough to describe the phenomenon. We can be aware of many things happening around us by observing them, and this, at least intuitively, is different from being aware of the things we are doing ourselves. Anscombe, for example, argues that it would strike us as very odd if someone were to say something along the lines of 'Let me see, what is this body bringing about?', and then observe what his body is doing (Anscombe, 1957, §43). Wittgenstein made a similar point when he noted "I do *not* say "See, my arm is going up!" when I raise it" (Wittgenstein, 1953, §627). Both examples suggest that the awareness relevant for intentionality in agency is not fed from observation. I am not entirely convinced we should trust our intuition and use of language on this matter, but this decision is a task for psychological research.

We could circumvent the troubles of awareness and sources of knowledge by using the notion of belief, rather than awareness. Notably, a reference to beliefs comes with its own peculiarities. Imagine we ask the sawer, 'What do you think you are doing?' She might answer, 'I believe I am sawing a plank.' The response is natural and satisfactory. However, when we point out 'Yes, but you are sawing *Frank's* plank', the sawer will certainly not respond 'Oh, I did not believe that'. Instead she will fall back on the notion of awareness or knowledge: 'Oh, I was not aware of that.' or 'Oh, I did not know that.' or even 'Oh, I know, so what?'. What does it mean that the sawer *believes* she is sawing a plank, but *knows*, or is *aware*, she is sawing Frank's plank. The positive role of belief for intentionality lies at the core of Davidson's predominant theory of action mainly developed in his paper "Actions, Reasons and Causes", and he gives an answer to the puzzle. Belief seems to pick out the knowledge that is relevant for the action from the perspective of the agent. Two of the relevant pieces of knowledge for the sawer are, first, she saws and second, it is a plank that she saws. Her knowledge of the plank being Frank's plank is irrelevant for what she does, and, therefore, not referred to as a belief in the context of her action. In conclusion, there is a notion of intentionality in agency involving awareness, knowledge or belief of what the agent is doing. This is the second agential feature associated with intentionality in agency:

> (EpiI) Intentionality in agency sometimes refers to awareness, knowledge or belief of what it is an agent is doing, where the description of the action from the agent's perspective picks out the intentional action over the things that the agent also happens to do with her action.

The first two inquiries about intentionality do not teach us much about what moved the agent. It settles the matter about what the agent actually has done intentionally in a physiologically and epistemic sense. An agent may well do some action A in the voluntary sense but not be aware that she is doing B by doing A as well. We would say that the agent did A intentionally, but did not do B intentionally, and it would be perfectly sensible despite there being no difference in the physical description of what is happening in A and B.

There are, of course, questions directed at an agent soliciting a more insightful response with respect to agency. We often ask, for example, "What did the agent want to achieve with this action". Usually, the answer will produce a goal of the agent. This is the idea of an 'intention with which' an agent acts. The goal usually is some direct effect or consequence of the action. Clearly, however, there are many things an action causes. Accordingly, the question often aims at singling out one of the many obvious effects as the goal of an action. Therefore, the question actually addresses two different aspects of intentionality: on the one hand, it may aims at finding out whether or not a certain effect was, indeed, the goal of the agent. On the other hand, it implicitly aims at finding out whether or not a certain effect was considered by the agent, but was not a goal of the action. A less implicit question would be "Did the agent consider the effect of her action beforehand". Thus, there are two different flavors of intentionality. The first case is the question for the goal of an action as seen by the agent. The latter case gives rise to the notorious discussion about the side-effect, which is often understood as something done intentionally in some sense (Knobe, 2003; Stoecker, 2014).

The two cases, both characterized as doing something intentionally in our everyday language, are very different. The first reveals to us, at least to some extent, what guided the agent in her action, while the second seems to be more about the agent's considerations of the effects of her action when deliberating about them.

However, for both cases, we tend to re-describe the action in terms of its effects, or what is supposed to be achieved by it without changing the notion of intentionality, i.e. we quite literally assume that we intend our action described by what we are doing (e.g., I turn on the light) in the same way we intend our action under the description of what is achieved or caused (e.g, I scare off the burglars). This is the strategy proposed by Joel Feinberg in his 1970 essay "Action and Responsibility." He coined the phrase 'accordion effect', which refers to the phenomenon that we view causal effects of an action as part of the agent's agency.

Another approach to extend the notion of intentionality to goals and effects, or another form of maybe the same approach, was chosen by Bratman in his essay "Shared Intentionality" from 1993. He points out that the objects of intention can be actions as indicated by the phrase 'intend to...', but also goals or some state of affairs as indicated by the phrase 'intend that...' (p.102). Both solutions allow for a wider range of things that can be intended. Both solutions, to me, seem valid as long as one remembers there are different notions of intentionality involved in the different expressions. These are the third and fourth agential features associated with intentionality in agency, respectively.

(EffI) Intentionality in agency sometimes refers to the ability to foresee the effects of actions and consider them in deliberation

(GoalI) Intentionality in agency sometimes refers to the idea that agents have goals, which are brought about as effects of their actions.

Goals and deliberation about other effects of actions reveal a lot more about the agent. By learning about the goal guiding an agent's actions, we usually learn something about the agent's desires or other meaningful attitudes. We also learn something about the agent's deliberation by finding out which consequences of her action she considered. The agent reveals to us a forward looking agency, which respects the side-constraints of her agential power. This is much more than simply knowing an agent acted voluntarily in a physiological sense and that she knew about certain aspects of her actions.

The notion of intentionality in agency, however, can be even more elaborate. Some of our actions are not only aimed at a direct effect, but serve a grander purpose; call it an end or, thinking back to Bratman, a plan. Bratman, as a reminder, builds on the notion of having a plan. He describes intentions as commitments to sub-plans in his planning theory of action, mostly laid out in his essays collected in, e.g., "Faces of Intention" (1990). The corresponding question in our everyday language would be something like 'Did the agent intend something beyond the obvious goal of her action?', or, certainly more commonly, 'What were you thinking?', or something similar. A positive answer reveals to us a very rich type agency, one in which the agent deliberates extensively about how her various actions fit together over time and space to achieve some greater purpose. It will not only tell us a lot about the agent's actions, but about the agent's life and personality. This is the fifth agential feature associated with intentionality in agency:

(PlanI) Intentionality in agency sometimes refers to plans that link the actions of an agent together over time and space in pursuit of some greater end.

Last but not least, there is the intention for the future also known as 'prior intention' or 'pure intention' (Davidson, 1963, 1978; Searle, 1979). The future-directedness, as a matter of fact, is not distinct for this aspect of intentionality in agency. Having a goal, for example, is future directed too. What is more important is the fact that intentions for the future have as objects not goal-states or elements of plans, but specific actions. Since the agent is not acting yet, it clearly is not the idea of intentionality in agency addressed by the first two questions: there simply is no qualitative experience or epistemic insight which we could ask about. The best description I can offer is that having such an intention for the future is the state an agent is in after she has decided to do something at a future point in time. Obviously, there is no reason why this sort of intention should vanish once the agent started the action but has not yet completed it. 'Pure' intentions, so it seems, last at least until an action is finished, but may exist well before. Accordingly, it is completely sensible to ask an agent 'What are you going to do?' to find out what action the agent is going to take in the future. It is equally sensible to ask 'What are you trying to do?' to find out what the agent intends to do at the moment of the question being asked. This is the sixth agential feature associated with intentionality in agency:

(ActI) Intentionality in agency sometimes refers to a standing decision to perform a specific action, possibly at a future point in time.

By looking at our everyday language about actions or introspection or common sense, I arrived at six agential features associated with intentionality in agency. The six features involve notions as different as can be: the physiological control of actions with the respective qualitative experience, awareness or belief, forward looking deliberation of effects, having a goal, having a plan in pursuit of a greater goal and, finally, having made a decision. Looking at the fundamentally different concepts involved, it strikes me as extraordinarily ambitious to set out and try to unify even two or three of them under one notion, let alone all six of them.

Naturally, I understand the scientific elegance of formulating one fundamental concept from which everything else with regard to agency flows, but we must be careful not to bend reality in doing so. A metaphor may help make this point clear: in cantinas, prepackaged meal boxes or outdoor adventure shops you might come across the very convenient 'sporks' or 'sporves'. Sporves are lengthy objects that have spoon-like scoops, fork tines and some sort of blade like a knife. Practical considerations led to the idea of sporves, but I am certain the idea for the sporf would have come up in philosophical discussions of human eating habits as well (if human eating habits were not such an easily observable matter). The fact about eating is that there are different pieces of cutlery for eating and not just the sporf. Theorizing about the cutlery of action, then, we should consider there is not this one thing called 'intentionality in agency', which somehow covers all, but take serious the whole stack of agential features needed to explain agency.

4.1.2 Unification challenge for intentionality in agency

Unifying the different agential features associated with intentionality in agency would be a great explanatory achievement, but I already expressed my doubts this is possible. I now discuss the most popular unification strategies and explain my doubts. As a starting point, I summarize the agential features relevant for intentionality in agency presented above in an interrogation-like conversation between two people after the agent in the example hit the very calm and thoughtful quizzer with his hand in the face:

(VolI)
Quizzer: Did you swing your arm up back then? (With a tone of surprise)
Agent: Yes.

(EpiI)
Quizzer: Did you know that what you did was hitting me?
Agent: Yes.

(EffI)
Quizzer: Did you know that this would hurt me?
Agent: Yes.

(GoalI)
Quizzer: Seriously? Did you actually want to hurt me?
Agent: Well, yes, it was my goal to hurt you, your pride if not your body, but that was not the sole purpose of hurting you.

(PlanI)
Quizzer: There better be a very, very good reason?!
Agent: I feel so stuck in this job, but my wife won't accept that I quit. If I get fired, on the other hand, because, say, I hit a colleague in the face who insulted my family–she won't be happy, but she'll accept that. So I decided to hit you in order to get fired. To soften the blow for my wife, I also prepared several applications for jobs I think are more for me.

(ActI)
Quizzer: Well, at least you thought it through. When did you come up with this?
Agent: Oh, I thought about it all week. Over the weekend I decided to hit you today, so I get fired by end of the month.
Quizzer: I am pretty sure that's going to happen. Now please get me a bandage.

What is immediately striking about this series of questions is a certain dependency. If the first question about the physiological voluntariness were negated, the second question about awareness of what exactly was done could not have the sense rendered by intentionality. Thus, we could not ask whether the agent did an action under a particular description, if she did not even have physiological control over her movements, e.g., the arm hitting the quizzer. Hence, the voluntary physiological control during acting is necessary, but not sufficient for being knowledgeable about what it is one is doing under any description.

If the second question were negated, the third question about the effects of the action could not make any sense, since the agent most certainly cannot be aware of an effect of an action that she did not think she was doing in the first place. With the example from above: If the hitter is not aware that she is hitting the quizzer, but, say, a cupboard next to the quizzer, she cannot know that her act of hitting causes pain to the quizzer. Hence, awareness of what is being done is necessary, but not sufficient for knowing the effects in question.

If the third question were negated, however, the fourth question about the goal of the agent is still potentially a good one. An agent might have the goal to hurt the quizzer by hitting him in the face, even though she does not know whether or not a hurtful experience will result from this. This need not strike us as irrational, but it could be an exploratory way of achieving one's goal–one simply looks at what happens after some action and compares it to what one intended to achieve. In most cases, however, we will not ask the fourth question, if the third is negated unless we suspect some irrational reasoning, e.g., in a child's behavior.

How little the first three and the fourth questions are logically related also becomes obvious if we allow the question not to refer to a *particular* action, e.g., a question along the lines of 'What does the agent want to achieve through his action(s)?'. For the question about the agent's goals to make sense, there does not need to be any specific action, let alone an action that has already been done or is going on at the moment of the question. We may simply have goals and not know how we are going to achieve them. In fact, in most cases the goal comes first, and only then do we come up with ways of achieving it. Hence, in between, there is no action for the goal. Yet, the agent is already committed to doing something to achieve it. For the fourth question to be affirmed, consequently, it is neither necessary nor sufficient to affirm any of the questions beforehand. For actions that already have been taken place, this is also true, but typically a negation of the third question implies the negation of the fourth question.

If the fourth question were negated–here the dependency stops even for actions that have already been performed–the fifth question about the agent's plans or greater purpose is still sensible given the first three questions were affirmed. If the agent denied her goal was to hurt the quizzer, but confirmed she knew her action would hurt the quizzer, the fifth question asks how the causing of pain fits into the agents plans. Two answers to the question are possible. First, the agent could refer to her actual goals or plans and relate the means of hurting the quizzer in a reasonable manner. If, secondly, the pain was not even a means, the agent is asked to present at least ethical considerations to justify his acceptance of the pain. Often enough, both types of reasoning come together. The first option I have discussed above. The second option returns to the discussion on the side-effects. I believe it is simply an ethical demand by other agents that morally relevant side-effects are considered by the agent, and, therefore, the agent must position herself when making a decision such that she cannot deny having caused the effects intentionally. Both, a reference to plans with interlocking means and considerations of relevant side-effects within those plans, indicate a very rich notion of agency, but are largely independent of the other notions of intentionality in agency.

The sixth question about the intention to act plays a more complicated role. None of the other questions need to be affirmed for it to make sense to ask the question and have it affirmed, i.e. the agent might have an intention at one point, but never follows through. It is equally possible, though very rare and quite puzzling, that the agent has the intention to act in a certain way, actually does act in a certain way, but negates the first question about doing it intentionally while affirming all others. The discussion of deviant causal chains displays striking examples regularly. Here is one discussed by Davidson in "Freedom to Act" (1973): Two mountaineers face a difficult situation, and one of them falls. The other mountaineer catches one of his friend's ropes and holds it tight only to realize that he will not be able to pull him up before he himself will fall due to the additional weight. He decides to let go off the rope, but it so happens that he does not let go the way he would expect. Instead, the mountaineer's hand releases the rope, because the thought of letting go, and essentially killing his friend, disturbed the mountaineer so much that his hands got sweaty causing the rope to simply slip through his fingers.

Less puzzling and more insightful is the fact that an affirmation of the question for an intention to act can be the starting point of an interrogation with hypothetical versions of the foregoing questions. Without the intended action ever having to take place, we may ask about its goals, its side-effects, and its role in greater plans and so on and so forth. This is interesting because the notion of future intention severs the tight connection between intentionality and action. It seems, as previously pointed out, intentionality also has to do with deliberation and making decisions, but this is neither sufficient nor necessary for an action to take place, which we would also call intentional on grounds of the other features.

The lack of consistent logical connections between the features associated with intentionality dampens the hope for unification, but at least they are not completely disconnected. The prospects of a unified theory are still tempting, but what routes are even available given the loose connections between the features?

The first attempt that comes to mind is the identification of intentionality in agency with one of the six features, or a sensible combination thereof. As we have seen from the lack of logical connections between the different notions of intentionality, it is hard to imagine how the left over features can be entailed. Thus, this approach would need to exclude most of the features of intentionality in agency. Such an *exclusive* account, therefore, fails to unify the different features, but simply reduces the scope of what we refer to when talking about intentionality in agency. This may be a valid strategy, and, in fact, we find it employed in more pragmatic approaches. The psychologist Tomasello, for example, simply defines individual intention in his 2005 study "Understanding and sharing intention: the origin of cultural cognition" as the means-end 'action plan' towards a goal employing the individuals knowledge and skills in its representation of the world. Simpler actions without such intentions are not accounted for and neither are more complex forms of agency evolving around long term plans and greater purpose á la Bratman. The upside of the exclusive approach is the cut down to a single pragmatic, usable concept. The downside, however, lies in the contingency of the definition of intentionality in agency and the inevitable misunderstandings coming with it. Take the very paper of Tomasello et al., where they define such a notion of intentionality: Tomasello et al. falsely identify their 'action plans' with the quite different sort of plans Bratman has in mind in his planning theory of agency[2] (p.676f.), which also aims at spelling out what intentionality means in a similarly exclusive manner. Thus, limiting the scope of intentionality of agency to one of the six features discussed above is certainly helpful in the discussion of specific aspects of agency, but it is arbitrary and does not help the academic discourse, in particular when interdisciplinary research is involved.

The second approach pushes forward a gradual understanding of intentionality in agency, where, on one end of the scale, we have intentionality just the way animals may display intentionality but cannot express them–this was brought forward by Anscombe herself in (Anscombe, 1957, §47). On the other end of the scale, we have full-blown intentionality as brought forward by Bratman, i.e. we

---

2 Tomasello et al. view 'action plans' as the specific way an agent chooses to change the environment out of the many possible ways the agent can interact with the environment to achieve a goal, e.g., switching on the light by pushing a button with the hand (rather the foot, the forehead or a stick). Intentions are the chosen 'action plans'. Bratman's plans, in contrast, are far more elaborate. They stretch in space and time over various actions (and possibly persons). Intentions are then elements of plans. Very simple entities can have 'action plans' á la Tomasello–only very elaborate entities can have Bratman-like plans.

have elaborate plans for the future, which characterize not only our actions but ourselves as persons(Bratman, 2015). We could also call it a pyramid approach to intentionality where important features are added on each level. We deliberate and deduce sub-plans or goals upon which we then commit and act upon. This involves both commitment to do things at a certain point in time and qualitative experience when doing them. This would fit with the time characteristics of the different features of intentionality: The time-span of having a plan covers all the time between formulating it and finishing it (or disbanding it). During this (plan) time - not before and not after - deliberation about sub-plans or formulations of sub-goals takes place, and having those goals covers all the time between formulating them and achieving them (or disbanding them). During this (goal) time - not before and not after - decisions for particular actions, which serve to achieve those goals, may be made, and having the corresponding future intentions covers all the time between having made the decision and finishing the action. During this (future intention) time - not before and not after - the action is done intentionally.

If the gradual account can be sensibly developed, it would have the appealing effect that almost everything ever written about intention can be smoothly merged into it. The concept of 'intentionality' would become a well-structured complex of the different features associated with it. It would make sense to differentiate the different grades of intention by introducing terms like, e.g., action-intention, goal-intention, effect-intention, plan-intention etc., much like I indicated above with (VolI), (EpiI), (EffI), (GoalI), (PlanI) and (ActI). A version of this type of account can be found in Elisabeth Pacherie's 2004 paper "Towards a Dynamic Theory of Intention." Pacherie introduces motor-intentions, present-directed intentions and future intentions at different levels within the psychology of a human agent, and she argues for upward and downward dynamics relating the different levels of intentionality.

Aside from the question, whether or not such an account actually unifies the different notions of intentionality, or merely puts identical name tags on otherwise distinct phenomena, the unfortunate downside would, again, be the inevitable difficulties in scientific discourse. Complicated concepts tend to be simplified by specialized disciplines to make research possible. Those simplifications then tend to dominate the understanding of the more complex context. Hence, psychologists will take one aspect of intentionality and frame it under 'intentionality per se'; social scientists will take another aspect from the range provided by the gradual concept of intentionality and also frame it under 'intention per se', and so will philosophers of ethics, language, mind and so on. Even worse, unless the philosopher or scientist has really wrapped her head around all the different aspects of intentionality, she will likely fall prey to her intuitive notions every now and then, and be rightly troubled by the contradictions and different points of view. A sound philosophical analysis of the concept of intentionality should avoid exactly this, but provide contrasted concepts enabling structured clear-cut discourse.

To see how important this is, it helps to note that even experts on the matter of intentionality require most of their capacities to answer questions, which may only be of relevance if the demand for unification is valid in the first place, be it within an exclusive or gradual account. To illustrate, recall my brief discussion of "Der Mythos des Singulären" by David Schweikard in the third chapter. In his book, we find a marvelous analysis about collective intentionality in groups. Schweikard breaks down differences in the approaches by, e.g., Tuomela, Searle, Gilbert and Miller, into differences in three aspects of intentions 'A intends that B does C': its subject (the 'A'), its mode (the 'B') and its content (the 'C'). On the one hand, this analysis assumes that intentions are something we have in our heads, much like the qualitative experience when exerting physiological control, or an attitude such as a belief when doing something. On the other hand, it respects that intentionality comes in many different variations and must, therefore, allow for quite different A's, B's and C's. An intricate discussion is set up to fit all notions of intentionality in agency in the formula 'A intends that B does C' and, thereby, hopefully, result in some intentional stance allowing us to say 'We intend that we do C', but still respect the inherently individual character of intentionality in agency. The analysis is brilliant, but also rather complex.

By comparison, almost anyone who ever had a social life, and in particular any philosopher who thinks about it, has no trouble admitting that several people, together, can have one and the same goal, can have one and the same plan, can come to decision together to bring about something in the future, and can foresee and know the effects of what they are doing. There is no obvious mystery. There would be a mystery, if we tried to claim they somehow, together, have one and the same qualitative experience, even a joint awareness or knowledge may trouble us.

Given the complications in communication and misleading focus of discussion, I propose to reject both the exclusive and the gradual account of intentionality in agency. But there are still more options for unification.

In a third approach, we could look for an additional concept that entails all six notions of intentionality, a concept which has slipped my analysis somehow as of yet. Unfortunately, the reason for such a slip is the fact that I do not know of any such inclusive concept. 'Doing something for a reason' might be considered a promising idea. In fact, the idea gave rise to Anscombe's analysis of the question 'Why?' in the first place. However, Anscombe correctly points out that a possibly sensible answer to the question is 'For no reason' (Anscombe, 1957, §18). The answer 'For no reason' implies that it is up to the agent to come up with reasons for her actions, i.e. reasons are something internal to the agent or, at least, the agent has to become aware of something that gives her reason to act. There is also a broader external understanding of reasons as advocated by, e.g., Rüdiger Bittner in his book "Doing things for reasons" (2001) according to which reasons are simply states of affairs in the world, and agents are merely responsive to the reasons the world presents to them. So far, I have found it somewhat difficult to recover the psychological phenomena attached to intentionality from such an external reason account. In particular, any attempt to spell out how exactly one particular state of affairs, out of the infinitely many states of affairs at any point in time, becomes a reason for some action will involve some reference back to the agent's psychological constitution. While an approach to agency based on external reasons is promising, it is unlikely to help with a theory of intentionality that recovers the different features associated with it. Ultimately, there may be some other inclusive account for intentionality in agency, but I simply fail to see it.

At least one other path to a unified theory of intentionality in agency remains. A fourth attempt suggests itself from the other-world argument of Anscombe (Anscombe, 1957, §21). Imagine a world in which there are no intentions with which people act. Would we still say they act intentionally, e.g., would the experience of acting still give rise to the notion of intentionality? Anscombe thinks not, and, consequently, gives intention with which one acts a superior status to acting intentionally. The notion of intention, so to say, is smeared over other phenomena related to action. The idea is a variant of the exclusive account discussed first. Consequently, it is not truly unifying the different features associated with intentionality, but explains that our talk of intentionality is mostly a linguistic phenomenon. The meaning of intentionality in agency is based on a primary feature for agency, but penetrates through to other concepts as well.

We find stronger versions of this approach, which are not in the spirit of an exclusive account. In his 1971 paper "Intentional Systems," Daniel Dennett developed the idea that entities or systems are intentional from the moment from which the explanation of their behavior as intentional is better than any other explanation. Indeed, we tend to describe the behavior of complex, yet, not even intelligent machines, the same way as we describe actions of human beings, viz. by reference to intentional states, such as beliefs, desires, goals, and so on and so forth. Following a strong linguistic account, we may discard the idea that there is something fundamental to the notion of intentionality entirely, and only talk about explanations, descriptions, expressions, intentional stance, etc. That approach, too, was foreshadowed by Anscombe, who primarily talks about expressions of intentions rather than intentions as a kind of mental entity, as was pointed out by Moran and Stone in (Moran and Stone, 2009). Moran and Stone claim that expressions of intentionality with regard to agency "are employable in action-explaining answers to the question "Why?"; they express forms of being on-the-way-to-but-not-yet having" acted (p.15). As such, expressions of intentions are not natural expressions of some mental state, but only conventional or linguistic.

A strong linguistic account denies there is an actual feature justifying the talk of intentionality, but claims that it is useful to talk about agency as if it were so. A weak linguistic account, in contrast, accepts there is some feature that gives rise to the primary notion of intentionality in agency, and contends this primary notion can be and is being extended to other phenomena as well.

It is hard to see, how a strong linguistic account of intentionality in agency can be consolidated with the results from empirical research about the development of understanding intentionality in monkeys, apes and small children. It seems children are capable of differentiating between inanimate happenings, animate behavior, goal-directed behavior and actions based on means-end analysis before they grasp an understanding of language, as I have discussed in the literature review in the third chapter (Tomasello et al., 2005). This suggests that the phenomena linked to intentionality in agency are independent from language use and understanding.

The weak linguistic account is open to such findings. In particular, empirical research may provide an answer for the question most central to the linguistic approach: which of the notions of intentionality is primary? Unfortunately, this is also where the account fails to generate true insight. First, the weak linguistic account seems to be rather arbitrary. Without any additional evidence, i.e. purely from within the account, we may pick any of the six features associated with intention, mark it as primary, and come up with very reasonable stories about how the primary notion formed our language to extend our reference to intentionality to related phenomena. With further insight, say from psychological experiments, the arbitrariness does not vanish from the account, but is merely camouflaged. Second, the results from the psychological experiments seem to recognize a variety of phenomena crucial for agency. Understanding other entities as animate agents seems to be an ability distinct from understanding the concept of a goal, which, in turn, is distinct from understanding the concept of reasoning behind a certain action. This is far from the premise of a weak linguistic account that there be one primary form of intentionality in agency. Neither a strong, nor weak linguistic accounts seem to be suited to provide a unifying theory of intention that explains to us the nature of intentionality in agency. They do, however, provide an explanatory alternative to introducing ontologically rich new concepts by referring to our way of talking about intentions.

4.1.3 Action theory diversified

In conclusion, all four discussed attempts to unify the different notions of intention fail. Importantly, they do not fail because they are completely unreasonable, but for other reasons. The exclusive and the gradual approach may be viable from a pragmatic perspective, but they further complicate the matter–in particular with respect to clarity of the scientific discourse. A promising inclusive account is not in sight, and the linguistic approach either fails to generate new insight, or is incompatible with empirical research. The chances for successful unification seem slim, which is to be expected given that so much research has been invested with no success up to now. Consequently, I suggest letting go of the idea of unification and the idea of a form of intentionality that arcs over all the different pieces of cutlery of action. In the end, it is action and agency we want to explain. Analyzing intentionality in agency helps us do so, but maybe not to the extent that we can build the entire theory. Still, we have to explain why intentionality is, in fact, attached to concepts like 'making a decision' or 'having a goal', which could perfectly stand for themselves. Formulating it the way I just did points at one possible route: instead of trying to merge 'having a goal' and other pieces of cutlery of action into the notion of intentionality itself, we should search for different relations between intentionality–whatever it stands for–and the different concepts.

What could this look like for central agential feature like 'having a goal'? Goals for actions arise from various sources: maybe I am hungry, and start to have the goal to find something to eat. Or I deliberate about how I can gain weight for an upcoming boxing match and arrive at the conclusion that finding something to eat would be a good first step. Or somebody else is really hungry and orders me to get something to eat, and I follow the order. In either case, having the goal alone does not imply that I act upon it in any particular way: I might be busy. I might have the goal to find something to eat; yet, I still want to finish what I am doing right now. Or I might not know how to find something to eat, and cannot come up with any action with which I could achieve the goal of finding something to eat. Or I just make a plan for the day listing all my goals for the day, while I do not know yet how many I will actually achieve, and how exactly I am going to act in order to achieve them. Notably, in such cases, we do not ask one another 'What are your intentions for the day?' but 'What are your goals for today?'. The talk changes the moment a specific action is planned or already executed. When a specific action is attached to a goal, we do indeed talk about intentions with which an agent is planning or doing them, and the content to which that intention refers to is identical to the content of the goal we previously talked about.

Following this, intentionality seems to come into play as soon as a particular action is planned or executed. On a quick assessment, this also seems to be true for the other five features associated with agency, which I discussed above: Decisions are not exclusively made to lead to action; we may decide which of two parties, who claim contradicting propositions, is correct. However, mysteriously, when we decide to do some particular action, we talk about intending to do something and refer to the decision. Predictions or knowledge of causal effects of actions is only a fraction of the overall set of predictions and knowledge of causal effects; yet, the former leads to ascription of intentionality, while the latter does not. Awareness or knowledge of what is going on is not restricted to the agent's own actions either, but it affects our judgment about the agent acting intentionally or not. As humans, we also have various qualitative experiences other than our voluntary bodily movements. We qualitatively experience seeing things and hearing things, but we only intentionally perform an action; we do not intentionally see or hear things.

How can we interpret the interplay of talk of intentionality and specific agential features? Yet another attempt at unification seems wearisome. More promising is an elucidation of how the different pieces of cutlery of action guide agents towards particular actions, and see how this applies to group activity as well. This provides an action theory with crisp and clear concepts, and, along the way, narrows down the possible roles that can be played by the notion of intentionality in agency. I focus on one of the concepts associated with intentionality in agency to provide a showcase of how this can be done. Since 'goals' were not only a key concept in the accounts for group activity, but also one of the most meaningful agential features associated with intentionality, the choice is easy. Incidentally, as mentioned earlier, most accounts using the concept of a goal provide only cursory notions of a 'goal' or 'having goals'. In the remainder of this chapter, thus, I will analyze the concepts of 'goal' and 'having goals', relate it to the idea of intentionality and draw conclusion for action theory of group activity and even action theory in general.

4.2 Goals in agency

I have shown that goals are a central concept for thinking about agency. In the previous chapter, I argued that having a common goal characterizes one of three basic types of acting together. In the review of models for acting together, goals were either used themselves as keys to understand group activity, or they were central elements in explaining what it is for several people to display intentionality. Additionally, as discussed in the previous section, having a goal is one of at least six agential features associated with intentionality in agency. Clearly, the concept 'goal' needs careful analysis given its outstanding role in action theory. Yet, it is hard to find in-depth analyses of goals and their relation to other key concepts of action theory. The search function in the Stanford Encyclopedia of Philosophy, for example, returns not a single explicit article for 'goal' while it returns multiple articles for 'intention', 'decision-making', 'choice', 'belief', 'desire', 'attention', 'will' and so on. Some in-depth discussions are found, however, in the literature on collective actions.

I propose an understanding of 'goals' and 'having goals' to close this research gap. I flesh out the notion of a goal as it appears in agency and discover it to be richer than often assumed. Goals are not simply states of affairs or outcomes, but, not surprisingly, show many characteristics usually attributed to intentions: goals cannot be thought without an entity to which they belong, they guide deliberation about how to achieve them and they are subject to rationality constraints for rational agents. Consequently, goals already have the functional properties usually reserved for intentions and with it the explanatory power required for agency.

I start by rejecting an overly simple conception of goals as akin to desires that seems to flow from a standard belief-desire model of action. The discussion helps introduce some important features of goals. On this, I build a first characterization of the concept of a goal. I leave several details open and focus on the functional roles of goals in agency instead.

4.2.1 Goals are not desires

Goals obviously play an important role for agency. When I asked a friendly philosopher of action theory about the nature of goals, he replied that goals are basically desires. This statement is certainly rooted in the standard account for intentional action as being based on a belief-desire pair (Davidson, 1963; Audi, 1973; Sinhababu, 2013). If we want to account for agency by means of beliefs and desires and, at the same time, respect the outstanding role of goals in agency, then the identification suggests itself. First, however, clearly not all desires are goals. I may desire it to be summer rather than winter, but this hardly qualifies as a goal in any sense. Secondly, in turn, not all goals seem to be desires; for I may have the goal of starting the snow cannon, even though I do not desire it at all—it may simply be my job as slope warden. Thirdly, however, I may desire that there be snow in this warm winter, and I might have the goal of making snow, and I do so by using the snow cannon. Thus, at least in some cases having a desire and having a goal look very alike.

So goals are not desires, but they seem to be related to desires more or less intimately, at least sometimes. Let me try to extract some insights about this from the three observations above.

First, the intuition that my desiring it be summer is not a goal may be related to the fact that there is no possible way to change anything about it being winter: we cannot twist the earth's axis to make it summer in any sense of 'can'; neither are we able to do so nor do we have the opportunity. Therefore, 'having a goal' may be different from 'having a desire' by the fact that the agent can actually bring about the goal. Unfortunately, this proposal quickly runs into trouble. On the one hand, we easily find cases of people having goals they cannot and never do achieve. Think of untrained Martin, who wants to win a marathon. Winning a marathon may be his goal, and we truly acknowledge this is his goal when we see him train hard. Yet, he may never reach a form to even complete a marathon, and he may even never seriously believe that he will reach such a form himself. So the requirement that the agent actually can achieve the goal shrinks, at best, to a *weak possibility requirement* that the agent believes it to be possible, in principle, to achieve her goal somehow:

> (WPRG) The weak possibility requirement for goals requires that the agent who has the goal believes it to be possible, at least in principle, that she can achieve the goal.

On the other hand, the fact alone that we can ensure or work towards the satisfaction of our desire does not automatically make the desire a goal. There are plenty of desires realizable within our abilities and opportunities, but only few of them become our goals. Thus, ability or opportunity to bring about what we desire is neither necessary nor sufficient for the transition from having a desire to actually having a corresponding goal.

On the plausible view that goals are some intermediate stage from merely having desires to actual action, we already see goals by themselves have important functional properties, which are usually discussed in the context of intentionality in agency. Indeed, discussions about an agent's beliefs related to his intentions, e.g., (Audi, 1973), are virtually identical to the discussion of the weak possibility requirement for goals (WPRG).

The second observation–that there are goals which are not present in the guise of desires–may be interpreted in different ways; two of which I would like to bring to attention. First, we might conjecture that, in fact, there is some other desire towards which repairing the snow cannon is directed, despite our desire that there be no snow, e.g., the desire to be good at our job. Hence, we find competing desires and only some of them transition into becoming goals. As Hugh McCann points out in his 1991 paper "Settled objectives and rationality constraints," this transition often comes with rationality demands: it would be odd if someone explained to us that his goals are both, to do his best at his job to make snow and that there be no snow. We do not demand consistency for desires, but we do so for goals. It should come as no surprise that similar rationality constraints are thought to be essential to, or even part of the very definition of, intentions as well. In "Two faces of Intention" (1984), Michael Bratman introduces the idea that we can differentiate intentions from other states of mind, like desires, by them being subject to rationality constraints, which is what McCann picks up on. Thus, again, goals by themselves already display an important functional property that enable agency without involving the idea of intentions or intentionality in agency:

> (RCG) Rationality constraints for goals require that an agent does not have an irrational set of goals from her perspective.

A second way to deal with the observation that there are goals without corresponding desires is to revisit the belief-desire conception of action. Davidson's original position presented in 1963 in "Actions, Reasons and Causes" did not refer to desires, but to 'pro-attitudes', i.e. there may be a variety of motivational states potentially leading to action other than desires, some of which may be ethical or social in nature or might even root in external force. Obviously, the statement that goals are essentially desires does not survive this shift, i.e. it does not make sense to claim that goals are essentially pro-attitudes. Pro-attitudes cover a great range of attitudes, some of which lead up to action in a very direct way, e.g., when we shout out some joyous expression after we had good fortune or success. Different pro-attitudes may simply provide distinct paths towards action. On the other hand, there might be a commonality worth exploring or at least a commonality for a great part of pro-attitudes. The starting statement turns into the weaker claim that goals are somehow determined by pro-attitudes. One promising way to make the claim work comes with the intuition that goals seem to be more content-based and less attached to the agent's emotional state. Following this intuition, we could claim the propositional contents of some pro-attitude, or the conditions of satisfaction for some pro-attitude, are extracted and put into the form of a goal, whatever its form may be. We may then sketch the remaining way towards action: the goals *guide our deliberation* up to an action decision, much like a riddle guides our thoughts in solving it. Naturally, we do not transition back into the original pro-attitude for motivation, but having the goal carries some sort of *commitment* towards the content and the actions plans resulting from our deliberation:

> (GDG) A goal serves as a guide or anchor for deliberation towards an action decision,

> (CG) having a goal implies a commitment towards achieving the goal.

Again, the functional roles of goals in agency expressed by guidance of deliberation (GDG) and commitment towards action (CG) are identical to the functional roles often ascribed to intentions. Simply replace 'goal' by 'intention' in (GDG) and (CG) and you have two of the key concepts in Bratman's account of intentionality in agency, as can be read off in several of his essays in his collection "Faces of Intention" (1999).

The third observation, desires and goals often seem to come together, has now already been illuminated. Desires and goals may be described by the same content, and the goal might even originate from a desire. But, despite those connections, it is obvious goals are neither desires, nor simply the propositional content of desires. Instead, goals and having goals show many of the characteristics usually ascribed to intentions: goals come with, at least, a weak possibility requirement (WPRG), goals must fulfill certain rationality constraints (RCG) for them to be goals of a rational agent, goals guide deliberation about how to achieve them (GDG), and they come with a commitment towards achieving the goal (CG).

The task at hand suggests itself: we should develop a clear concept of what it means to have a goal (or be a goal) from the perspective of action theory, and discuss what is left to be a genuine characteristic of intentionality, rather than goals themselves. I start with the development of a concept of a goal, which mainly derives from different sources in the literature on action theory. I follow up with a brief overview of relevant discussions of intentions, each of which somehow features the notion of goals. Finally, I will develop a proposal that weaves the concept of a goal into a theory of action, which—as a consequence—need not rely on the notion of intentionality.

4.2.2 The concept of a goal

The literature on action theory for individuals contains astonishingly little explicit discussion of the concept of a 'goal'. Surprisingly, the arguably more complicated area of action theory for group activity provides more insight as I have reviewed in the third chapter. Philosophers hesitate less to ascribe goals to a group, compared to intentions and, therefore, tend to use the notion of a goal more explicitly. Correspondingly, 'goals' and 'having goals' are taken to be much simpler phenomena than intentions. Velleman goes as far as to state that 'having goals' and 'sharing goals' "is of little philosophical interest" (Velleman, 1997, p.36); yet, he develops some thoughts on goals in his 1997 paper "How to share an intention". According to him, goals and intentions differ in that intentions resolve what one will do, while goals do not (p.32f.) Velleman shares the idea that goals motivate us to exercise deliberation and planning, and argues that sharing a goal comes down to having one and the same outcome as a goal (p.35). Put together, a goal is an outcome that motivates the agent to figure out what plan or action to pursue, but does not resolve what one will do in some sense.

If a goal is an outcome, a valid question is what it is an outcome of. If we accept (GDG) as Velleman does, i.e. that goals guide deliberation about what plan or action to pursue, then goals cannot be outcomes of particular actions. A goal cannot be the guide for deliberation that results in a decision to act in a particular way and, at the same time, literally be the outcome of that action. At best, goals are outcomes of some yet to be specified actions, or an outcome of how the world develops between now and then. Outcomes of this sort, however, are not really outcomes in a meaningful sense–they do not result from something specific–but they are simply states of affairs. Thus, I suggest the sensible interpretation of Velleman's goal conception is that a goal is a state of affairs to be brought about by an agent's actions, and they have a guiding function in deliberation and planning.

In this reading, it is also clear why sharing goals appears to be easy: states of affairs are out there, and agents are out there. Bring two agents together to contribute towards one and the same state of affairs and you have a shared goal. Additionally, this idea captures our everyday language about goals. Goals are achieved or reached; implying that there is some actual state of the world, which we can bring about and can be identified with the goal. In German language, even actual objects are identified with a goal or 'Ziel' in German: the finish line of a race, for example, is called 'Ziel'. It actually is sensible to say that one 'reached the goal in a race'; meaning, one physically crossed the finish line. The same is true for other locations like travel destinations. In English, this is not possible, but intuitively we might still identify goals with actual states, i.e. world states brought about by the owner of the goal. At the same time, we often talk about 'having goals'. This, too, suggests that goals are something external that can be had, and having it simply means we are motivated to achieve or reach them. Unfortunately, this intuitively appealing idea quickly proves to be less helpful than expected.

First of all, we need a clear distinction between 'states of affairs' and 'states of the world'. On this point, we find an important insight in the discussion of collective action in Kutz' outstanding paper "Acting together" from 2000. Kutz points out it is very unlikely that two or more people have the exact same goals, and he proposes "two agents share a goal if there is at least one [...] outcome, [...] whose [...] realization would satisfy the intentions of each" (p.5). As it stands, the proposal is somewhat unclear because there is no clear distinction between goals and intentions, but Kutz extracts the insight that goals of agents only need to 'overlap' to count as shared goals. The notion of 'overlap' of goals forces us to fully acknowledge there is not a one-on-one relation between a goal and an actual world state. Indeed, we can immediately accept that one and the same world state may realize multiple goals, e.g. my cooking pasta realizes both, my goal to kill time (no matter how) and my goal of eating something (no matter what). In this sense, my goal to kill time 'overlaps' with my goal of eating with respect to the world in which I cook pasta. Equally, one and the same goal may be realized by different world states. I need not cook pasta to kill time or eat something; I may also watch a TV show to kill time and put a pizza into the oven to get something to eat. Thus, goals cannot be specific aspects of particular world states either because many other world states may satisfy the specific aspect as well. The relation between goals and world states, thus, is the same relation that states of affairs have to world states (Textor, 2016). If anything, then goals are states of affairs, not states of the world.

In seeming contradiction with this, it is true we refer to world states as goals in retrospection, i.e. we might say things like 'X was her goal' with X being some state of the world, but it is important to note that X *was* her goal. Indeed, the agent stopped having her goal the moment it was satisfied by bringing about X. There is nothing that can be properly called the goal of the agent after it has been achieved, despite the fact that state X may still persist. Therefore, I propose we do not call world states like X 'goals', but 'goal states' or 'target states', which is an equally common alternative in common language.

Second, even with a proper distinction of 'state of affairs' and 'world states', it is clear that not just any state of affairs is also a goal. In fact, the vast majority of states of affairs are not goals. How do we tell apart the states of affairs that are goals from those that are not? It is hopeless to look for the answer by looking at a state of affairs itself. Nothing about it will tell us whether or not it is a goal. This is very different from most other concepts explained by this schematic. We could say, for example, a tree is a plant. Clearly, not all plants are trees, so we need a way to identify trees among the plants. To do so, we specify the properties of plants that make them trees. The same does not work with goals and states of affairs: nothing about the state of affairs will tell us whether or not it is a goal. If, however, goals cannot be specified to be states of affairs by any feature of the states of affairs, we have good reason to reject the claim that goals are states of affairs in the first place.

Theodor Ebert discusses the concepts of ‚means' and 'ends' in his 1977 paper "Zwecke und Mittel: Zur Klärung einiger Grundbegriffe der Handlungstheorie." While he does not use the German word for 'goal' directly, one can identify goals as one of three types of 'Zwecke' (ends) defined by him. About those he writes, "Zwecke in diesem Sinn gibt es gar nicht außerhalb eines auf sie gerichteten Erreichen-Wollens" (p.35) and "Zwecke sind erhoffte, erwünschte, kurz: vorgestellte Wirkungen [..., und] *vorgestellte* Wirkungen eines Handelns [...] sind [...] eine Unterklasse der Vorstellungen des Handelnden" (p.36). Here, Ebert offers a solution to the problem that we cannot look at states of affairs to identify them as goals:

goals do not exist without the wish to achieve them, and, he continues, goals are consequences we hope for or wish for, in short: they are envisioned consequences, but envisioned consequences are a subclass of the agent's visions. We need not take this as an ontological statement, but the important point Ebert makes is that, in order to tell goals apart from mere states of affairs, we must not look at the states of affairs, but at the agent who has the goal.

More precisely, we have to look at the agent's mental life. I addressed this idea in the literature review when I discussed Tomasello's intriguing 2005 work on "Understanding and sharing intention: The origin of cultural cognition," in which a goal is a representation of the future world next to a representation of the current world in an agent's head. Tomasello et al. refer to this representation as the "internal goal" as opposed to the "external goal," which actually is a future state of the world (p.676). Following these thoughts, I conclude goals are not states of affairs, but they are connected to states of affairs. In fact, they are representations of states of affairs. Unfortunately, sharing representations is by no means simple, especially when they are supposed to be in an agent's head. A minimum requirement for a shared goal, thus, has to involve some externalization of the representation. Incidentally, external realization of agential features is exactly what I identified to be the key to understanding group activity.

Third and closely related to the previous point, to say that something is a goal already implies there is an entity to which it belongs. The necessary link to a subject is an idea found in one of the most popular discussions of joint action by Margaret Gilbert in her 1990 paper "Walking together: A paradigmatic social phenomenon." While Gilbert seems to take it as given that joint action necessarily requires a shared goal, she realizes goals are necessarily bound to a subject. That insight, I believe, is one of the major reasons why she introduces 'plural subjects' as carriers of common goals in contrast to merely shared personal goals. We need not accept the notion of 'plural subjects', however, to agree to the important insight about goals: a 'goal' necessarily belongs to an entity that 'has the goal'.

Indeed, this becomes obvious when it is not clear to whom the goal belongs, and how odd it is to identify a state of affairs to be a goal in such situations. Imagine a friend, whom you know well, states a goal that does not fit with any of her interests, something like 'Look, the goal is that in one year from now crystal meth has replaced crack as the number one drug among students of philosophy.' Not believing this is the goal of your friend, you would be lost with this statement until your friend states whose goal this is supposed to be. Every inquiry would either assume somebody to be the owner of the goal or explicitly or implicitly ask for the owner of the goal. The elliptical character of statements of goals becomes even more obvious when there is nothing that could possibly have that goal, e.g., 'the goal is that the black hole completely absorbs the star'. Again, these observations push away the idea that goals are states of affairs, but suggest that goals belong to entities: what it takes to *be* a goal cannot be answered without answering what it takes for an agent to *have* a goal.

The discussion from the relation of goals and desires and the insights of Velleman's, Kutz', Ebert's, Tomasello's and Gilbert's positions allow to synthesize the concept 'goal': from Gilbert's position, I take it to be true that goals belong to agents. What it is to be a 'goal' cannot be said unless we know what it is for an agent to 'have a goal'. From Tomasello's position, I take it to be true that 'having a goal' essentially means to have a representation, but what is represented is not a world state. Rather, following, Ebert's position, what is represented is a 'state of affairs'. The future world state that actually satisfies the goal, so I argue, should be explicitly called a 'goal state', rather than a 'goal' itself to account for the possibility of 'overlapping' goals suggested by Kutz. From Velleman's position, I take it to be true that goals guide an agent's deliberation and provide some sort of motivation to go through with it. Both of these functional properties already came up in the discussion of the relation of goals and desires. I also include the other properties and functions from that analysis.

Thus, I propose to characterize goals in agency by:

(G) A goal is a representation of a state of affairs that belongs to an agent with the functional properties as outlined in the weak possibility requirement (WPRG), the rationality constraints for goals (RCG), the guidance of deliberation of goals (GDG) and the commitment towards achieving the goal (CG).

So far, I have only talked about goals in the context of agency, but goals might also belong to entities that are not agents. Being able to have a goal certainly is an important agential feature, but is it not also available to entities other than agents? The answer depends on (i) what kind of representation is involved and (ii) how demanding the functional properties (WPRG), (RCG), (GDG) and (CG) really are.

With regard to (i), the type of representation in (G), it is not important what the nature of the representation is, but simply the insight that a goal cannot be identified with an existing object or state in the world; it must be some sort of representation thereof. In action theory, where human agents are mostly at the center of research, 'having a goal' often means the agent has a mental representation, i.e. a representation realized in whatever form the human mental faculties represent states of affairs. On the one hand, states of affairs can be represented by much simpler entities in a different way. In the discussion of the account of List and Pettit in the third chapter, I already mentioned their example of a small robot, which puts up small cylinders (List and Pettit, 2013, p.19). The fact that goals are representations does not exclude this kind of robot from having goals. On the other hand, states of affairs may also be symbolically represented on a sheet of paper: I might give you a list with the comment, 'Here are my goals.' This is a sensible thing to say and do. If I seek your advice, for example, we might actually sit and discuss the sheet of paper. When you start thinking and share your thoughts, you will likely come back to the sheet several times to check whether or not your advice makes sense. You will likely point to different items, think of ways they can be realized in one stroke, and point out ones that must be treated separately and so on and so forth. In the second chapter, I discussed diffusion and alienation using the examples of means and goals of the group activity. In complex group activity, goals are written down in contracts and tracked on white-boards; documents are prepared for meetings; protocols are written and so on and so forth. That being said, I believe the specifics of the representation relevant for (G) are largely irrelevant. Thus, the fact (G) involves a representation of a state of affairs does not make it overly restrictive with respect to the entities that have goals.

With regard to the functional properties of goals, I propose a similarly broad understanding: the requirement that the entity, which has a goal, in some way deems it possible to achieve the goal need not be realized within a complex mental structure featuring beliefs or statistic reasoning. In fact, even with proper agents, the possibility condition is rarely satisfied by way of explicit beliefs. Instead, agents may see other agents achieve something and aim for the same by way of similarity, or they simply have already achieved similar goals in the past. Goals chosen in this way are chosen partly on the implicit assumption that the goal can be achieved. In extreme cases, there may even be an explicit disbelief in achieving the goal: the agent might know it is virtually impossible to achieve her goal, but hopes for divine intervention or some miraculous way of chance. In either case, the weak possibility requirement for goals (WPRG) is not overly restrictive with respect to the entities that may have goals.

The rationality constraints for goals (RCG), too, must be understood relative to the entity having the goal. Even with human agents, there is great variance when it comes to rational capabilities. One agent may immediately see that two of her desires are not co-realizable and decides from which to form her goal. However, another agent may not see it and starts to pursue two contradicting goals and only recognizes this at a later point in time. When it comes to simpler entities, the rationality constraints may even be automatically fulfilled. Think of an entity that can only have one goal at a time. Clearly, when you have only one goal, its pursuit cannot contradict the pursuit of other goals.

The guidance of deliberation (GDG) provided by goals has two aspects. First, the agent needs to deduce what goal state she wants to bring about that satisfies her goal, and, second, she needs to think of how to bring it about. The two aspects are closely related in human agency, as is shown by Csibra and Gergely in several co-authored papers: when we understand that agents have goals, we are also able to interpret and predict other agent's behavior in these terms. However, our observation only gives us information about observed end-states, observed obstacles and observed behavior–not about goals, action constraints and actions. Infants of 12 months of age already are able to translate these observations into a teleological trinity of actions as means to goals under given constraints, i.e. "the future state will become encoded as the goal" (Csibra et al., 2003, p.114). They, too, claim that "a goal represents a state" and take care to call the states goal-states, rather than goals themselves (Csibra and Gergely, 2006, p.61). However, the interesting point is that they explicitly ask how the transition from merely observing end-states to goals is done, for there are many aspects of an end-state that can be the goal. They introduce the notion of a "principle of rational action[, which] presupposes that (1) *actions* function to bring about future *goal states*, and (2) goal states are realized by the most rational action available to the actor within the *constraints of the situation*." (Gergely and Gergely, 2003, p.298). In human agency, thus, the understanding of goal-directed action not only guides deliberation towards the respective goal state and actions as means to achieve the goal states, but it does so in a practically rational manner.

Indeed, it seems impossible to think of goals in human agency that do not feature this sort of guidance when it comes to human agency. Imagine Nikki states she wants to see Niagara Falls, and, if asked about how to do this, Nikki answers: 'Why do you ask?' or 'It never crossed my mind to think about that'. We would be confused by such an answer and likely start to think of 'seeing Niagara Falls' merely as Nikki's wish, or hope or less. Furthermore, if Nikki were to tell us she booked a flight to Berlin, and if we knew Nikki is as rational as most of us, we would conclude that Nikki is not flying to Berlin to achieve the goal of seeing Niagara Falls. However, if we knew Nikki is not as rational as most of us, maybe Nikki is a 3-year old child or mentally challenged, we may still acknowledge she has the goal of seeing Niagara Falls, but she chooses the means to do so erratically. The point is that deliberation to achieve a goal need not be rational, in general. Deliberation in human agency certainly often works this way, but this is a property of human deliberation–not an implication of 'having a goal', in general.

Instead, I propose to read the guidance of deliberation of goals in the much weaker sense that the entity having the goal uses the methods of finding a solution to the challenge of achieving the goal available to it. For simplicity, I call 'methods of finding a solution to the challenge of achieving the goal' deliberation. Deliberation, understood in this broad sense, is not overly restrictive with respect to the entities that can have goals.

Finally, the commitment towards goals (CG) is well-known from human agency as well. If Nikki, who stated her goal is to see Niagara Falls, continues to say something along the lines of 'I just want to see Niagara Falls. I won't do anything about it, though', we, again, would not take her seriously in having the goal of seeing Niagara Falls. We would, at best, ascribe to her a strong, unreflected desire or, at worst, a take-what-you-can-get attitude. The reason we would not believe Nikki has the goal she states to have is because she is not trying to do anything to achieve it. The commitment that comes with a goal, whatever that is in detail, results in trying to achieve it. If we characterize the commitment towards a goal by the fact that it results in trying to achieve the goal, commitment can take different forms for many entities. In human agency, it may be the motivation inherited from the original pro-attitude that drives us to trying. For mechanical or digital entities, it may be hard-wired or coded to try to achieve the goal once it receives relevant input, i.e. machines or software cannot help but be committed towards their goals. For groups of agents, contracts, incentive systems and established procedures ensure that they try to achieve certain goals as a group. In conclusion, commitment towards goals (CG) need not be understood in an overly restrictive way with respect to the entities that can have a goal.

Overall, the discussion of goals in agency can be generalized to explain why entities other than agents have goals. The functional roles are variable enough to allow for completely different realizations and depth or quality of the resulting functional capabilities. This being so, the characterization of the concept of a goal (G) is a good first step, but it needs refinement depending on the particular entity it applies to. Even one and the same entity may have goals in different variations. Human agents, for example, may sometimes have goals with the most developed functional properties, i.e. well-grounded beliefs in the reachability of a goal (whatever 'a belief' actually is), a coherent set of different goals that potentially interlock in a hierarchical structure, logical reasoning and statistical evaluation of possible solutions and an elaborate commitment with clear parameters for reconsideration. Most of the time, however, human agents have but a hunch if they can achieve something, do not notice an immediate conflict with other goals at the time being, simply do what they always do in similar situations to achieve the goal, and a loose commitment that is little more than an urge. In both scenarios, the human agent has a goal, but she has so by way of quite different realizations of the typical functional properties of the goals, which are likely featured by equally different aspects of her mental and physical constitution.

Nonetheless, I think I have come far in revealing the core features of goals and rejecting optimistically simple notions of goals as mere states of affairs or even world states. Most importantly, the discussion of goals and their role in agency confirms how similar the idea 'goals' and 'having goals' is to intentionality in agency. In fact, (G) could just as well describe the concept of an 'intention with which' an agent acts. Therefore, I now look at how goals and intentionality in agency can possibly be related.

4.2.3 Goals and intentionality in agency

In the previous subsection, the analysis of goals revealed that goals have properties and functions usually attributed to intentions. My reason for looking at goals in the first place was its natural relevance in the discussion of intentionality and, of course, its outstanding role in group activity. The strong connection between goals and intentionality and agency, not surprisingly, was again confirmed by the previous analysis. Consequently, it is now time to look at the relationship between goals and intentionality in agency more explicitly.

Instead of looking at individual agents, however, I will again draw on insight generated from action theories for group activity simply because the discussion of goals and intentionality is most transparent in these accounts.

The first remarkable point about goals in group activity is that almost any account claims 'common goals' and 'having common goals', or some similar notion, are a necessary element for collective agency. This is so surprising because there is no comparable claim in individual action theory *for goals*. *For intentions*, on the other hand, it is often assumed they are the key element in individual agency. As much as it is surprising, it is also wrong. I have already shown common goals are, in fact, *not* necessary for acting together. Indeed, two or more individual agents may bring about a world state satisfying their personal, distinct goals. This only requires that the agents realize that their respective goals might be satisfied by one and the same world state and, consequently, they decide to coordinate their actions towards this state. The resulting world state is *not* their goal, but merely the goal state that satisfies their personal goals. In light of this, the idea that goals are necessary for group activity sticks out even more and deserves explanation.

The explanation, I believe, must refer to the outstanding role of intentionality in individual agency, and intentions in particular. On the one hand, intentions are viewed as the mark of agency for individual agents. On the other hand, intentions are often pictured as some sort of 'mental state', or belonging to the realm of the 'mind' in general. Unfortunately, it is not clear how 'mental states' can be shared or how 'minds' can be merged; yet, we would like a similar mark of agency for group activity. Consequently, we must look for an alternative for intentions in group activity that, both, serves as a mark of agency, but can be easily shared. The unreflected notion of a goal seems to provide exactly that. In particular, were we to believe that goals are actual world states or external states of affairs, then we could claim agents can easily share them. The reference to external goals, thus, provides the binding force for group activity. Group agency, so we may continue, is the combination of a goal on the group level and some mental phenomenon on the individual level that embeds the group goal into a form of intentionality in agency resulting in a concept of 'group intentionality', which necessarily requires the notion of a common goal.

Clearly, the strategy is not compatible with the understanding of goals I provided before, but the key idea may still be valid. It may be possible to add a 'mental' phenomenon to the notion of a goal on the individual level in order to somehow embed goals into the intentionality of agency. The only problem is: what shall this extra 'something' be? I have already argued that, for individual human agency, goals are realized within the mental faculties themselves with functional properties crucial for exercising agency. What else is needed?

The notorious problem of the mental versus the external surfaces in another way during the discourse about group activity. Most accounts assume implicitly or explicitly that goals are actual or possible states of affairs, or an outcome. When multiple agents have a goal together, they need to know something about the other person, namely, that the other person knows about this 'external' goal as well. This *common knowledge condition* can be found in most accounts of collective action in stronger or weaker forms. Notably, however, we find no analogue in individual action theory, i.e. it is not explicitly required that an agent knows her goal. This suggests an intimate relation between an agent and her goals making an explicit knowledge condition superfluous. That, however, leads to a paradoxical understanding of goals: in collective action theory, goals are often used because they are assumed to be just states of affairs with no particular relation to an agent– at best they can be ascribed to an agent. This allows sharing them easily without mysterious ways of mind-merging, as long as the agents relate to the goal by knowing it. In individual action theory, in contrast, the relation between an agent and an agent's goals seems to assume having a goal already implies knowing about the goal. My analysis of goals suggests the latter is true. As a conclusion, the motivation to replace intentions with goals for a simpler theory of group activity is mute. The strategy to split the 'mental' intentionality from the 'external' goal runs into a dead end. Goals, at least as they come in individual human agency, are no less mental than intentions.

Next to a distinction between the 'mental' on the individual level accounting for intentionality, and the 'external' by way of goals, there is a second insightful tendency in the discussion of group activity that sets apart agency and action execution. In group activity, goals are thought to affect and be affected by multiple agents. In particular, the guidance of the agents' deliberation and actions is not a matter of one agent alone, but of several agents. Some agents might not even have a say in how their goals are to be achieved, given the group is organized hierarchically. Some agents may not even know about the goal. At the same time, however, the execution of the actions is thought to remain on the individual level. Indeed, everyone seems to agree that a group cannot act intentionally in the literal sense of intentional action execution: in the end, the individual agents act–not the group somehow itself. The group does not have a 'body' it can control in order to achieve the goals set on a group level. Consequently, the notion of intentional action is separated on the individual level by way of, e.g., doing ones part (Kutz, 2000), or meshing subplans that belong to the individual agency as Bratman would put it (Bratman, 1992), while the corresponding goals are somehow fixed on the group level.

As before, thus, the idea is to view goals as something external that can be easily shared on a group level, but it needs individual agents who act intentionally to embed the goals into agency. This implies that intentionality in agency does not come with goals alone, but that there need to be some sort of control, typically involved in acting intentionally. I briefly discussed the notion of control in the reflections on intentionality in agency, and noted that we may differentiate two dimensions: one dimension is simply control over one's execution of an action–this corresponds more to the idea of intentional action; the other dimension is control over what the agent is supposed to do in the first place–this corresponds more to the idea of goals and the respective deliberation. Usually, in individual action theory, the second dimension is thought to be more relevant to agency (Frankfurt, 1997, e.g.,), while mere execution control seems to be contingent. In group activity, for some reason, the roles are reversed when we insist that, ultimately, the individual agents act, and not the group. Intentionality in group activity, thus, is recovered by referring to 'intentional actions' of the individuals who actually have a body to do so.

In conclusion, two major strategies to integrate goals into intentionality in agency can be identified from the discussion of group activity. First, we may claim goals need to be complemented with some sort of mental phenomenon. Given that we know agency mainly from our own human agency, and that human agency heavily relies on our 'minds', this is intuitively sensible, but it is unclear what exactly this mental phenomenon is supposed to be. Second, we may claim goals need to be complemented with actual intentional action to account for intentionality. Again, we know from our own human agency that we have a body and intentional control over it. Somehow, this rounds out the idea of goals and intentionality in agency.

Neither strategy is convincing, so I claim, but they touch upon two fundamental preconceptions with regard to intentionality and agency in general; namely, that agency requires a 'mind' and a 'body'. These are powerful preconceptions that immediately block any form of agency other than what we know from human agency. They deserve a thorough rejection, and I will do so in the next chapter. What is important to note about both strategies is that the notion of 'having a goal' carries most of the explanatory weight, while the integration into the notion of 'intentionality' is somewhat ad-hoc. We need some mental phenomenon or some profound notion of intentional action to keep the idea of intentionality relevant.

Naturally, a third option suggests itself: simply let go of the idea of intentionality in agency, whenever goals or other agential features can do the explanatory work.

4.3 Insights from intentionality and goals in agency

The analysis of intentionality in action theory resulted in six different features of agency associated with it–the cutlery of agency, so to speak. The features turned out to be distinct, i.e. not reducible to one another or some other feature. While the different phenomena often play tightly connected roles in agency, trying to merge them into one phenomenon named 'intention' or 'intentionality', so I argued, is not helpful. Consequently, I proposed to take the concepts themselves more seriously in action theory and take the focus off intentionality in agency.

As a showcase of this proposal, I have analyzed the concept of a 'goal' mostly with help from accounts for group activity. As it turns out, 'goals' indeed display much of the properties and functionality needed for agency already. So much, in fact, it is hard to find a role for intentionality in goal-based agency. If intentionality in action theory is to mean something, it should not mean 'having goals'.

Without looking at the other notions associated with intentionality in action theory, I now make the bold assumption that the same will be true for *all* of them. Consequently, instead of focusing on a single concept of intentionality in action theory, I propose to accept the diversity in agency and rethink action theory accordingly. The relevant features need not be limited to the ones associated with intentionality, but different sets of *agential features* may be viable.

In the literature review for accounts of group activity, I have pointed out the assumptions concerning individual action theory vary greatly. On the one extreme, we have philosophers like List and Pettit who assume primitive robots constructed to autonomously bring cylinders into an upright position already display a minimal form of agency. On the other extreme, philosophers like Bratman put up strong rationality demands and complex cognitive abilities to account for coordinated, temporally extended action plans in order to display proper agency. The view on agency as proposed offers a simple solution to these seemingly contradictory positions. Agency comes in varying degrees of complexity depending on which agential features are actually employed. The idea of a sharp line between agency and simpler forms of behavior in the guise of 'intentionality' does not fit the reality of agency.

Given this insight, how do we best describe agency? What are the relevant agential features? Is there a minimal set of agential features required for agency, or do we need different sets of agential features allowing for different grades of agency? Philosophy of action has to revisit those questions, and I am convinced the answers will result in a more discursive, concept-driven theory of agency without the obstacles posed by the idea of intentionality as the single mark of agency.

As far as the idea of agency in group activity is concerned, the discussion of the role of goals and intentionality in agency revealed two powerful preconceptions that challenge any type of agency other than individual human agency on a fundamental level, viz. that agency requires a mind and a body. This finds its expression in the focus on intentionality as mental entities 'intentions' and physiologically inspired notions of 'intentional action'. In the final chapter, I reject both claims and, thereby, open up the possibility of different kinds of agency, including group agency.

5 Kinds of agency

What started out as an inquiry about agency in group activity has led to the discussion of specific concepts relevant for agency in general. I concluded that agency is constituted by a variety of agential features in possibly multiple ways. It is only natural that the subjects of agency, viz. agents, may also be constituted in ways very different from human agency. So far, however, the only entities that are agents beyond any doubt are human beings. Notably, this is not a conclusion from some basic action theoretic principles. Rather, it is a pragmatically justified constraint on action theory that human beings are agents, or, at least, capable of performing actions in a reasonable number of circumstances. If an action theory contradicts this strongly intuitive perception of ours, it should be and usually is quickly rejected.

The idea that human beings are agents compared to other non-agential entities is, I assume, grounded in the introspective difference between types of doings. We know very well that we sometimes only react to things from instinct, let ourselves go, even do things without even being aware of them, and we observe other creatures displaying similar patterns of *behavior*. However, we also know very well that we sometimes do things in a very different manner: we do not merely behave, we act. The explanation of this difference is, of course, the goal of action theory. I have reviewed that the difference is often thought to be marked by some sort of 'intentionality', but the discussion of goals and intentionality revealed two basic pre-conceptions behind this distinction: what almost every approach to agency has in common is a reference to our mental faculties in some way or another. Be it our ability to act based on reason (Anscombe, 1957), willingly guide our doings (Frankfurt, 1997), a special combination of beliefs and desires (Davidson, 1963; Sinhababu, 2013), fundamental mental states called 'intentions' (Searle, 1979), or our ability to make and have plans (Harman, 1976; Bratman, 1999) and so on and so forth. Indeed, where else would we look for a difference other than in our mental faculties? This is how our species apparently differs significantly from other species. Consequently, mind and agency are thought to belong together. This is the 'mind-agency-paradigm'.

The mind-agency paradigm, i.e. the close connection between having a sufficiently complex mind and being an agent, is often used to shut out any other form of agency than individual human agency. Machines cannot be agents because they do not have a mind. Animals may have a mind, but it is not sufficiently complex to support agency in most animals. And, of course, groups clearly do not have a mind and, so, cannot display agency. The idea that human beings are agents and that action theory should at least account for this fact is turned into the idea that human beings are the only agents.

https://doi.org/10.1515/9783110628623-005

The usual response to this conclusion from the mind-agency paradigm is that the functional requirements for agency are multiply realizable without necessarily involving a constitution similar to the human mind (List and Pettit, 2013). Velleman, for example, even turns the entire argument around and claims that whether or not something 'has a mind' should be judged by its functional capabilities, i.e. if a group has group level features functionally equivalent to human intentions, then this group has a mental component (Velleman, 1997). List and Pettit follow the same strategy culminating in the catch phrase "Groups with minds of their own" (Pettit, 2003). The characterization of agency in terms of functional requirements is a popular and powerful response to the mind-agency paradigm, but I favor a more direct response to the idea that individual human agency is the only type of agency. After all, the functional requirements may be chosen such that they can only be fulfilled by the human mental faculties and the evasive maneuver does not work anymore.

To do so, I review empirical research results about the 'prototype' of agency, i.e. individual human agency. Psychological research has unveiled some of the mechanisms involved in acting, and the results are rather disenchanting. Taking human agency as a blue-print for agency in general becomes a questionable strategy in light of these discoveries. This is not particularly unusual. Think of the human eye as a prototype for visual perception. It is remarkable, no doubt, but it also has a large blind spot not far from the center of our visual field. The visual spectrum is only a tiny fraction of the electromagnetic spectrum. Adjustment to different intensities of light takes long and the eye is quite damageable. In short, the human eye is far from perfect. This is, of course, no new insight and true of essentially everything about us. We are biologically evolved creatures shaped by ecological pressures. All our features are adapted not to approach perfection, but to be better at reproduction than other creatures in our habitat.

When thinking about agency, we have to be aware that human beings presumably only display imperfect agency, just like we only have imperfect vision. In fact, on the assumption that agency is something special beyond 'mere behavior', we are one of the first creatures to have evolved into agents, and it is to be expected that we are not particularly 'good' at it. This is all the more reason to abstract from the specific way agency is realized in human beings. As a result, the mind-agency paradigm might still hold in some form, e.g., in a functionalist sense, but its details may not rely on the specifics of the human mental faculties.

When it comes to groups, the lack of a mind is only one of two troublesome preconceptions for group agency. Agents are usually thought to be able to actually execute actions in a way controlled by the agents themselves. To do so, the agent needs a body. This 'body-agency paradigm' seems so obvious that its validity is rarely challenged. At best, the discussion of the 'body-agency paradigm' is about the specific relation of the body and agency in terms of, e.g., bodily movements as basic actions that generate all other actions (Davidson, 1971; Haddock, 2005; Mele, 2003; Taylor, 1973).

Considering groups, a simple conclusion from the body-agency paradigm suggests itself: not only do groups not have a mind, they have no body either. If a group is 'doing' something, it is ultimately a human being or a machine doing something. This seems to imply the group never has full control of what is done, but only individual humans have (or machines, which are constructed and controlled by humans). Hence, groups cannot display agency beyond what the individual human agents do (Kelsen, 1945; Ludwig, 2014; Margolis, 1974; Velasquez, 1983, for similar versions of this argument).

In the discussion of authority and authorization in the third chapter, a solution for this restriction has already offered itself. We know from human agency that human agents may order others to do their bidding or authorize them to do something in their name, thus, lifting the restriction that an agent has to have a body with which she controls her actions. Obviously, however, this is not the common way of executing one's actions, and it might be exclusive to entities with a mind and the ability to communicate, which also happens to require a body. This solution to overcome the body-agency paradigm, therefore, is immediately challenged. Instead, I would like to focus on what this 'common' way actually is. As with the empirical research about some of the mental aspects of human agency, research into human action execution is no less surprising and potentially counter-intuitive. The common way does not look so common up close, and the body-agency paradigm needs to be reformulated just as radically as the mind-agency paradigm.

Ultimately, so I argue, the specifics of human decision making and action execution are not suitable as a basis for a general concept of agency. Instead, human agency should be viewed as one specific and even potentially flawed way to realize agency. A more abstract action theory needs to overcome simple versions of the mind-agency paradigm and body-agency paradigm. The general action theory may then be used, for example, to identify or create other entities that display agency without a mind or body in the intuitive sense. The principle of external realization of agential features, in particular, offers itself to explain agency on a group level, which I will argue for in the last part of this chapter.

5.1 Human agents as prototype agents

Human beings are agents, at least most adult human beings most of the time. This does not mean they always display agency, but they are certainly capable of agency if nothing interferes with how things commonly are. Naturally, our intuitive view on agency as well as our theoretical considerations are strongly shaped by human agency. Many famous characterizations of agency, accordingly, rely on introspectively graspable notions. Anscombe, for example, made it one of the key features of agency that agents know what they are doing without observation (Anscombe, 1957, §8/9). Without introspection, such ideas are much less comprehensible.

There are obvious disadvantages to this strategy[1]. I would like to point out one not so obvious concern. Human beings certainly are amazing creatures at times, but when looking at ourselves, we are also somewhat self-opinionated–we like to put ourselves in a better light than we actually are. Normally, at least when it matters, most of us are likely to think of ourselves as independent agents, thinking *our* reasons for our actions through, making decisions that reflect who we are as persons and being in full control of our actions. Upon honest introspection, this high standard rarely applies. Even in big life decisions, I know many including myself who wonder for days, weeks or months and finally make a decision more on gut feeling than anything else. Introspection is a guide in philosophical inquiry, but it must be critically evaluated, and even then it might not be a good guide.

In light of scientific progress, especially in psychology, the reliance on intuition and introspection is, fortunately, increasingly unnecessary and can be replaced by the respective scientifically validated insights. For action theoretic considerations, this requires an interdisciplinary approach. I highlight some selected results, and their implications for action theory for two particularly relevant aspects of agency. The first aspect concerns the mental faculties involved in human decision making and challenges the mind-agency paradigm, while the second is about action execution as a challenge to the body-agency paradigm.

I start with a closer look at decision making, which is deemed crucial for most actions. Psychology has studied many cases in human decision making that display patterns which are far from ideal compared to typical action theoretic claims on rationality in agency. While this does not mean human agents are incapable of rational decision making, it certainly supports the claim that many of the specifics of human agency may not serve as blueprints for agency in general. Second, I evaluate action control in the sense of execution control. As it turns out, reasonable models of execution control link together predefined motor programs, observational clues and high level action guidance on an unconscious level. It becomes clear that human agency relies on various mechanisms hidden to introspection,

---

1 Introspection and intuition are highly subjective and, consequently, hard to measure objectively. Introspection and intuition are known to be deceptive in many areas, e.g., optical illusions, logical reasoning, retrospective rationalization, social adaptation, sprituality. Introspection and intuition are also culturally influenced, e.g., when it comes to questions about right and wrong (Pust, 2017; Schwitzgebel, 2016, for a comprehensive overview).

and those mechanisms seem to be contingent realizations of agential features. Other forms of agency may rely on completely different realizations no less and no more special.

5.1.1 Decision making in human agency

Making decisions is a key element in our intuitive picture of agency, but it is not unambiguous. On the one hand, making a decision seems to be something done at a specific point in time that initiates action. It is a *choice* between different courses of actions or doing nothing. On the other hand, making a decision often means to entail the reasoning that led to the choice. It is this second notion of decision making that inspires elaborate action concepts. An agent *deliberates rationally* what courses of action are available and how they fulfill the agent's goals. The choice itself, ideally, follows their best judgment resulting from deliberation. Davidson called this type of judgment an "all things considered judgment" or "all-out judgment" (Davidson, 1978, p.99).

It is important to note that making choices and deliberation are, in fact, distinct parts that can easily fall apart. An agent may deliberate meticulously and rationally not to buy a pack of cigarettes and light a smoke only to find herself smoking a cigarette from the pack she just bought against her previous judgment a few minutes earlier. Cases of 'weakness of will' or 'acrasia' have a long history in philosophical discussion (Plato, 1967, 351b-369a)(Aristotle, 350, 1045a15-1052a36)(Ainslie, 1992; Bratman, 1996; Davidson, 1970; Hare, 1963; Wolf, 1985) and they show how our idealized conception of decision making in agency does not match reality. As a consequence, those cases are often regarded as cases that do not display agency or only some distorted variation of it.

Cases of weakness of will feature a rational judgment about what to do and a consequent action that counteracts exactly this judgment. There are, however, also actions that are not preceded by any deliberation at all, let alone a rational one. Rosalinde Hursthouse gave some examples of "Arational actions" in her so titled paper from 1991. Such actions may be emotionally triggered, habituated or done in a reflex-like manner. This, too, suggests a clear distinction between rational deliberation associated with decision making and making choices associated with decision making.

'Making a choice' is a very interesting action theoretic concept. It seems to be a non-rational element enabling agents to initiate action. Rational deliberation is one way to support making a choice between different possible actions and, thus, make a decision. However, given rational deliberation and making a choice for action are not hard-wired as shown by cases of weak will and arational actions, it is possible that what looks like a choice based on rational deliberation might only be contingent with rational deliberation, and the actual reason for the choice is not given by rational arguments. In fact, we know cases in which we create rational explanations of our choices only after we made them—we 'rationalize' our actions, but is this also possible when everything seems according to our ideal picture of agency? Surely, it would be odd if our deliberation had no effect whatsoever on our choices, but the choices may not be determined by our deliberation alone. Rational deliberation may only be one factor among others.

There are several results from psychological research that, indeed, suggest the choices we make are often influenced by various other factors, even when the agents think they rely only on rational considerations.

5.1.1.1 Halo effect

Salomon Ash was one of the first to discover what is now known as the *Halo* effect. He devised a series of experiments in which the participants had to provide a character description based on a selection of adjectives provided to them. In one of the experiments, the adjectives read:

A. intelligent–industrious–impulsive–critical–stubborn–envious

B. envious–stubborn–critical–impulsive–industrious–intelligent (Ash, 1946, p.270)

The adjectives for A and B are identical, but reversed in order. The suggested attributes are largely incommensurable. Thus, there is no natural order. A person's intelligence is usually independent of her impulsiveness or stubbornness. From a rational point of view, just given the two lists of adjectives with no sensible ordering, character descriptions based on the lists should show no significant difference. Yet, "[t]he impression produced by A is predominantly that of an able person who possesses certain shortcomings [...], while] B impresses the majority as a "problem," whose abilities are hampered by his serious difficulties" (ibd.) Just by different ordering, therefore, the judgment of character greatly differs, and it seems that the *first* impression leads to a significant different interpretation of the following character traits. After we have made a first judgment about a person, thus, additional information about the person is interpreted more negatively or positively depending on the first impression.

The "tendency to like (or dislike) everything about a person—including things you have not observed—is known as the halo effect" (Kahneman, 2011, p.82), and its practical implications are disturbing. The psychologist Kahneman, for example, changed his method of judging student's essays in order to avoid the halo effect. He was tasked with grading two essays for his students. Instead of reading a single student's essays in order, he shuffled and anonymized them. As a result, "When I [Kahneman] was disappointed with a student's second essay and went to the back page of the booklet to enter a poor grade, I occasionally discovered that I had given a top grade to the same student's first essay [...] The lack of coherence left me uncertain and frustrated." He then describes how he was even tempted to change the grades accordingly (p.69).

As if this was not enough, experiments conducted by Forgas showed the magnitude of the halo effect is mood dependent: "positive mood can increase and negative mood can eliminate halo effects" (Forgas, 2011, p.816). Not only are judgments about other persons unjustifiably tilted towards our overall first impression of them, but it also depends on whether or not we have good day.

Clearly, the halo effect leaves a significant dent in the conception of human agents exercising rational deliberation. This does not mean, however, the halo effect is always a bad thing. In a critical analysis of the halo effect in general, Murphy et al. note the halo effect "may actually increase the accuracy and validity of ratings, especially accuracy and validity in distinguishing between ratees" (Murphy et al., 1993, p.220). Said differently, the halo effect creates greater contrast in our judgments of others and, therefore, simplifies our choices. In general, the halo effect also furthers coherence of a person's views and coherence clearly is an aspect of rationality. The way in which the halo effect creates coherence, however, can only be characterized as flawed from the perspective of an idealized rational agent.

5.1.1.2 Priming

Another interesting psychological mechanism is 'priming'. According to one of the most famous studies, priming "refers to the incidental activation of knowledge structures, such as trait concepts and stereotypes, by the current situational context" (Bargh et al., 1996, p.230). More importantly, the "automatic activation of stereotypes should make the perceiver him- or herself more likely to act in accordance with the [respective] trait concepts" (p.233). Indeed, Bargh et al. have shown in a series of experiments that participants primed with words associated with elderly people actually reduced their walking speed on a completely unrelated occasion a few minutes later (p.237f.) After priming participants with words typically associated with impoliteness, they interrupted a conversation between the experimenter and a confederate more often. Furthermore, they showed more hostile behavior when primed with pictures of Afro-Americans. In the last case, the pictures were shown only subliminally, i.e. the participants did not even consciously notice the priming.

These and many more experiments established it as "virtually axiomatic among social psychologists that the mere exposure to socially relevant stimuli can facilitate, or *prime*, a host of impressions, judgments, goals, and actions, often even outside of people's intention or awareness" (Molden, 2014, p.1). Kahnemann presents a host of such experiments in his book "Thinking Fast and Slow".

The research on priming shows that deliberate and conscious decisions, such as interrupting others in a talk, are significantly shaped by completely non-rational and even unconscious factors. These factors will outweigh rational considerations sometimes and, thus, potentially lead to irrational behavior. As with the halo effect, however, priming does not necessarily produce bad behavior. It is easy to imagine how priming improves our performance as agents. When confronted with a new situation, we pick up clues from our environment and immediately prepare our cognitive apparatus to deal with events likely to correspond with these clues and behave accordingly. Since we are not in control of the priming effect, however, it will sometimes apply to inappropriate situations as well.

Both, halo and priming, thus, can be sensible methods to govern action in many circumstances in a fast and economical manner effectively resulting in an evolutionary advantage over using other methods. This advantage is weighed against possible misapplications of halo and priming mechanisms in situations where, e.g., a more rational type of deliberation would produce better results with more effort and less speed.

The choice between rational deliberation and other practical decision mechanisms, so we might hope, feeds from a conscious judgment. In particular, we might hope that we act on conscious, rational deliberation in situations with high stakes. Situations that matter most to us are, for example, situations with a significant ethical dimension. Psychology looked at those as well, and the results tell the same story.

Schnall et al. asked the participants of their study to morally judge a selection of actions in dilemma situations, e.g., eating one's dog when starving, but primed them previously with notions of either disgust or cleanliness (Schnall et al., 2008). Their results show that "incidental feelings of disgust can influence moral judgments and make them more severe," while "cleanliness can reduce the severity of moral judgments" (p.1). In a similar experiment, Valdesolo et al. find that "heightened positivity increased the odds of selecting the appropriate (i.e. utilitarian) response to the footbridge dilemma" after watching a "5-min comedy clip taken from "Saturday Night Live""(Valdesolo and DeSteno, 2006, p.477). It does not matter here that the experimenters judge the utilitarian response to the footbridge dilemma as the positive one, what matters is that watching a completely unrelated comedy clip from a night show apparently has a significant impact on how people judge actions in a profound moral dilemma. People live or die because someone made a good joke just before.

5.1.1.3 Confirmation bias

Maybe moral situations are also not suited to talk about rationality since, usually, intuition is a strong guide in ethical questions. Intuition, in turn, is undoubtedly influenced by various factors other than rational deliberation. The psychological research repertoire also includes experiments in which the participants are confronted with explicitly rational or, at least, purely cognitive tasks. Such tasks would be, for example, finding a rule to a pattern or checking the validity of a rule when presented with evidence. As it turns out, human beings are prone to a severe "*Confirmation bias* [..., which] connotes the seeking or interpretation of evidence in ways that are partial to existing beliefs, expectations, or a hypotheses in hand" (Nickerson, 1998, p.175).

One of the first researchers to discover the confirmation bias was P. C. Wason. He presented a number of cards to the participants of his study and the rule that "*if a card has a vowel on one side then it has an even number on the other side*" (Wason, 1966, p.146). The participants were asked which cards they have to turn around in order to verify the rule. From a logical point of view, it is clear that you need to turn around cards displaying a vowel or an uneven number to check the validity of the rule. For example, if the cards show A-B-1-2, then the backsides of cards B and 2 are irrelevant, while you would need to check whether there really is an even number on the back of the A-card and a consonant on the back of the 1-card. Yet, a majority of the participants turned around cards that showed vowels and *even* numbers, i.e. they picked the cards that would show couples that positively confirmed the rule and ignored one of the cards that could potentially disconfirm the rule.

One might object that the logical structure of if-then statements is different in everyday understanding, e.g., that 'if p, then q' also implies 'if not p, then not q', and, therefore, the choice of an even number is correct. However, following this desperate argument, the participants would be expected to turn around *every* card in order to verify the rule and the real problem becomes even more apparent: human beings have a confirmation bias that makes us ignore even simple logical rules unless we are specifically trained otherwise.

As with the halo effect, the confirmation bias as part of human reasoning could be interpreted as a warrant for coherence. If we already have a belief or hypothesis, we tend to look for evidence that supports it in order to create a harmonic view of the world. Coherence is, among other things, one of the criteria for a set of rational beliefs. Thus, while the reasoning shaped by the confirmation bias is a display of flawed rationality, it may be a mechanism for human beings to arrive at a rationally coherent system of beliefs. Nonetheless, confirmation bias supports the claim that our rational capacities are incomplete and fail even at simple rational tasks.

5.1.1.4 Anchoring effect

Last but not least, I invoke the 'anchoring effect' that generates brute irrationality. When presented with estimations tasks, it turns out that "different starting points yield different estimates, which are biased toward the initial values." This does not sound particularly spectacular at first, but Tversky and Kahnemann showed that this effect occurs even if the initial value is "a number [..] determined by spinning a wheel of fortune in the subjects' presence," and the task was to estimate the percentage of African states in the UN. Participants who had seen a high number on the wheel of fortune estimated an average that was 20% higher than that of participants who had seen a low number (Tversky and Kahneman, 1974, p.1128). Thus, a completely arbitrary number has a tremendous effect on an estimate that should be based on various, actually relevant information.

Again, one might object that making an estimate in a laboratory setting may not induce a heightened sense of relevance, but Mussweiler et al. show even "accomplished trial judges with an average of more than 15 years of experience" who were asked to provide a serious judgment "were influenced by sentencing demands, even if the demands were made by non-experts. [...] A difference of 8 months in prison for the identical crime" (Mussweiler et al., 2004, p.184 and references therein). In a general review, Mussweiler furthermore notes that anchoring is independent of the reliability of the anchor as seen with the wheel fortune, the plausibility of the anchor, e.g., when ridiculously large numbers are chosen as initial value, the motivation and expertise of the estimator and the time between presenting the anchor and the estimate (p.186)

The anchoring effect is, so far, probably the most disturbing research result of psychology when it comes to rational deliberation and, consequently, decision making. Completely arbitrary unrelated information drastically influences estimates that figure in our judgments and decision making. In many situations in which the anchor is not arbitrary, the effect is likely to be useful to get fast, sufficiently accurate estimates, but its persistence in more elaborate situations is quite astonishing. What are we to conclude from these observations?

5.1.1.5 Conclusions from empirical research of human decision making

The review above only highlights a fraction of the research results. Many more can be found in the references and the references therein. While there are critical works on established phenomena as well, they are usually only critical with respect to methodological aspects, categorization of the phenomena or the origins of the observed effects. The overarching picture, however, is unambiguous.

The psychological research shows that various arational factors influence our decision making. In many of these cases, we are not even aware of these factors. Rational, conscious decision making, thus, only captures a small part of how human beings come up with action choices.

Yet, most of the time we are very successful decision makers. Accordingly, the effects discussed in the psychological research come with practical advantages, which ensure exactly this success at least in common situations. Our limited mental capacities and time constraints often do not allow for long periods of rational deliberation, let alone gathering all required information. The arational mechanisms, in contrast, are fast and readily available. More than that, they are also fairly reliable in common situations, and it has been argued they even produce better results than, e.g., elaborate statistical procedures in realistic scenarios (Wübben and von Wangenheim, 2008). From this, it can be argued that–given human limitations, effort of decision making and complex environmental factors and uncertainties– the psychological mechanisms in human decision making produce optimal results despite not following idealized rational procedures. Exactly this is claimed by one of the leading contemporary psychologists on this topic, Gerd Gigerenzer. He proposes to leave behind the dogma that the psychological mechanisms in decision making, called 'heuristics', are "associated with errors and contrasted with logical and statistical rules that were believed to define rational thinking," but he acknowledges they "can often be more accurate than complex "rational" strategies" (Gigerenzer and Gaissmaier, 2001, p.473). This challenges the role of idealized rationality in decision making quite generally, because any entity is presumably better off with an appropriate balance of fast, heuristic decision making and rational decision making based on logic and statistics. From a designers' perspective, thus, creating an agent only capable of rational decision making is likely to be irrational.

It has now become clear that decision making is highly dependent not only on the environment, but on the entity doing the decision making as well. Human beings, in particular, have a specific set of cognitive capabilities, a specific set of psychological mechanisms to provide fast and mostly appropriate solutions and a specific history of past decision making both, evolutionarily as well as individually. In light of this, any claim that human decision making can and should be taken as a general blue-print for decision making faces a serious body of evidence suggesting otherwise. Rather, an entity with different capacities and different history will rely on a different set of decision making tools fitting its specific pragmatic needs. Artificial intelligence endowed with extensive logical capabilities and cheap, fast information processing, for example, will most certainly not require a mechanism that enhances the coherence of its views resulting in a confirmation bias. A generalization of decision making in agency as it is done in human beings, thus, is not sensible. Instead, we must abstract from the specifics of human agency and use concepts that are not specific to human beings.

The mind-agency paradigm, too, is deeply challenged. Given the introspective and often inaccessible decision processes in human decision making, our intuition about agency derived from our own experience is not trustworthy. The plausibility of the mind-agency paradigm hinges on the question of whether or not the mechanism required for decision making really requires a mind in the form known from human agency. The way we make decisions, as suggested by the psychological research, often relies on effective and efficient mechanisms that do not display particularly 'mindful' behavior. So often in fact, that an exclusion of these mechanisms from a theory of human action would render human beings non-agents most of the time. If we embrace those mechanisms for human agency, on the other hand, the fact that they are biologically realized in a human mind is but contingent.

5.1.2 Execution control in human agency

I will now look at a second aspect of human agency usually thought to be central to agency in general. Many things we do are usually not thought to be proper actions. While some activities originate from our body, they seem to happen to us rather than being done by us. All sorts of reflexes and bodily movements are examples, but we may also find ourselves doing more elaborate activities without a 'sense of agency'. Most of us have started painting some meaningless sketches in our notebooks during a boring lecture or when circling around a completely unrelated topic in our minds. Musicians know that during improvisation you may start wandering off and the music just keeps appearing, yet, the musicians exercise quite intricate movements producing non-arbitrary sounds. Sleep walkers find themselves doing what looks like the result of proper action when they wake up. It is not clear whether or not such cases should be described as cases of agency because a crucial element seems to be missing–control.

The topic of control, like decision making, is not unambiguous in action theory. On the one hand, there is control on a high level. Frankfurt calls it 'guidance control' in the context of the debate on free will. Guidance control ensures we are doing only those actions we actually want to do upon reflection. In order to understand this notion of control, one needs to understand what it means to perform actions we actually 'want to do upon reflection'. Frankfurt argued for a hierarchical structure of volitions, in which second order volitions may have our first order volitions as objects, i.e. they tell us what we want to want. If the volitional structure behind an action is in harmony, the agent is in control in the sense that her decisions are genuinely *her* decisions (Frankfurt, 1997). Even if she is not, however, she might still act–she just does not act freely based on her own decision. To do so, the agent still needs to be in control in a less sophisticated sense.

The latter type of control, on the other hand, is control of the execution of an action. Usually, we are in control of our bodily movements, but our actions are rarely achieved by consciously controlling the specifics of our bodily movements. In fact, when we start to explicitly control our bodily movements, our overall movements usually slow down significantly and become less reliable. Think about writing some word by hand. It takes longer and usually looks worse when you start focusing on your hand and finger movements and control them explicitly in order to write. Similarly, walking or even just standing still feels awkward when you try to explicitly control your limb movements. This suggests execution control must be split in at least two further levels. First, the control of our specific bodily movements, which is something we rarely do on a conscious level. Second, the things we actually control or do–our actions–display a level of control with a light teleological character: agents move their arms and put their hands around things in order to grasp them, but what they are doing is simply grasping things; certainly agents move their legs and feet so as to walk upstairs, but what they are doing is simply walking upstairs.

Thus, even a brief discussion of control in the context of agency reveals three distinct phenomena. High level control ensures we are doing what we actually want to do, e.g., this medicine tastes disgusting, but I drink it anyways in order to get well. Additionally, low level execution control of our actions is required, e.g., putting the medicine in my mouth and swallowing it with some water. Finally, a low level execution control of our specific bodily movements is needed, e.g. moving my fingers of the one hand to grab the small cup with medicine, moving the arm up to my mouth to empty the cup into my mouth, grasping a glass of water with my other hand afterwards, lifting it to my mouth and then tilting my head accordingly to swallow. Only the first two types of control seem to be exercised consciously most of the time, while the latter usually is not controlled consciously.

Control in agency, consequently, is far more complicated than it might appear at first glance. A host of questions immediately arises. How many different levels or types of control are revealed when we look at human agency in more detail? How do they relate to each other? Are they always necessary for proper display of agency? Is there a sufficient set of different control mechanisms for agency? How are the different types of control physically realized? How reliable are they? How do they figure in the phenomenology of action and so on and so forth? Each question requires detailed research philosophically, psychologically and physiologically.

The topic of phenomenology of action control, for example, is addressed by Elisabeth Pacherie in her 2007 paper "The Sense of Control and the Sense of Agency." She, too, suggests that when talking about control–and about the phenomenology of control in particular–the phenomenology and corresponding concepts of control must be further differentiated. Inspired by her three tier model of intentionality, she proposes to talk of "the sense of motor control, the sense of situational control and the sense of rational control" (p.19). She further provides a host of empirical research results to underpin this distinction and additional philosophical theses.

For a discussion of high level control as discussed in the free will debate, a good starting point is Shield's selective review and critical discussion of research in neuro-science in "Neuroscience and conscious causation: Has Neuroscience shown that we cannot control our own actions" from 2014. This, too, shows the wide array of research required to shed light on these questions.

For the argument I propose here, fortunately, a smaller scope suffices. I merely need to find examples for concepts that are deemed crucial for agency, while their actual realization in human agency is not suited for generalization, or at least calls for a different understanding. I showed this for decision making in human agency, and I now turn to low level execution control.

5.1.2.1 Motor programs

It seems intuitively obvious that we, human beings, are capable of controlling our bodily movements on all levels. I can move my arm and my fingers, I can walk, write words, move my tongue to form words and so on and so forth. Next to this, it is also everyday experience that many of our movements unfold without controlling them explicitly. I scratch my head; I reposition in my chair every now and then; I drive a car largely without attending to my movements and so on and so forth. On the other hand, every now and then, each of us is faced with situations that require new motor skills, and it is usually a quite challenging experience. Carrying a newborn for the first time needs practice as does brushing your teeth with your less dominant hand because your dominant hand is occupied. Learning a new sport or a new technique usually comes with extensive training and so on and so forth. Finally, cases of lack of control are also abundant; a silly staring contest is usually ended by one of the contesters losing control over his eye lids. Various reflexes produce bodily movements leaving us with little to no control to avoid them. Many people also have ticks that they have a hard time to control, such as twitching, wrinkling one's nose or nail biting.

From introspection, thus, it is clear our control over our body is far from perfect but ranges from non-existent to masterful and all flavors in between. Fortunately, the way we control our body is a proper subject of empirical research. The results indicate that the specifics of our actions are controlled largely by unconscious processes and are partly fixed in advance with little conscious influence.

Simple, but non-arbitrary movements have been used to study the direct control of our bodily movements. In their 1979 paper "Control of fast goal-directed arm movements," Wadman et al. present experiments in which they asked participants to perform a fast arm movement towards a specific target and manipulated the execution in different ways, including completely blocking the arm movement. Their study finds that muscle activity is independent of such manipulations at least for a short duration. Wadman et al. conclude "that a kind of 'action program' is used for controlling a fast goal-directed movement." In particular, these 'programs' seem to shut out "direct control of muscle activity during these movements" for short periods of time after initiation despite the fact that information about unexpected changes, e.g. a blocking of the movement, is available (Wadman et al., 1979, p.5). At least for the duration of 100msec, neither consciously nor unconsciously available information is used to control movements (p.15).

The same principle was shown to hold for less abrupt movements. Denier van der Gon conducted a series of experiments studying hand writing. From the results, they concluded "feedback is used in some parts of the writing mechanism and as an overall control. Adjustments by this control have a delay not less than about 100msec" (Denier van der Gon and Thuring, 1965, p.146). The delays are usually not perceived in everyday introspection. We usually feel like we are 'in touch' with our bodily movements without such a motor echo. In reality, so it seems, our active control based on internal and external feedback, however, is not synchronous with the execution. To ensure fluent movement despite delayed control, movements are planned ahead and executed automatically.

This works extraordinary well, even for tasks involving a high degree of motor coordination such as throwing something which involves well coordinated movements of hand, arm, shoulder, back and legs, i.e. almost the entire body. This is in stark contrast, however, to equally or even less demanding tasks subjects are not used to performing. Accordingly, Schmidt notes that "At one level, people seem able to produce coordinated actions easily, almost trivially. [...] Yet, at another level, the laboratory data (and a few everyday examples) suggest remarkable interference [...] Well-known cases involve patting one's head while rubbing one's tummy. [...] Other examples [...] showed that not one of 100 subjects was able to recite a nursery rhyme with proper rhythmic intonation while tapping a 1-3-123 rhythm. Summers et al. (1993) provide evidence about difficulties in tapping different rhythms with two hands" (Schmidt et al., 1998, p.330, references therein).

Motor programs, so it seems, are not only relevant for short movements, but they enable a smooth performance of complex tasks as well. Without them, e.g., when facing new tasks for which we have not yet developed the respective programs, or when they fail, e.g., when unusual external factors disturb our movements, we perform poorly. The idea that we in some way consciously directly control our bodily movements, thus, needs to be reevaluated. Even for rather elaborate activities like walking, writing, throwing and so on, we do not necessarily control the specifics of our bodily movements. Rather, our conscious control seems to have a teleological character: in everyday performance, we focus on the goals and relevant intermediate stages of our actions, while unconscious processes take care of the specifics of execution.

This means we do not usually, for example, move our hand and fingers in a specific manner in order to write a word, but we just write a word, and that is all we are consciously doing. We do not usually make a left turn with our car by turning the steering wheel–we just make a left turn. This, I believe, is in accordance with most peoples' intuition, and it is not new to philosophy of action either. Elisabeth Anscombe provided this insightful example: if you were to keep an object level at a constant height by quickly tapping it from below with your arm, e.g., a light balloon, you would, at first, have some trouble and actively control your arm movements in order to keep the object level. In this learning period, i.e. a low skill scenario, it is correct that you keep the object level by doing something else, viz. tapping the object from below. Once you have mastered the skill, however, you will stop consciously controlling your arm movements. Instead, you just keep the object level (Anscombe, 1957, §30).

Motor programs, thus, explain why we do not usually control our specific bodily movements, yet, perform our actions well in most situations. But they also show how restricted conscious control over our body really is. Were we to rely on conscious control in everyday action, we would not only be overwhelmed by the cognitive demands, but we would perform poorly and regularly fail to achieve our goals. Maybe, one might wonder, conscious control is still needed for the fine tuning of our movements. After all, if we focus on a task at hand, we often perform better.

5.1.2.2 Conscious control of skilled actions

For skilled actions, a focus on the task at hand often is perceived as helpful. What we focus on, however, is not the specifics of our bodily movements. Quite to the opposite, research suggests expert performance is characterized by the absence of conscious attention, let alone control. The focus required for expert performance, thus, cannot be the focus on the fine tuning of our bodily movements, but maybe a focus on the situation in general to prevent distraction, for example. To capture this point, Michael Brownstein cites the essayist David Foster Wallace in his 2014 paper "Rationalizing flow: Agency in skilled unreflective action", who writes: "what goes through a great player's mind as he stands at the center of hostile crowd noise and lines up the free-throw that will decide the game might well be: *nothing at all*" and "those who receive and act out of the gift of athletic genius must, per force, be blind and dumb about it [...] because they are its essence" (Wallace, 2005, p.155). While this sounds somewhat harsh, this is exactly what research suggests.

Flegal and Andersen put participants of different skill levels through a small golf course. After a little bit of training, they asked some of the athletes to describe how exactly they perform the task and then repeat the task. "Strikingly, describing their putting experience significantly impaired higher skill golfers' ability to re-achieve the putting criterion, compared with higher skill golfers who performed the irrelevant verbal activity" (Flegal and Anderson, 2008, p.927). Just because the golfers with high skill consciously thought about what exactly they were doing, "they took twice as many putts to re-achieve the putting criterion on a later test than did control participants." It is noteworthy, however, the "verbal description by itself does not impair skill execution, unless the performer possesses a higher degree of proceduralized knowledge" (p.930). Said differently, the more skilled we are, the less we consciously think about what we are doing, and it even harms our performance when we do it nonetheless. Only when faced with new motor challenges, our conscious observations and plans of action seem to positively affect our performance.

The loss of conscious control in human agency can go even further without losing agency. In a neuro-scientific study on musical improvisation, Charles Limb and Allen Brown note that "[s]pontaneous artistic creativity is often considered one of the most mysterious forms of creative behavior, frequently described as occurring in an altered state of mind beyond conscious awareness or control" (Limb and Braun, 2008, p.1). In line with this intuitive idea, they observe specific patterns of brain activity in their experiments that "reflect a combination of psychological processes required for spontaneous improvisation, in which internally motivated, stimulus-independent behaviors unfold in the absence of central processes that typically mediate self-monitoring and conscious volitional control of ongoing performance" (p.1). They conclude "[m]usical creativity vis-à-vis improvisation may be a result of the combination of intentional, internally generated self-expression [...] with the suspension of self-monitoring and related processes [...] that typically regulate conscious control of goal-directed, predictable, or planned actions" (p.5).

Human action execution, consequently, is not about conscious control of low level execution in any detail of our bodily movements. At best, we guide our actions from a teleological perspective, and even this is not always the case, as shown by the examination of musical improvisation. Obviously, this does not mean we only focus on an overarching goal, but the granularity of consciously planned execution steps is far coarser than the physiological execution. The level of granularity depends on the specifics of our biological constitution and various other factors. In today's technologized world, the specifics of execution often even go beyond our own biological mechanisms. When a human agent drives a car, no one would seriously doubt it is the human agent who is making a turn or braking. In modern cars, however, the technology goes far beyond a mechanical translation of turning the steering wheel into turning the car or pressing down a pedal to brake the wheels. Electric power assisted steering in cars, for example, automatically adjusts steering force depending on the driving conditions and eventually triggers electronic stability control, another safety system, to individually slow down the wheels to improve stability. Anti-lock braking systems (ABS) prevent the wheels from locking up and maintain tractive contact with the road surface. The specifics of turning a corner or braking in difficult driving conditions are not controlled by the driver at all. Even if the driver wanted to, it is physically impossible for her to perform the tasks the assistant systems are performing. Yet, she is the one making a turn or braking.

The car example also demonstrates that the specifics of human action control cannot be simply generalized. Today's robots, to take the technology example further, have an array of sensors and information processing units available that are usually less versatile and only provide very specific information compared to the human senses, but they often are extremely fast and enable robots to actually monitor and adjust their movements far below a threshold of 100 msec. If there are robotic agents in the future, they will most likely control their actions on different granularity levels and use different mechanisms. If we want to learn something from human agency for agency in general, we should start by looking at the specifics, but we must then abstract from it and ask what is actually relevant for agency–execution control does not seem to be a good candidate for a simple generalization. Given the teleological character of action execution in human agency, execution control on the level of specific movements might not even be relevant for agency at all.

5.1.2.3 Forward and inverse models

The lack of instant control of our bodily movements once they are initiated, neither consciously nor unconsciously, has one wondering why we perceive our execution as being under continuous control and how it is possible we perform so well even in complex motor tasks. For one, we are usually not aware of motor programs that pre-plan our movements, and do not feel the delay in control though it should be perfectly recognizable by our proprioception, i.e. our internal sense of our body. This poses a challenge to the phenomenology of action as is discussed in more detail in Pacherie's paper (Pacherie, 2007) from a philosophical perspective, or, for example, in Frith's 2005 psychological review "The self in action: Lessons from delusions of control." Another explanatory problem is the obvious quality of our performance. We are able to perform demanding motor tasks and adjust our movements. More than this, we are capable of coordinating different parts of our body not only with respect to each other, but also with respect the changes we bring about in the environment. If our left hand throws a ball to our right hand in a quick manner, then it cannot be the case that we observe the result of our left hand's throwing movement and move our right hand accordingly to catch the ball. We are too slow to do such things. This is the simple pragmatic question of how we are able to perform well, including adjustments and coordination of our bodily movements without instant feedback driven control.

To address these issues, the key concept of 'internal modeling' emerged from empirical studies. Daniel M. Wolpert et al. conclude "[t]here are two varieties of the internal models: (i) forward models, which mimic the causal flow of a process by predicting its next state (for example, position and velocity) given the current state and the motor command; and (ii) inverse models, which invert the causal flow by estimating the motor command that caused a particular state transition" in their 1995 paper "An Internal Model for Sensorimotor Integration" (p.1880). The crucial advantage of forward models is that "the outcome of an action can be estimated and used before sensory feedback is available" (ibd.) Forward models, thus, provide the solution for the problem of movement control by predicting the outcomes of our motor programs and adjust or coordinate our movements accordingly. Naturally, we cannot 'see' these models working in our brains–so how are Wolpert and others so sure about their existence.

The idea is to take the basic concept of internal modeling and create an actual model working with the same principles and compare it to behavioral studies. Wolpert at al., for example, asked the participants of their study to estimate their arm's position after moving it in the dark (p.1880). As it turns out, the participants mostly overestimated the distance their arm had traveled. More importantly, this bias shows a characteristic curve depending on the duration of the movement: the bias is greatest for short movements and becomes more accurate for longer movements. This characteristic curve is best explained by a model that uses a forward model for initial estimation and uses sensory information to improve the estimate when it is available. While there seems to be a bias in the forward model dominating the estimate in short movements, the more accurate sensory information reduces the bias after a short time, thus, "the peaking and gradual decline in bias is a consequence of a trade-off between the inaccuracies accumulating in the internal simulation of the arm's dynamics and the feedback of actual sensory information" (p.1882).

This dynamic of the results of internal forward models and proprioceptive sensory information explains how it is possible for us to have a continuous experience of action control and actually adapt to immediate changes in our environment. Predictions of forward models bridge the gap between action initiation and sensory feedback and take into account how the environment changes during our movement–at least in normal circumstances without unexpected effects.

Mitsuo Kawato wrote a review on internal models and their empirical plausibility and also comes to a positive result in "Internal models for motor control and trajectory planning" from 1999. In particular, he believes that "[t]he most convincing set of data for the existence of forward models comes from studies on coordination between reaching and grasping" (p.719), which, incidentally, is exactly what his experiments are about. The idea is roughly this: when grasping an object between the finger tips and moving it around, not only must the arm perform the respective movements, but the grip force of the fingers must be adjusted so the object does not slip. The use of inverse and forward models readily explains how this is possible without inhumanly fast control of the finger movements: the inverse model for the desired arm movement prompts a motor command for the arm. A copy of the motor command, the so called 'efference' copy, is then fed into a forward model that deduces the behavior of the object in the grip of the fingers, i.e. it models how the desired arm movement affects the environment. This information is then used to properly adjust the grip force applied by the finger tips so the object does not slip during the arm movement. This explains how we are able to coordinate our bodily movements respecting changes in the environment without actually observing these changes. For additional supporting evidence for internal models, Kawato cites a host of further behavioral studies as well as some neurophysiological studies that have shown the validity of this approach (Kawato, 1999).

One particularly popular series of experiments investigated the tickliness of self-produced compared to externally produced stimulation. In "Spatio-Temporal Prediction Modulates the Perception of Self-Produced Stimuli" from 1999, Sarah J. Blakemore, Chris D. Frith and Daniel M. Wolpert asked participants to tickle their right hand with their left hand and compared it to tickling from an external source (Blakemore et al., 1996). They found that "[s]ubjects consistently rated self-produced tactile sensation as being less tickly than when it was externally produced" (p.551). The sensation produced by essentially identical stimulus, thus, differs greatly between self-produced and an external stimulus. The reason is thought to lie in the predictions of forward models when a human agent initiates movement. The results of the left hand's movement are predicted, and the right hand is prepared for the stimulus which reduces the tickle sensations. To support the model further, they manipulated the left hand's movement instead of just replacing it by an external stimulus and found the "tickliness rating increased with increasing degrees of delay and trajectory perturbation between the actions of the left hand and the resultant tactile stimulus on the right hand" (p.554). They conclude from this that "the extent to which self-produced tactile sensation is attenuated (i.e., its tickliness) is proportional to the error between the sensory feedback predicted by an internal forward model of the motor system and the actual sensory feedback produced by the movement" (p.551). Inverse and forward models, thus, ensure we are prepared for the immediate consequences of our movements and adjust not only further movements, but also our perception and interpretation of sensory information.

Internal models solve the practical challenges posed by non-instant control of our movements and generate a sense of continuity without delay or motor echoes. As with motor programs, we are not aware of the internal modeling. Consequently, it is a challenge to fit them into our intuitive picture of agency, which usually features conscious actions and all sorts of elaborate concepts like rational deliberation about means to our goals, planning for the future and so on and so forth. The conscious control in the sense that we set our goals and, at least roughly, the means to achieve them somehow transforms into unconscious movement plans calculated by internal models and triggered by motor programs. There is no conscious control of our actions down to the very movements of our body.

While the idea of internal modeling is universally applicable to entities with a body, the specific models in human agency are clearly tailored to the human physiology and shaped by every individual's experience. On the one hand, it is conceivable that an entity with quasi-instant processing of sensory information does not require forward models; it may even do without inverse models by using rapid trial and error mechanisms. Robots with appropriate sensor and information processing could possibly perform this way. On the other hand, it is equally thinkable that an entity outsources the internal models to another entity, but remains in control of the teleological component. In fact, human beings are already doing this. Navigation systems in cars, to stick with the example from above, only require a target destination of the driver. They use their GPS-sensors in combination with stored maps to run an algorithm that calculates a viable route. For this route, a simple model then calculates the driving duration and includes information about traffic jams and road works and adjusts the route accordingly. Such navigation systems could then feed into an autonomous driving system to actually navigate the car along this route without human intervention. Nothing of this would change the fact that the person in the car traveled to the target destination as part of her agency.

5.1.2.4 Affordances and pragmatic representations

Next to actually planning bodily movements, coordinating different body parts and then executing the movement, an important aspect of control is to choose the specific way we perform actions. Empirical research makes a strong case that inverse and forward models make the planning and coordination of bodily movements, while motor programs trigger the actual execution. But how do these mechanisms include the various possibilities of how a goal can be achieved. When I think about how to drive a nail into a piece of wood, I can consciously look around for something I can use as a hammer, but for many activities I do not have a similar thought consciously. For example, when I want to open a door, I usually do not consciously look for a door handle, and then say to myself 'Oh, let's use the door handle to open that door'. How am I still regularly finding myself opening doors without this cognitive step?

One answer to this question once more leads into a serious challenge for our intuitive understanding of how we act. Research in perception suggests we do not only perceive abstract physical properties of objects like color, size, position and so on, but our perception is shaped by the actions that can be performed with the perceived objects. In "The ecological approach to perception," James J. Gibson introduces the term 'affordance': "The *affordances* of the environment are what it *offers* the animal, what it *provides* or *furnishes*, either for good or ill," for example, "the surface *affords support*. [...] It is stand-on-able, permitting an upright posture for quadrupeds and bipeds. It is therefore walk-on-able and run-over-able. It is not sink-into-able" (Gibson, 1986, p.127).

Perception, according to this theory, not only contains abstract physical properties, but immediately delivers an array of actions available to us in our environment. For opening a door, we do not need to consciously remember the function of a door handle and its relation to the door, we just perceive the door handle as 'press-to-open-able'. If we want to open the door, our internal models already have all information needed to come up with a solid solution.

While the Gibsonian theory of affordances takes a quite radical, contested form in rejecting any representational states in favor of direct perception (Millikan, 2004; Nanay, 2013, discussion and references therein), a less radical variant of this approach was developed and is being refined by Bence Nanay. In "Between perception and action" from 2013, Nanay defines the notion of a 'pragmatic representation' as the "representational components of the immediate mental antecedents of actions" that mediate between sensory input and motor output (p.13). In particular, "[p]ragmatic representations are genuine mental representations: they represent objects as having a number of properties that are relevant to performing the action" (p.18). Where Gibson claims we directly perceive affordances, i.e. something akin to action possibilities, Nanay only claims that our pragmatic representations "attribute properties, the representation of which is necessary for the performance of an action," and he calls these properties "action properties" (p.39).

The empirical evidence for such theories is not rock-solid, but the general direction is promising. For visual perception, it has been shown there are two more or less distinct visual subsystems: "the ventral and dorsal streams. To put it simply, the ventral stream is responsible for identification and recognition, whereas the function of the dorsal stream is the visual control of our motor actions" (p.63). However, it is unclear how distinct the two systems really are, whether or not a similar distinction exists for our other senses, and how all of this is connected to pragmatic representations or affordances in general (Nanay, 2013, ch. 3).

Whatever the details of perception turn out to be, it seems clear our perception is shaped by our agency. It is not the case that we perceive the world as realistic as possible, but as pragmatic as possible. Our perception is tailored to our specific pragmatic needs. We do not perceive door handles in a way to paint them or reconstruct them perfectly, but we perceive door handles in a way optimal for the possibility of pushing them and using them to open doors. This implies that our perception and our motor system are mutually dependent. Clearly, our bodily movements depend on what we perceive, but our perception also depends on what we are able to do. As a consequence, perception, as with all the concepts before, in human agency is specific to the human physiology and history.

5.1.2.5 Conclusions from empirical research on human execution control

Human execution control turns out to be quite different from what one may expect. Our specific bodily movements are rarely controlled consciously, but follow motor programs that resist not only conscious control, but any control at least for short periods of time. The coordination, fine tuning and adjustment of movements lasting longer than 100 *msec* are rarely controlled consciously either: While conscious control does play a role in motor learning, it decreases our performance of skilled actions. Highly skilled actions are even characterized by the absence of conscious control. Instead, internal models create motor programs, predict the movement consequences in the environment and make adjustments accordingly. This allows for complex, coordinated bodily movements to be successful at a speed not possible with conscious control. All of this is enabled by a pragmatically optimized perception of our environment.

The actual execution of our actions in terms of bodily movements, as a consequence, may completely by-pass conscious control. Our perception subconsciously delivers pragmatically relevant information to our internal models, which subconsciously creates motor programs and predictions for possibly complex, coordinated movements.

Obviously, however, many of our actions are consciously controlled in a way relevant to our sense of agency: I open the door, and the fact that I do does not bypass my consciousness at all. While I do not consciously control the specifics of my bodily movements in order to open the door, I do consciously control my action on a coarser level. Conscious human action control, thus, is teleological in character, i.e. the choice of an action goal and, presumably, the decision to actually start execution is consciously controlled. The level at which we exert our conscious control seems to depend on various factors; one of which is our skill level as seen above.

All of this is specific to human beings. Motor programs, whatever form they actually take, are tailored to an individual's physiology. Internal models are shaped by evolution, individual experience and external factors of the situation. This is also true for perception which further depends on the human specific sensory input and so on and so forth.

The manner in which action execution works in human agency also casts doubt on the body-agency paradigm in general. For human agency, the details for actual execution seem irrelevant: low level control of bodily movements largely bypasses our consciousness, and, more importantly, our conscious influence on our bodily movements is severely limited. We are not able to control our movements at all for short periods of time after initiation, and when we do, the performance quality drops drastically. The control relevant for agency has a teleological character, but teleological action control does not necessarily require a body capable of action execution.

5.2 Insights from empirical research on human agency

The selective review of empirical insights on human decision making and human execution control makes it clear that a generalization of human agency to agency in general is a difficult task. It is to be expected that empirical research on other agential features has revealed or will reveal exactly the same problem. Human agency is very specific to the human organism. Our intuitive picture of central agential features is hard to recognize, or simply contradicted by closer inspection. The idea of agency as involving rational deliberation as a key element, for example, would render many of our doings as non-actions. This may not be as dramatic as it sounds. If there is a distinct form of behavior called 'agency', then human beings are one of the first creatures to have evolved into agents, and it is likely we are far from perfect agents. One would have to argue that important elements of agency rarely reveal themselves in our everyday activities, but this would be merely an evasive maneuver to avoid a contradiction with empirical research. I prefer a more open-minded response.

In light of the specifics of human agency, not only should we reject human agency as a blue print for agency, but also critically re-evaluate both the mind-agency paradigm and the body-agency paradigm. As suggested above, an agent does not need a body in the conventional sense, and neither does an agent need a mind like a human mind. What agents need in terms of decision making and control are sensible methods to make action choices and teleological control. These agential features should be analyzed and detailed conceptually independent of human agency.

Functionalism is one way to do this, but it often only goes half way. The idea of functionalism, in general, is to describe the features relevant for action in terms of their functions and their relations to each other. Bratman's plans, for example, are defined mostly by their function to guide deliberation, provide stability against reconsideration and so on. Additionally, they must fulfill normative demands, e.g., rationality demands of consistency and coherence with respect to other plans, but also to other beliefs held by the individual. Somewhere along this functional specification, however, Bratman identifies elements of these plans with 'intentions' ontologically on par with beliefs and desires (Bratman, 1999). In light of the psychological research, it appears highly speculative to postulate mental states in our brain that can and should be characterized by the outlined functional and normative properties. Even if there are such mental states, it is wholly unclear how they relate to the mechanisms already discovered by psychology.

I wonder why functionalists often fall back on the ideas of specific mental states. Why not simply leave it as a functional description of externally observable agential features? To stay with Bratman's account, it is completely satisfactory to have a functional characterization of plans and observe that human beings usually make plans–they talk about them, sometimes they write them down, discuss them, adjust them, they follow them, or abandon them; it is not as if there was no proof of the existence of plans and their relevance in agency. There is no need to underpin their existence with any sort of mental states. In fact, functionalism makes itself unnecessarily vulnerable by postulating such states.

Paul Churchland's eliminative materialism is an example of one of the most vicious attacks on functionalism based exactly on the postulation of, from his perspective, unreasonable mental states (Churchland, 2008). If functionalism is understood as a tactical maneuver in order to save the claim of certain mental states regardless of their empirical plausibility, then the rejection of functionalism is almost unavoidable.

Philosophers who take psychological research into account seem to follow this idea and reject the classical view of mental states like beliefs, desires and intentions. Bence Nanay, for example, rejects the belief-desire model–even for "highly deliberative human actions" that he actually calls "decision-making" (Nanay, 2013, p.87)–on the grounds of psychological research as just presented. Instead, Nanay takes the positive results from psychology of perception and applies them to human agency.

It is important to note, however, Nanay as well as Churchland have a passion for explaining *human* agency. Indeed, looking at the empirical evidence, we have only begun to understand how human agency works in detail, but we have already sufficient proof there is only minor overlap with our ideal, presumably naive conception of human agency as rational and controlled accordingly. However, if we are about to generalize agency and, potentially, create new agents either by forming corporations or creating artificial agents, it would be outright madness to implement the same, potentially flawed mechanisms. Naturally, we should try to overcome human specific agency and focus on creating 'better' agents. This, I believe, is the true normative dimension of action theory, and it is here where functionalism can help.

In conclusion, functionalism or any way of abstraction from human agency to agency in general should not be understood as a defense of an empirically implausible psychology, but as a way to extract or single out agential features in human agency in order to generalize them for application to other entities if needed. This is completely in line with my earlier demand for a diversified understanding of agency. I can now readily make sense of group activity and how it creates a new form of agency.

5.3 Conclusion–Agency in groups

This work started with statements of the form "Group G did action A" (GA). Such statements suggest groups do things as if they were agents. The analysis up to this point took a recursive path following insights from both action theory for group activity and individuals as well as their impact on each other. In the last section, I concluded human agency is a helpful starting point to develop a general concept of agency, but little more. In particular, looking at two specific aspects of how the human mind and physiology work, two paradigmatic preconceptions about agency lost their plausibility. The mind-agency paradigm is not plausible if it means agency requires rational, conscious decision making realized in a biological mind. The body-agency paradigm, too, is not plausible if it means agency requires direct, conscious control of action execution realized in a biological body. The empirical insights suggest we must let go of these introspectively appealing, but wrong ideas about human agency. Our psychology and physiology is full of effective shortcuts and even flaws and most of them completely bypass our conscious experience of agency.

The study of group activity, on the other hand, revealed potent concepts to explain the kind of agency we value. The key principle of agency in group activity, so I argue, is the observation that features of agency are realized by some mechanisms, processes or structures external to individual agents (ERAF). This principle is independent of what exactly we choose to be the essential features for agency, as long as they can be externally realized. These agential features on a group level come with a crucial advantage over agential features of human agents: we do not need introspection or intuition to theorize about them; they are out in the open and require externally observable mechanisms to be established.

I discussed several of these mechanisms in the second chapter, where I found that it is often impossible for individual agents to be responsible for the results of group activity by way of their individual agency. Agential features are externally realized in group activity to enable interaction. This starts with linking the individual's actions by simply sharing information, which already helps split a task into individually executed sub-tasks. In individual agency, there is also a requirement to link the movements of our different body-parts, but the links are internally realized by, e.g. motor programs, forward and inverse models and some type of perceptual affordances. The specifics at work are very different, but the principle is the same: an information flow is required to effectively coordinate different parts of the overall activity. Clearly, however, a mere information flow between agents does not justify the introduction of a new kind of agency.

For actual agency, a number of features are required. Many of them are merely necessary and also required for what can be called 'mere behavior'. The challenge of action theory in general is to figure out what makes 'action' go beyond lower forms of activity and provide convincing concepts to characterize agency. Ever since the ground breaking works by Elisabeth Anscombe (Anscombe, 1957) and Donald Davidson (Davidson, 1963), intentionality in agency is generally thought to be at the very core of agency. Over more than half a century now, a wealth of philosophical research has been dedicated solely to understanding intentionality in agency, most often in terms of mental states or attitudes called 'intentions'. Not surprisingly, the same focus is dominant in providing explanations for group activity and, ultimately, group agency. I have shown that this focus is unjustified not only with respect to group activity, but for action theory in general.

Intentionality at the individual level, so I argued, is associated with at least six different features of agency, namely, voluntariness (VolI), epistemic access (EpiI), cause-effect consideration (EffI), goal-directedness (GoalI), planning (PlanI) and action decisions (ActI). The unification of these features is the unreached pinnacle of philosophical action theory, but I argue that it is not only unreached but, indeed, unreachable. The features associated with intentionality are partly related to one another within agency. By themselves, however, they are distinct, and it is futile to attempt to reduce them to a single phenomenon. The best one can do is explain our use of expressions of intentionality from a linguistic perspective, i.e. viewing "intentionality" as some sort of conceptional glue allowing simple descriptions and ascriptions of agency and agency-like behavior. Beyond that, I propose to let go the idea that there be one single mark of agency, but accept a diversified view on agency matching the complexities of reality.

An alternative suggests itself, when looking at attempts to explain intentionality on a group level. Since intentionality for group activity cannot be explained with recourse to introspection or speculative mental states, philosophers have tried to spell out what it means to share an intention, have collective or joint intentions and so on. As a result, more basic or, at least, more accessible concepts have been used to do the explanatory work like goals, plans, decision structures and more. The reference back to intentionality often remains to suggest continuity between action theory for individuals and groups. However, given the powerful concepts used to explain group activity, the direction of continuity should be the other way around: we should take serious the insights from group activity and rethink action theory in general to accommodate individual agency in this picture as well.

According to this line of thought, agency is not marked by a single phenomenon, but a variety of agential features are required for agency. As a consequence, there is not one type of agency characterized by a single phenomenon, but many types of agency characterized by different agential features. Indeed, this is what we observe in individual agency: we know of spontaneous actions, habituated actions, carefully deliberated actions, expressive actions and so on and so forth. Accordingly, there are many different variations of group activity that depend mainly on how many and to what degree agential features are externally realized. This insight immediately opens up a convincing approach to group agency. A group displays agency if agential features are externally realized that are essential to agency.

To exemplify this strategy, I chose one particularly important and fundamental concept in agency. The idea that an agent has goals and pursues these goals is undeniably a core feature of agency. Surprisingly, explicit discussion of the concepts 'goal' and 'having a goal' are not easy to come by. In action theory for individuals, the concepts are taken as self-explanatory, probably because we are so familiar with having goals as part of our agency. In action theory for group activity, in contrast, philosophers are more aware that the idea of 'having (common) goals' requires explanation, but the explanations given of what it is to 'have a goal' (mental attitudes?, commitments?, intentions?) or 'be a goal' (states of mind?, states of affairs?, outcomes?, representations of world states?) differ greatly and even contradict each other. Consequently, I explored the notion of a 'goal' in more depth and made interesting discoveries relevant for both individual action theory and group activity.

To start with, the concept 'goal' already entails the notion of 'having a goal'. A goal cannot be thought without an entity to which it belongs. Acknowledging this, it is no surprise that goals are not actual states of the world, let alone outcomes of actions or alike. 'Goals' come before actions and before thinking about actions. They are some sort of representations of states of affairs guiding an agent not only in thinking about what actual state of the world she wants to bring about, but also what actions she chooses to do so. In doing so, we expect the agent not to knowingly choose actions preventing her from achieving her goals. If she does, we will start to doubt that her goal is really her goal. The concept of a 'goal', thus, is much richer than one intuitively suspects. More importantly, the richness much resembles the richness of intentionality in agency. In fact, goals already do a large part of the explanatory work in goal-directed agency, and there is little left to add for 'intentionality'.

The fact that goals are more complex than we usually think challenges an assumption often made when talking about group activity. It is not clear that goals can be easily 'shared' by multiple agents. In particular, the kind of representations involved in having a goal are most likely mental representations in the case of human agency. A group, clearly, cannot have a mental representation.

This is the point where we have to challenge our preconceptions about agency rooted in our experience as human agents. Fortunately, we have already seen that empirical research encourages to reject human agency as a general blue print for agency. We are, thus, free to ask whether or not a group can have a goal independent of its individual agents. Using the terms introduced in this work, the question is whether or not the agential feature 'having a goal' can be externally realized in a way that it cannot be ascribed to the individuals any longer, but must be ascribed to the group as a whole. I discussed two mechanisms that, indeed, do so in a convincing way and potentially create a new form of agency in group activity.

First, a goal of group activity can be *diffused* over the group. That means the goal is split into various sub goals and means and subsequently divided into overlapping units that can be achieved more or less independently. Different members of the group then take care of the different units, potentially without even knowing what the other units are, what the other members are doing and how it all fits together. This, indeed, is the typical situation in today's big companies. It is important to note that diffusion is not only a horizontal phenomenon, i.e. if you think of the means-goal structure as a pyramid with many means at the base and the one or few goals at the top, diffusion works horizontally *and* vertically. A top manager is likely to know virtually nothing about what is going on in a shop floor other than whether or not they deliver what she needs for her tasks. Everything else would simply overburden any human being if the group is large, and it would be ineffective in every circumstance.

Second, a goal can be *alienated* from the agents of the group. If you are part of a diffused group activity, you might recognize the goals of your particular unit, but you might fail to identify with them. A lack of motivation is inevitable unless you find an alternative source of motivation. A lack of motivation on the individual level is, indeed, a serious problem for group activity and eventually leads to its demise. A popular counter measure is the introduction of explicit incentive systems. Monetary compensation in the form of salary or bonuses is often something that people are willing to work for, but also social status, power and other non-monetary benefits can be given to individuals as alternative goals. As an effect, however, the members of such a group do not engage in the group activity in pursuit of a common goal, but in pursuit of personal goals. A shadow structure of personal goals is smartly constructed so that the individuals participate in the group activity accordingly.

With diffusion and alienation of goals and respective means in place, it is hard to argue the goals still belong to the individuals. The best one could reasonably claim is there always needs to be *some* individuals in the group who have the actual goals of the group activity. This argument would have to show that it is impossible to replace these individual goals by personal goals, which are only linked to the group goals. I do not know of any such argument.

It is not immediately clear, on the other hand, that the goals belong to the group either. For a group to have a goal, the group needs to be able to represent states of affairs; it needs to be able to form decisions about what to do to achieve the goal; and it needs a way to actually do it. All three aspects, I believe, are easy to come by. An incentive system and a proper means-goal structure for diffusion already require a communication of the goals to the respective agents. Thus, there already need to be representations of the respective states of affairs either in spoken language, or written down in a group's manifest, evaluation systems, work contracts and so on and so forth.

When it comes to decision making in groups, there is a wealth of literature accounting for this. I reviewed, for example, List and Pettit's account of collective rationality and French's idea of a corporate internal decision structure or Schweikard's practical integrity. They not only show how decision making works in group activity, but also that it eventually transcends the individual level.

For the actual control of actions towards a goal, we should remember how this is done in human agency. It is not the case that human beings exert direct, conscious control over their actual movements, but rather have teleological control. We have conscious control over what actions we want to take, but our sub-conscious psycho-physical systems largely take care of the rest. I discussed several ways how groups gain comparable control. On the one hand, there are standards, automated processes and even computerization prescribing what action to take at a very low level of execution. On the other hand, positions in groups often come with authority and authorization. Individuals who occupy these positions are authorized to act on behalf of the group, and they may use their authority to order other members to do specific tasks for the group.

With all of this, I have shown that groups have agential features. The extent to which some groups have agential features, furthermore, leads to group activity that cannot be understood only with reference to individual agents and agency anymore. Only both, the agential features on the individual level and the agential features realized at a group level, explain agency in group activity. I proposed to use the term corporate agency for this new form of agency. Corporations, consequently, are not complete agents independent of the individual member's, but neither are individual members complete agents without the agential features realized on the group level. Such is the nature of group agency.

Bibliography

Accenture (2016). The New Delivery Reality. https://www.accenture.com/us-en/new-delivery-reality-post-parcel-players-index. Last accessed on: 8/8/2019.

Ainslie, George (1992). *Picoeconomics: The Strategic Interaction of Successive Motivational States within the Person*. Cambridge University Press, Cambridge.

Anscombe, Gertrude E. M. (1957). *Intention*. Harvard University Press, Cambridge, Massachusetts, 2. aufl. edition.

Aristotle (350). *Nicomachean Ethics*. the Internet Classics Archive.

Arnold, Denis G. (2006). Collective Moral Agency. In French and Wettstein (2006), pages 279–291.

Arrow, Kenneth J. (1952, [2nd ed. 1963]). *Social Choice and Individual Values*. John Wiley & Sons, New York, 1st edition.

Ash, Salomon E. (1946). Forming impressions of personality. *The Journal of Abnormal and Social Psychology*, 41(3):258–290.

Audi, Robert (1973). Intending. *Journal of Philosophy*, 70(13):387–403.

Austin, J. L. (1956). A Plea for Excuses. *Proceedings of the Aristotelian Society*, 57:1–30.

Bacharach, Michael (1999). Interactive team reasoning: A contribution to the theory of co-operation. *Research in Economics*, 53(2):117–147.

Bacharach, Michael (2006). *Beyond Individual Choice: Teams and Frames in Game Theory*. Princeton University Press.

Bargh, John A., Chen, Mark, and Burrows, Lara (1996). Automaticity of Social Behavior: Direct Effects of Trait Construct and Stereotype Activation on Action. *Journal of Personality and Social Psychology*, 71(2):230–244.

Bentham, Jeremy (1988). *The Principles of Morals and Legislation*. Great books in philosophy. Prometheus Books.

Birnbacher, Dieter (1996). Tun Und Unterlassen. *Zeitschrift für Philosophische Forschung*, 50(3):506–510.

Bittner, Rüdiger (2001). *Doing Things for Reasons*. Oxford University Press.

Björnsson, Gunnar (2011). Joint Responsibility Without Individual Control: Applying the Explanation Hypothesis. In van den Hoven, Jeroen, van de Poel, Ibo, and Vincent, Nicole, eds., *Moral Responsibility: beyond free will and determinism*. Springer.

Blakemore, Sarah-J., Frith, Chris D., and M., Wolpert Daniel (1996). Spatio-Temporal Prediction Modulates the Perception of Self-Produced Stimuli. *Journal of Personality and Social Psychology*, 71(2):230–244.

Botelho, Greg, Brascia, Lorenza, and Martinez, Michael (2016). Anger, praise for Apple for rebuffing FBI over San Bernardino killer's phone. http://edition.cnn.com/2016/02/18/us/san-bernardino-shooter-phone-apple-reaction/. Last accessed on: 08/08/2019.

Botelho, Greg and Starr, Barbara (2016). 49 killed in U.S. airstrike targeting terrorists in Libya. http://edition.cnn.com/2016/02/19/africa/libya-us-airstrike-isis/. Last accessed on: 08/08/2019.

Braham, Matthew and van Hees, Martin (2011). Responsibility Voids. *Philosophical Quarterly*, 61(242):6–15.

Bratman, Michael E. (1984). Two Faces of Intention. *Philosophical Review*, 93(3):375–405.

https://doi.org/10.1515/9783110628623-006

Bratman, Michael E. (1992). Shared Cooperative Activity. *The Philosophical Review*, 101(2):327–341.

Bratman, Michael E. (1993). Shared Intention. *Ethics*, 104(1):97–113.

Bratman, Michael E. (1996). Planning and Temptation. In Friedman, Marilyn F., Clark, Andy, and May, Larry, eds., *Mind and morals - essays on cognitive science and ethics*, pages 65–75. MIT Press, Cambridge.

Bratman, Michael E. (1997a). I Intend That We J. In Holmström-Hintikka, Ghita and Tuomela, R., eds., *Contemporary Action Theory -*, volume 2, pages 49–63. Kluwer Academic Pub.

Bratman, Michael E. (1997b). Responsibility and Planning. *The Journal of Ethics*, 1(1):27–43.

Bratman, Michael E. (1999). *Faces of Intention - Selected Essays on Intention and Agency*. Cambridge University Press, Cambridge.

Bratman, Michael E. (2006a). Dynamics of Sociality. In French and Wettstein (2006), pages 1–15.

Bratman, Michael E. (2006b). What is the Accordion Effect? *Journal of Ethics*, 10(1-2):5–19.

Bratman, Michael E. (2014). *Shared Agency - A Planning Theory of Acting Together*. Oxford University Press, New York.

Bratman, Michael E. (2015). The Fecundity of Planning Agency. In Shoemaker, David, ed., *Oxford Studies in Agency and Responsibility*. Oxford University Press, Oxford.

Brewer, Marilynn B. and Gardner, Wendi (1996). Who Is This "We"? Levels of Collective Identity and Self Representations. *Journal of Personality and Social Psychology*, 71:83–93.

Brownell, Celia A. (2011). Early Developments in Joint Action. *Review of Philosophy and Psychology*, 2(2):193–211.

Brownstein, Michael (2014). Rationalizing flow: agency in skilled unreflective action. *Philosophical Studies*, 168(2):545–568.

Butterfill, Stephen Andrew (2012). Joint Action and Development. *Philosophical Quarterly*, 61(246):23–47.

Chant, Sara Rachel, Hindriks, Frank, and Preyer, Gerhard (2014). Introduction - Beyond the Big Four and the Big Five. In Chant, Sara Rachel, Hindriks, Frank, and Preyer, Gerhard, eds., *From individual to collective intentionality*, pages 1–33. Oxford University Press, New York.

Churchland, Paul M. (2008). Eliminative Materialism and the Propositional Attitudes. In Lycan, William G. and Prinz, Jesse, eds., *Mind and Cognition*. Blackwell, Malden.

Collective Intentionality X (2016). http://enposs.eu/events/conference-collective-intentionality-x/. Last accessed on: 8/8/2019.

Condorcet, Marie-Jean-Antoine-Nicolas de Caritat de (1785). *Essai sur l'application de l'analyse à la probabilité des décisions rendues à la pluralité des voix*. Imprimerie royale, Paris.

Copp, David (1979). Collective Actions and Secondary Actions. *American Philosophical Quarterly*, 16(3):177–186.

Csibra, Gergely, Bíró, Szilvia, Koós, Orsolya, and Gergely, György (2003). One-Year-Old Infants Use Teleological Representations of Actions Productively. *Cognitive Science*, 27(1):111–133.

Csibra, Gergely and Gergely, György (2006). 'Obsessed with goals': Functions and mechanisms of teleological interpretation of actions in humans. *Acta Psychologica*, 124:60–78.

Davidson, Donald (1963). Actions, Reasons, and Causes. *Journal of Philosophy*, 60(23):685–700.

Davidson, Donald (1970). How Is Weakness of the Will Possible? In Feinberg, Joel, ed., *Moral Concepts*. Oxford University Press.

Davidson, Donald (1971). Agency. In Binkley, Robert Williams, Bronaugh, Richard N., and Marras, Ausonio, eds., *Agent, Action and Reason*, pages 3–25. University of Toronto Press, Boston, MA & Oxford, UK.

Davidson, Donald (1973). Freedom to Act. In Honderich, T., ed., *Essays on Freedom of Action*. Routledge AND Kegan Paul.

Davidson, Donald (1978). Intending. In Yovel, Yirmiyahu, ed., *Philosophy of History and Action*. D. Reidel, Dordrecht.

Davidson, Donald (1985). *Handlung und Ereignis*. Suhrkamp, Frankfurt am Main, deutsche erstausgabe edition.

Denier van der Gon, J.J. and Thuring, J. Ph. (1965). The guiding of human writing movements. *Kybernetik*, 2(4):145–148.

Dennett, Daniel C. (1971). Intentional Systems. *Journal of Philosophy*, 68(February):87–106.

Dunfield, Kristen A. and Kuhlmeier, Valerie A. (2010). Intention-Mediated Selective Helping in Infancy. *Psychological Science*, 21(4):523–527. PMID: 20424094.

Ebert, Theodor (1977). Zweck und Mittel. Zur Klᶠarung einiger Grundbegriffe der Handlungstheorie. *Allgemeine Zeitschrift für Philosohpie*, 2(2):21–39.

Fagan, Melinda Bonnie (2014). Do Groups Have Scientific Knowledge? In Chant, Sara Rachel, Hindriks, Frank, and Preyer, Gerhard, eds., *From individual to collective intentionality*, pages 163–186. Oxford University Press, New York.

Feinberg, Joel (1970). Action and Responsibility. In Feinberg, Joel, ed., *Doing & Deserving; Essays in the Theory of Responsibility*. Princeton University Press, Princeton, N.J.

Fischer, John Martin and Ravizza, Mark (1998). *Responsibility and Control: A Theory of Moral Responsibility*. Cambridge University Press.

Flegal, Kristin E. and Anderson, Michael C. (2008). Overthinking skilled motor performance: Or why those who teach can't do. *Psychonomic Bulletin & Review*, 15(5):927–932.

Foot, Philippa (1967). The Problem of Abortion and the Doctrine of Double Effect. *Oxford Review*, 5:5–15.

Forgas, Joseph P. (2011). She just doesn't look like a philosopher...? Affective influences on the halo effect in impression formation. *European Journal of Social Psychology*, 41:812–817.

Frankfurt, Harry G. (1971). Freedom of the Will and the Concept of a Person. *The Journal of Philosophy*, 68(1):5–20.

Frankfurt, Harry G. (1997). The Problem of Action. In Mele, Alfred R., ed., *American Philosophical Quarterly*, pages 157–62. Oxford University Press.

French, Peter A. (1979). The Corporation as a Moral Person. *American Philosophical Quarterly*, 6(3):207–215.

French, Peter A. (1995). *Corporate Ethics*. Harcourt Brace College Publishers, Fort Worth.

French, Peter A. and Wettstein, Howard K. (2006). *Shared Intentions and Collective Responsibility*. Midwest Studies in Philosophy Volume No. XXX. Blackwell Publishing, Boston, MA & Oxford, UK.

Frith, Chris (2002). The self in action: Lessons from delusions of control. *Consciousness and Cognition*, 14:752–770.

Gergely, György and Gergely, Csibra (2003). Teleological Reasoning in Infancy: The Naıve Theory of Rational Action. *Trends in Cognitive Sciences*, pages 287–292.

Gibson, James J. (1986). *The ecological approach to visual perception*. Lawrence Erlbaum Associates, Hillsdale, New Jersey.

Gigerenzer, Gerd and Gaissmaier, Wolfgang (2001). Heuristic Decision Making. *Annual Review of Psychology*, 62(2):451–482.

Gilbert, Margaret (2006). Who's to Blame? Collective moral Responsibility and Its Implications for Group Members. In French and Wettstein (2006), pages 94–114.

Gilbert, Margaret P. (1990). Walking Together: A Paradigmatic Social Phenomenon. *Midwest Studies in Philosophy*, 15(1):1–14.

Goldman, Alvin I. (1970). *A Theory of Human Action.* Princeton University Press, Englewood Cliffs.

Gräfenhain, M., Behne, T., Carpenter, M., and Tomasello, M. (2009). Young children's understanding of joint commitments. *Developmental Psychology*, 45(5):1430–1443.

Haddock, Adrian (2005). At One with Our Actions, but at Two with Our Bodies. *Philosophical Explorations*, 8(2):157–172.

Hamann, Katharina, Warneken, Felix, and Tomasello, Michael (2012). Children's Developing Commitments to Joint Goals. *Child Development*, 83(1):137–145.

Hamlin, J. Kiley, Wynn, Karen, and Bloom, Paul (2007). Social evaluation by preverbal infants. *Nature*, 450:557–559.

Hare, R. M. (1963). *Freedom and Reason.* Oxford, Clarendon Press.

Harman, Gilbert (1976). Practical Reasoning. *The Review of Metaphysics*, 29(3):431–463.

Held, Virginia (1970). Can a Random Collection of Individuals Be Morally Responsible? *Journal of Philosophy*, 67(14):471–481.

Hobbes, Thomas (1909). *Hobbe's Leviathan.* Oxford University Press, New York, first edition.

Hodson, Hal (2014). The AI boss that deploys Hong Kong's subway engineers. *NewScientist*, 2976.

Hursthouse, Rosalind (1991). Arational Actions. *Journal of Philosophy*, 88(2):57–68.

Isodore, Chris (2016). Ford plans four new SUV models. http://money.cnn.com/2016/02/12/autos/ford-suvs/. Last accessed on: 08/08/2019.

Kahneman, Daniel (2011). *Thinking fast and slow.* Macmillan, New York.

Kawato, Mitsuo (1999). Internal models for motor control and trajectory planning. *Current Opinion in neurobiology*, 9(6):718–27.

Kelsen, Hans (1945). *General Theory of Law and State.* Lawbook Exchange.

Knobe, Joshua (2003). Intentional Action in Folk Psychology: An Experimental Investigation. *Philosophical Psychology*, 16(2):309–325.

Kornhauser, Lewis A. and Sager, Lawrence G. (1993). The One and the Many: Adjudication in Collegial Courts. *California Law Review*, 81(1):1–59.

Kutz, Christopher (2000). Acting Together. *Philosophy and Phenomenological Research*, 61(1):1–31.

Lewis, David (1973). Causation. *Journal of Philosophy*, 70(17):556–567.

Limb, Charles J. and Braun, Allen R. (2008). Neural Substrates of Spontaneous Musical Performance: An fMRI Study of Jazz Improvisation. *PLos ONE*, 3(2).

List, Christian and Pettit, Philip (2013). *Group Agency.* OUP Oxford, New York, London.

Ludwig, Kirk (2014). The Ontology of Collective Action. In Chant, Sara Rachel, Hindriks, Frank, and Preyer, Gerhard, eds., *From individual to collective intentionality*, pages 112–33. Oxford University Press, New York.

Mackie, John L. (1977). *Ethics: Inventing Right and Wrong.* Pelican Books, reprint edition.

Margolis, Joseph (1974). War and ideology. In Held, Virginia, Morgenbesser, Sidney, and Nagel, Thomas, eds., *Philosophy, Morality and International Affairs*, pages 246–265. Oxford University Press.

Matthias, Andreas (2004). The Responsibility Gap: Ascribing Responsibility for the Actions of Learning Automata. *Ethics and Information Technology*, 6(3):175–183.

McCann, Hugh J. (1991). Settled Objectives and Rational Constraints. *American Philosophical Quarterly*, 28(1):25–36.

McIntyre, Alison (2019). Doctrine of Double Effect. In Zalta, Edward N., ed., *The Stanford Encyclopedia of Philosophy*. Metaphysics Research Lab, Stanford University, spring 2019 edition.

McLaughlin, Erin (2016). How ISIS recruits children, then kills them. http://edition.cnn.com/2016/02/19/middleeast/isis-child-soldiers/. Last accessed on: 08/08/2019.

Mele, Alfred R. (2003). *Motivation and Agency*. Oxford University Press.

Miller, Seumas (2006). Collective Moral Responsibility: An Individualist Account. In French and Wettstein (2006), pages 176–193.

Miller, Seuma and Makela, Pekka (2005). The Collectivist Approach to Moral Responsibility. *Metaphilosophy*, 36(5):634–651.

Millikan, Ruth G. (2004). *Varieties of Meaning*. MIT Press.

Molden, Daniel C. (2014). Understanding priming effects in social psychology: What is "social priming" and how does it occur? *Social Cognition*, 32:1–11.

Moran, Richard and Stone, Martin J. (2009). Anscombe on Expression of Intention. In *New Essays on the Explanation of Action*, pages 132–168. Palgrave Macmillan.

Morreau, Michael (2016). Arrow's Theorem. In Zalta, Edward N., ed., *The Stanford Encyclopedia of Philosophy*. Metaphysics Research Lab, Stanford University, winter 2016 edition.

Murphy, Kevin R., Jako, Robert A., and Anhalt, Rebecca L. (1993). Nature and Consequences of Halo Error: A Critical Analysis. *Journal of Applied Psychology*, 78(2):218–225.

Mussweiler, Thomas, Englich, Birte, and Strack, Fritz (2004). Anchoring effect. In Pohl, Rüdiger F., ed., *Cognitive Illusions: A Handbook on Fallacies and Biases in Thinking, Judgment and Memory*. Psychology Press, Hove, UK.

Nanay, Bence (2013). *Between Perception and Action*. Oup Oxford.

Neuhäuser, Christian (2011). *Unternehmen als moralische Akteure*. Suhrkamp, Frankfurt am Main, originalausgabe edition.

Nickerson, Rymond S. (1998). Confirmation Bias: A Ubiquitous Phenomenon in Many Guises. *Review of General Psychology*, 2(2):175–220.

Pacherie, Elisabeth (2004). Toward a Dynamic Theory of Intentions. In Pockett, Susan, ed., *Does Consciousness Cause Behaviour?* Mit Press.

Pacherie, Elisabeth (2007). The Sense of Control and the Sense of Agency. *Psyche*, 13(1):1–30.

Pacherie, Elisabeth (2013). Intentional Joint Agency: Shared Intention Lite. *Synthese*, 190(10):1817–1839.

Pettit, Philip (2001). Deliberative Democracy and the Discursive Dilemma. *Noûs*, 35(s1):268–299.

Pettit, Philipp (2003). Groups with Minds of Their Own. In Schmitt, Frederick F., ed., *Socializing Metaphysics: The Nature of Social Reality*, pages 93–167. Rowman & Littlefield, New York.

Plato (1967). *Plato in Twelve Volumes - Protagoras*, volume 3. Harvard University Press, Cambridge, MA.

Plutarch, Gilbert (75). *Theseus*. Hutchinson.

Pust, Joel (2017). Intuition. In Zalta, Edward N., ed., *The Stanford Encyclopedia of Philosophy*. Metaphysics Research Lab, Stanford University, summer 2017 edition.

Rakoczy, Hannes, Warneken, Felix, and Tomasello, Michael (2008). The Sources of Normativity: Young Children's Awareness of the Normative Structure of Games. *Developmental psychology*, 44:875–81.

Roth, Abraham Sesshu (2014). Prediction, Authority, and Entitlement in Shared Activity. *Noûs*, 48(4):626–652.

Roth, Abraham Sesshu (2017). Shared Agency. In Zalta, Edward N., ed., *The Stanford Encyclopedia of Philosophy*. Metaphysics Research Lab, Stanford University, summer 2017 edition.

Schmidt, Richard A., Heuer, Herbert, Ghodsian, Dina, and Young, Douglas E. (1998). Generalized Motor Programs and Units of Action in Bimanual Coordination. In Latasch, Mark L, ed., *Progress in Motor Control*, volume 1, pages 329–360. Human Kinetics, Champaign, Kanada.

Schnall, Simone, Benton, Jennifer, and Harvey, Sophie (2008). With a Clean Conscience. *Psychological Science*, 19(12):1219–1222.

Schweikard, David P. (2011). *Der Mythos des Singulären - eine Untersuchung zur Struktur kollektiven Handelns*. Mentis-Verlag, Paderborn, 1. edition.

Schwitzgebel, Eric (2016). Introspection. In Zalta, Edward N., ed., *The Stanford Encyclopedia of Philosophy*. Metaphysics Research Lab, Stanford University, winter 2016 edition.

Searle, John R. (1979). The Intentionality of Intention and Action. *Inquiry*, 22(1-4):253–280.

Searle, John R. (1990). Collective Intentions and Actions. In Cohen, Philip R., Morgan, Jerry, and Pollack, Martha, eds., *Intentions in Communication*, pages 401–415. MIT Press.

Setiya, Kieran (2011). Intention. In Zalta, Edward N., ed., *The Stanford Encyclopedia of Philosophy*. Spring 2011 edition.

Shields, Grant S. (2014). Neuroscience and Conscious Causation: Has Neuroscience Shown that we cannot Control Our Own Actions? *Rev. Phil. Psych.*, 5:565–582.

Simon, Herbert (1979). *Models of Thought*. Yale University Press, New Haven, London.

Sinhababu, Neil (2013). The Desire Belief Account of Intention Explains Everything. *Noûs*, 47(4):680–696.

Stoecker, Ralf (2008). Action and Responsibility–A Second Look at Ascriptivism. In Lumer, Christoph and Nannini, Sandro, eds., *Practical Identity and Narrative Agency*. Routledge.

Stoecker, Ralf (2014). Handlungen, Absichten und der Nebeneffekt-Effekt. In Grundmann, Thomas, Horvath, Joachim, and Kipper, Jens, eds., *Die experimentelle Philosophie in der Diskussion*, volume 2094, pages 259–278. Suhrkamp.

Taylor, Richard (1973). *Action and purpose*. Humanities Press.

Textor, Mark (2016). States of Affairs. In Zalta, Edward N., ed., *The Stanford Encyclopedia of Philosophy*. Winter 2016 edition.

Thomson, Judith Jarvis (1976). Killing, Letting Die, and the Trolley Problem. *The Monist*, 59(2):204–217.

Tomasello, Michael, Carpenter, Malinda, Call, Josep, Behne, Tanya, and Moll, Henrike (2005). Understanding and Sharing Intentions: The Origins of Cultural Cognition. *Behavioral and Brain Sciences*, 28(5):675–691.

Tuomela, Raimo (1984). *A Theory of Social Action*. D. Reidel Publishing Company.

Tuomela, Raimo (2006). Joint Intention, We-Mode and I-Mode. In French and Wettstein (2006), pages 35–58.

Tuomela, Raimo and Miller, Kaarlo (1988). We-Intentions. *Philosophical Studies*, 53(3):367–389.

Tuomela, Raimo and Miller, Kaarlo (2014). Collective Goals Analyzed. In Chant, Sara Rachel, Hindriks, Frank, and Preyer, Gerhard, eds., *From individual to collective intentionality*, pages 34–60. Oxford University Press, New York.

Tversky, Amos and Kahneman, Daniel (1974). Judgment under Uncertainty: Heuristics and Biases. *Science*, 185(4157):1124–1131.

Vaish, Amrisha, Carpenter, Malinda, and Tomasello, Michael (2010). Young Children Selectively Avoid Helping People With Harmful Intentions. *Child Development*, 81(6):1661–1669.

Valdesolo, Piercarlo and DeSteno, David (2006). Manipulations of Emotional Context Shape Moral Judgment. *Psychological Science*, 17(6):476–477.

Velasquez, Manuel G. (1983). Why Corporations Are Not Morally Responsible for Anything They Do. *Business and Professional Ethics Journal*, 2(3):1–18.

Velleman, David J. (1997). How To Share An Intention. *Philosophy and Phenomenological Research*, 57(1):29–50.

Wadman, W.J., Denier van der Gon, J.J., Geuze, R. H., and Mol, C.R. (1979). Control of fast goal-directed arm movements. *Journal of Human Movement Studies*, 5:3–17.

Wallace, D. F. (2005). *Consider the lobster*. Little, Brown and Co.

Warneken, Felix, Chen, Frances, and Tomasello, Michael (2006). Cooperative Activities in Young Children and Chimpanzees. *Child Development*, 77(3):640–663.

Warneken, Felix and Tomasello, Michael (2007). Helping and Cooperation at 14 Months of Age. *Infancy*, 11(3):271–294.

Wason, P. C. (1966). Reasoning. In Foss, Brian M. and Dodwell, Peter C., eds., *New horizons in psychology*, volume 1, pages 135–151. Penguin Books, New York City.

Watson, Gary (1975). Free Agency. *The Journal of Philsophy*, 72(8):205–220.

Weirich, Paul (2014). Collective Rationality's Roots. In Chant, Sara Rachel, Hindriks, Frank, and Preyer, Gerhard, eds., *From individual to collective intentionality*, pages 187–206. Oxford University Press, New York.

Wimmer, Heinz M. and Perner, Josef (1983). Beliefs about beliefs: Representation and con-straining function of wrong beliefs in young children's understanding of deception. *Cognition*, 12(1):103–128.

Wittgenstein, Ludwig (2010, [1953]). *Philosophical Investigations*. John Wiley & Sons.

Wolf, Ursula (1985). Zum Problem der Willensschwäche. *Zeitschrift für Philosophische Forschung*, 39(1):21–33.

Wolpert, Daniel M., Ghahramani, Zoubin, and Jordan, Michael I. (1995). An Internal Model for Sensorimotor Integration. *Science*, 269(5232):1880–1882.

Wübben, M. and von Wangenheim, F. (2008). Instant Customer base analysis: managerial heuristics often "get it right.". *Journal of Marketing*, 72:82–93.

Yan, Sophia (2016). Uber is losing $1 billion a year in China. http://money.cnn.com/2016/02/19/technology/uber-losing-1-billion-china/. Last accessed on: 08/08/2019.

General index

https://doi.org/10.1515/9783110628623-007

Index of technical terms

https://doi.org/10.1515/9783110628623-008